The
Forsaken Son

The
Forsaken Son

*Child Murder and Atonement
in Modern American Fiction*

✦

Joshua Pederson

NORTHWESTERN UNIVERSITY PRESS
EVANSTON, ILLINOIS

Northwestern University Press
www.nupress.northwestern.edu

Printed in the United States of America

10 9 8 7 6 5 4 3 2 1

Library of Congress Cataloging-in-Publication Data

Names: Pederson, Joshua, author.
Title: The forsaken son : child murder and atonement in modern American fiction /
    Joshua Pederson.
Description: Evanston, Illinois : Northwestern University Press, 2016. | Includes
    bibliographical references and index.
Identifiers: LCCN 2016007589 | ISBN 9780810132276 (pbk. : alk. paper) | ISBN
    9780810132283 (cloth : alk. paper) | ISBN 9780810132290 (e-book)
Subjects: LCSH: American fiction—20th century—History and criticism. |
    Infanticide in literature. | Infanticide—Religious aspects—Christianity. |
    Atonement in literature.
Classification: LCC PS374.I495 P43 2016 | DDC 813.5409355—dc23
LC record available at http://lccn.loc.gov/2016007589

"A dead baby's not a pretty thing," Katz said. "I mean, presumably you guys aren't advocating infanticide."

—Jonathan Franzen

What kind of father is it who would rather his son were slaughtered than forgive his ill-advised creatures who have been corrupted by his precious Satan? What is supposed to be demonstrated by this gruesome and archaic sacrifice of the son? God's love, perhaps? Or his implacability? . . . Yahweh has a tendency to employ such means as the killing of the son and the first-born.

—Carl Jung

At three o'clock Jesus cried out with a loud voice, "Eloi, Eloi, lema sabachthani?" which means, "My God, my God, why have you forsaken me?"

—Mark 15:34

How *can* one do theology in the presence of one million burning children?

—David Blumenthal

CONTENTS

ACKNOWLEDGMENTS

A project as big as this isn't finished without help, and I am grateful to all the friends, family, teachers, and colleagues who gave encouragement and aid along the way.

My graduate school mentors remain invaluable sources of support to me even now. Peter Hawkins is the scholar after whom I pattern myself to this day. He is a model teacher, author, and guide, and I count myself incredibly fortunate to have studied under him. I also offer humble thanks to Susan Mizruchi for introducing me to some of the authors addressed here, for encouraging me to run with this idea in its early stages, and for offering excellent advice as I crafted the prospectus.

My wonderful colleagues at Boston University's College of General Studies also gave fine counsel as this project came together. Sheila Cordner, Davida Pines, Adam Sweeting, Meg Tyler, and Robert Wexelblatt all read pieces of the work in progress, and the final product is markedly better as a result of their sensitive, insightful commentary. I am very grateful to Natalie McKnight, who has fought so tenaciously for me as I strive to advance in academia. I also thank the crew in suite 419—John Lyons, John Fawell, and Tom Whalen—for making sure I never win our NCAA basketball pool; the victory would surely go to my head. It's a pleasure and an honor to work with them all.

I also owe special thanks to all the fine people at Northwestern University Press for helping me bring this project to term. I am especially grateful to Henry Carrigan for taking a chance on a first-time author, to Nathan Mac-Brien for editing so insightfully, and to Gianna Mosser for responding to my many questions with patience and grace.

Most get by with help from their friends, and I'm no different. So I send thanks to Rebecca Aviel, Louis Bosso, Karin Denison, Jodi Elliott, Paul Furlow, Sara Gothard, Christopher Ives, Mishy Lesser, John and Shannon Mackey, and Justin Marceau. I am grateful to them all for sharing ideas and cocktails.

Few get more support from their families than I do. I can never thank my parents enough for their perpetual love and care. My mother gave me my passion for literature, and my father taught me to think critically about faith. I am forever grateful. Lukas is my brother and my best friend. I am not worthy. Further, special thanks go to David and Mary Blohm for making a Midwesterner feel more at home in New England.

Last, I send all my love to my beautiful wife, Jessica. And to my new son, Judah. This book has absolutely nothing to do with him.

The
Forsaken Son

Chapter 1

"Rachel Weeping"

✦

Atonement Theology and Forsaken Children

> We wanted theology to offer healing. We were convinced
> Christianity could not promise healing for victims of intimate
> violence as long as its central image was a divine parent who
> required the death of his child.
> —Rita Nakashima Brock and Rebecca Parker

For Christians, Jesus dies on the cross to save us from our sins. Or he dies to set an example of love and self-sacrifice. Or he dies to defeat the devil. But no matter the reason Jesus perishes, Christians are generally sure that his death "atones": it rectifies, reconciles, or saves. But for Jean-Baptiste Clamence, the idiosyncratic hero of Camus's *The Fall*, Jesus dies because he can't bear living with his own guilt. Clamence explains: "he must have heard of a certain Slaughter of the Innocents. The children of Judea massacred while his parents were taking him to a safe place—why did they die if not because of him? Those blood-spattered soldiers, those infants cut in two filled him with horror."[1] The "Slaughter" Clamence mentions is described in the second chapter of the Gospel of Matthew. King Herod, governor of Judea, learns from wise men that the Messiah is to be born in Bethlehem, so he sends them to scout the location. Yet the men are warned in a dream of Herod's evil intentions, so they visit Jesus but never report back to Jerusalem. Enraged, Herod orders the execution of every baby in Bethlehem. God is quicker than Herod, though, and he sends an angel to Joseph in a dream to warn him. However, the other parents of Bethlehem receive no similar warning, and while Jesus and his parents escape to safety, the infants from the city and the surrounding area are cut down. According to the evangelist, the massacre fulfills a prophecy foretold in the book of Jeremiah:

> A voice was heard in Ramah,
> wailing and loud lamentation,
> Rachel weeping for her children;
> she refused to be consoled, because they are no more. (Jer. 2:18)

That prophecy predicts the Slaughter of Innocents suggests that this mass killing of babies is and always has been part of the divine order. And Jesus, it seems, cannot bear being part of that order if his life is bought with the death of children—many children. Thus, Clamence continues, when Jesus yells from the cross, "Why hast thou forsaken me? . . . it was a seditious cry"[2]—a last-minute call to insurrection that Clamence believes is cut from some gospels to staunch the radical spirit it represents. "Yes, it was the third evangelist [Luke]," says Clamence, "who first suppressed his complaint . . . Well, then, the scissors!"[3] The author of John follows suit.

Of course, Camus's book is fiction—and heterodox fiction at that—and Christianity does not share his theory of the cross. The great Swiss theologian Hans Urs von Balthasar seems untroubled by Christ's lament, explaining that "the Son could not be abandoned by the Father" and claiming that his cry of forsakenness is not "sedition" but a kind of role-play: Jesus "has taken on our curse and our forsakenness, not as if he had actually been or become these things himself, but by taking on the role . . . and making himself like us."[4] Yet the questions Clamence's exegesis provokes don't die so easily: is the Slaughter of Innocents a necessary part of the divine plan? Does the Christian God really demand the death of children? Jesus's suffering doesn't *feel* like role-playing; is it? And if Jesus is "forsaken" on the cross, why would God ever forsake *his own* child? These are difficult challenges, and especially thorny ones for believers. Yet they are also substantive, legitimate, and based on an honest reading of scripture. After all, it's not Clamence's Jesus who is "forsaken"; it's the Christ of the Gospel of Mark. And Camus doesn't invent the Slaughter of Innocents; Matthew recounts it. Further, for Christians, God both inspires and presides over both texts. This book is about that God—a God who arrays angels, shepherds, and traveling kings around one manger in Bethlehem while lining others with blood. It's about a God who gives us his son only to have him tacked up on rough lumber to bleed out. And it's about the violence our salvation seems to require, a violence that too often includes the murder of children, even God's own. Further, this project is about a group of theologians and novelists who amplify Christ's complaint—"Why hast thou forsaken me?"—and who will not forsake the children whose lives God seemingly demands.

The Fall is the seed from which this project grows, because in the years after I read it, I began to see in American literature the same chilling confluence of Christianity and child murder that Clamence observes in the gospels. In recent American fiction, Edward Albee, William Faulkner, Toni Morrison, John Updike, Flannery O'Connor, Joyce Carol Oates, Bernard Malamud, Vladimir Nabokov, William Styron, Cormac McCarthy, Sam Shepard, and others have written works that prominently feature infanticide. Yet many of these books are also liberally spiked with the language of Christian devotion. McCarthy's *Outer Dark*—about a father who tries to kill his infant child by exposure—features dozens of allusions to scripture. In Oates's *My Sister,*

My Love, a mother explains her rationale for killing her daughter using the language of evangelical Christianity. O'Connor's *The Violent Bear It Away* features a young man whose murder of a disabled child sparks a prophetic mission. And the titles of all three are taken directly from Christian scripture.

Of course, child murder and Christianity do not often come up together in polite conversation. Aren't they anathema, the one to the other? The Bible includes persuasive evidence not only that God has an especial love for children but—as if it needs even be written—that he strenuously objects to their murder. In the gospel of Matthew, Jesus proves his affection for the young when he reprimands his disciples for keeping them away: "Let the little children come to me, and do not stop them; for it is to such as these that the kingdom of heaven belongs" (19:14). This passage inspired the nineteenth-century Chicago preacher Clare Woolston to write the classic Sunday school hymn, "Jesus Loves the Little Children." More pointedly, many traditional interpretations of the story of the binding of Isaac in Genesis 22 suggest that Abraham's near-murder of his son is actually a dramatic *rejection* of child sacrifice. After all, though God commands Abraham to kill his own child, God also—in cliffhanger fashion—stays his servant's hand. According to this reading, Yahweh speaks a forceful message in the story of the *akedah*: unlike other ancient Mesopotamian faiths, Judaism *does not require* the death of children to placate the deity.[5] But given Jesus's affection for children and God's putative rejection of child murder, the Lord's inability to protect children causes some to despair. In *The Brothers Karamazov*, Ivan famously cites as reason for his unbelief his contention that no good God could allow the suffering death of a child. For Ivan, the fact that child murder even *exists* invalidates the language and promise of the Christian faith.[6] Given this tension, how do we explain the combination of the wrenching violence of child murder and Christian theological language in American fiction?

This book is an effort to answer that question, to explain the provocative coincidence of the vocabularies of infanticide and Christianity in six modern American novels: Flannery O'Connor's *The Violent Bear It Away*, the first two installments of John Updike's *Rabbit* tetralogy, Toni Morrison's *Beloved*, Joyce Carol Oates's *My Sister, My Love*, and Cormac McCarthy's *Outer Dark*. To do so, I turn to recent discussions of atonement. Atonement theology is Christianity's answer to the question, why does God send his son to die a painful death on the cross? That answer—or set of answers—has proven remarkably durable, holding up for centuries. Yet since the 1950s, especially in American theological circles, these answers have become either less satisfying or downright objectionable. And as atonement theology shows signs of wear, the cross reverts from saving grace to trauma—or even crime. More bluntly, without atonement, the cross comes to resemble a filicide, in which God forces his son to die for no apparent reason. Here, then, I argue that the novels about child murder discussed likewise give voice to modern skepticism about traditional atonement theology. And they all develop a single, dark metaphor: the murdered children are also Christ figures, dying for reasons that seem less and less clear, in moments that feel increasingly tragic. This metaphor then allows these novelists to effectively extend modern theology's critique of atonement, interrogating the theories that underlie it, the tropes and themes that relate to it, and the behaviors it inspires.

In sum, it is my contention that these fictions partake in a changing theological discourse on the nature of the death of Jesus in which Christ's execution comes to look more like an avoidable tragedy and less like an atoning sacrifice. In these novels, every time a child is killed, we are tempted to cast a skeptical gaze back on Christianity's traditional interpretation of the cross, thinking, surely these sons and daughters do not have to die—does Jesus?

For most believers, the message of the crucifixion is hope, redemption, and salvation. The third chapter of John—the latest of the four canonical gospels—captures this message succinctly in what has become the bumper-sticker summary of American Christianity: "For God so loved the world that he gave his only Son, so that everyone who believes in him may not perish but may have eternal life" (3:16). The evangelist continues, "Indeed, God did not send the Son into the world to condemn the world, but in order that the world *might be saved* through him" (John 3:17, italics mine). It is Jesus him-self who speaks all these words, and one senses that the John author writes them with confidence, sure of the salvific power of his Christ's life, death, and works. A hint of that confidence carries over even to the cross, on which Jesus arranges for the care of his mother, asks for wine, and offers crisp, concise last words, "It is finished" (John 19:27–30). The evangelist concludes, "Then he bowed his head and gave up his spirit" (19:30). The active form of the last verb—"gave" in the English—indicates that Jesus maintains agency even to his last breath.

By contrast, Mark, the earliest gospel, comes to a close much less cleanly. One hesitates to overplay the contrasts between Mark and John; indeed, they share as much as they keep to themselves. Yet it's hard not to get the sense that Mark's author, who writes his text decades (or even a century) before John, is less comfortable with the crucifixion—and that John's relative assuredness is only the result of difficult reflection by the first generations of Christian believers. Paula Fredriksen describes the mood of Mark as one of "nervous anticipation" amplified by one simple question: "Who is this man, and what will he do next?"[7] It's a question even Jesus sometimes cannot answer. On the cross, Mark's Christ seems hesitant, afraid, even abandoned. It is Mark who first gives us the dying call that Camus calls "seditious": "My God, my God, why have you forsaken me?" (15:34)[8] Jesus has only one more utterance, a "loud cry" that immediately precedes his death (15:37). The gospel's conclu-sion just a few verses later is equally unsettling.[9] Mary Magdalene, Mary the mother of Jesus, and a third woman named Salome arrive at Jesus's tomb to find the covering stone removed. Upon entering, having noticed that the corpse is missing, they are confronted by a mysterious young man who tells them simply that Jesus "has been raised" and "is not here" (16:6). In response, the women flee "from the tomb, for terror and amazement had seized them; and they said nothing to anyone, for they were afraid" (16:8). The text ends with an unexpected word—"afraid"—and the earliest of the four canonical gospels closes with flight, fear, and silence. Serene Jones argues that the last word of the Greek original—the preposition *gar* (roughly, "for")—leaves the reader even more unsettled; it is as if the evangelist trails off mid-sentence.[10] Jones continues, "At the very moment when we, as readers of the Gospel, are in need of the greatest relief . . . Mark does not give it to us. . . . He allows the Gospel story to run away from us. Instead of pulling it together, he leaves us peering into the gaping space of an ending that never comes."[11] For Mark, the death of the man who would be the messiah is a ragged wound that is slow to heal, and it's difficult to discern what Jesus's death means—if it means anything at all.

Perhaps one of the best ways to think of atonement, then, is as a set of theologies designed to put Mark's fears to rest—to assure the disciples fleeing the tomb not only that Jesus's death is meaningful, but miraculous. Though there is no single orthodox theology of atonement, all the prominent theories take part in Christology—the systematic effort to explain the purpose of Jesus's birth, life, and death. John Sanders describes atonement by noting that while most Christians agree *that* Jesus saves, there is a variety of opinions as to *how* he does so.[12] Atonement theology attempts to answer that very question: how does Jesus's death function? Or, more broadly, what does Jesus's death *do*? This was a crucial question for first-century Christians, many of whom were deeply invested in the idea that Jesus was the Jewish messiah—a powerful earthly leader who would restore Israel and confirm God's divine preference for the Israelites. The messiah was to be a king, an emperor, or a strong military commander. And when Jesus dies the ignominious death of a criminal, pinned to a cross under a mocking placard, his followers' disappointment couldn't be more devastating. The authors of the New Testament, then, have a daunting task: they must characterize Jesus's death not only as explicable, but as desirable. They must convince their readers that the crucifixion is part of the plan—and that it has a salutary function. The John author offers one simple effort to do so: he argues simply and emphatically that Jesus's death *saves*. And the confidence of John's Jesus springs in part from the fact that the author can explain the import of Christ's death so forcefully. But the work of atonement theology begins even before the composition of John. As Martin Hengel argues, we find the first recorded theologies of atonement in the letters of Paul, the earliest of which were likely written in the middle of the first century.[13] Paul's efforts at articulating the atoning power of the crucifixion are multiple and sundry; he offers numerous solutions to the mystery of Jesus's death, and he seems content to let that variety of answers stand without ever lifting one up over the others. But while the Christian church never professes one dogmatic version of atonement, two medieval saints developed the most influential models. In *Cur Deus Homo*, Saint Anselm proposed the satisfaction model—the most prominent version of what would come to be known as "objective" atonement. In it, humans sin and in the process incur a debt to God that they cannot repay. That debt is an unacceptable affront to God's honor. To settle the account, a sinless man (Jesus) must die, in effect accepting the punishment that would otherwise be required of humans. Thus, sin is appropriately met with punishment, debt is paid, and divine honor is restored. Just a few years later, Anselm's near-contemporary Peter Abelard, in his "Exposition of the Epistle to the Romans," put forth a competing, "subjective" atonement model sometimes called the moral example theory. For Abelard, Jesus instantiates ideal human behavior. In his death, he teaches humans obedience to the divine will, self-sacrifice, and steadfastness in the face of suffering. Abelard's atonement fits into the *imitatio Christi* tradition, a devotional mode that emphasizes the joy and fulfillment that can be had from modeling one's own actions after Christ's. To this day, these two theories remain the closest thing Christianity has to an orthodox theology of atonement and the most prominent explanations of Jesus's death.

That Anselm and Abelard's models of atonement were more or less unchallenged for eight hundred years is testament to their durability and ingenuity. However, in the early twentieth century, Gustaf Aulén initiated an influential critique of both in the process of attempting to renovate a third, even older theory of atonement. In *Christus Victor*, he argued that Abelardian and Anselmian theologies are "discontinuous." In such models, God stands apart from Jesus in the moment of the Son's crucifixion, overseeing or observing Christ's suffering death: "according to the [discontinuous] view, the act of Atonement has indeed its origin in God's will, but is, in its carrying-out, an offering made to God by Christ as man and on man's behalf."[14] Discontinuous atonement theories portray God as requesting or demanding Jesus's crucifixion without participating in (or "feeling") it and thus open God to charges of cruelty, distance, or even murder. Such is the case in Anselm and Abelard, both of whom separate Jesus from God in the moment of the crucifixion while the former does the work of reconciliation by dying at the latter's command. Further, Jesus's cry on the cross in Matthew 27 and Mark 15—"My God, my God, why have you forsaken me?"—allows for the possibility that the Son is not a willing participant in this transaction. Aulén is a forerunner of subsequent generations of American theologians and religious writers who mounted convincing critiques of discontinuous atonement models, among them René Girard, James H. Cone, Robert J. Daly, Delores S. Williams, and, more recently, S. Mark Heim, J. Denny Weaver, Stephen Finlan, Rita Nakashima Brock, and Rebecca Ann Parker. Many of these authors also argue that atonement may not merely cast God as a killer; it also could encourage bad behavior in believers by bolstering ideologies of oppression.

Simply, traditional models of atonement give perpetrators a theological rationale for promulgating racism, misogyny, and abuse by suggesting that God allows for the transferability of punishment from one individual or group to another and by implying that God encourages the passive endurance of unjust suffering. (I will expand on both these arguments in chapter 2). Thus, discontinuous atonement theories provide compelling reasons for the death of Jesus, but they do so at a steep and perhaps unconscionable price: the universal loving-kindness of God and the good behavior of Christians. In brief, from the perspective of its critics, the God of traditional atonement theology looks less like a compassionate redeemer and more like an abuser—or a homicide willing to, in J. Denny Weaver's words, "[arrange] the death of one child for the benefit of the others."[15] For Weaver and the rest, God is neither strong ruler, just arbiter, nor good shepherd; he is a menace and a cold-blooded killer.

This grisly portrait of the deity is my subject in this book, and I contend that the murderous God of atonement stalks the pages of American theology and fiction in and around the turn of this millennium. In what follows, I trace the development of this dark divinity and his forsaken son through creative and religious writing in the hopes of demonstrating the dangers of atonement models that spawn a potentially filicidal God. I also ask, with the theologians at work in this area, where we go from here. If a deep reading of traditional atonement refigures the cross as a crime scene, how do we solve its mystery? Can Christianity appropriate such a disturbing truth at its core? Are there acceptable alternatives? Does the atonement inspire undesirable conduct in those who accept its insights? Can the devout worship a God who "arranges" his son's unwilling death? If not, can Christian theology survive without atonement?

These are troubling questions that believers have only begun to address. This book takes them past the boundaries of theology in hopes that fiction may provide a more appropriate venue for honestly addressing them. By and large, the theologians considered here strive to "fix" atonement in hopes of saving one of Christianity's central symbols. By contrast, creative writers have no such responsibility; if in religion, one is bound by doctrine, literature has no dogma. In his recent book *Hating God*, Bernard Schweitzer writes of the freedom fiction grants authors to challenge church teaching, test heresy, or even speak blasphemy. He thus suggests that literature provides a perfect field for wrestling with the Godhead: "literature is *the* principal conduit for expressions of animosity against the Almighty." He attributes this fact to the

> make-believe potential, the *as if* factor of literature, which has served as a defense against public prosecution of authors from Flaubert to Joyce and Nabokov. But literature has another incomparable advantage over straightforward nonfictional discourse when it comes to the hostility against God: the imaginative scope of literature allows one

to toy creatively with an idea that is both troubling and difficult to
act upon. Indeed, only in fiction is it really possible to wrestle with
God with any degree of realism, since God cannot be compelled to
face off with his opponents in the real world.[16]

I write this book under Schweitzer's banner, engaging novelists who develop
the ghoulish trope of child murder in order to wrestle with a frightening God.
O'Connor, Updike, Morrison, Oates, and McCarthy use religious language
to depict infanticides that recall the crucifixion. This typological echo allows
them to reassess the cross—and to question the God who would send his own
Son to death.

These authors' critical engagement with the logics of atonement springs
in part from what is, for each writer, a deep and honest struggle with Christianity. Hence, this book also explores the personal faith journeys of five
prominent modern American novelists and posits that an understanding of
each writer's religious background is important to the ways we read their
work. All five authors were brought up Christian, yet each grapples with the
religion he or she has inherited. This battle drives some away from Christianity (Oates and McCarthy) while deepening the faith of others (O'Connor
and Updike). (Morrison rests somewhere in between.) Yet whether believers,
atheists, bitter Christians, or lapsed Catholics, they all are Biblically literate,
and their novels feature direct meditations on the gospel texts pertinent to
the development of atonement. Another part of my job in what follows, then,
is the unpacking of these scriptural references. Thus, I use source criticism
to demonstrate the ways in which these writers use scripture to interro-
gate Christian doctrine.[17] Finally, some of these writers, notably O'Connor,
Updike, and Oates, are also quite familiar with both American and continen-
tal theology; thus, I identify and expand on relevant allusions to theological
literature when appropriate.

A few crucial questions remain before we begin. Why now, why here, and
why does this trend play out in major ways in modern American literature?
Why has a critique of traditional interpretations of the crucifixion sprung
up among a group of authors writing nearly 2,000 years after the fact, thou-
sands of miles away from Jerusalem? Let me offer a few explanations.

First, these authors' willingness to consider the cross as crime opens them
to the possibility that the crucifixion is a moment of victimization or of
trauma. And such a characterization partakes in a new, widespread appre-
ciation of the pain of victimhood in the last six decades. More simply, my
project is part of the growing field of trauma studies and a piece that testifies
to the status of Jesus as victim of violence.

Recent years have seen a marked rise in attention to trauma and victimhood. Elie Wiesel has argued that "if the Greeks invented tragedy, the
Romans the epistle, and the Renaissance the sonnet, our generation invented

a new literature, that of testimony."[18] Wieviorka notes that the last fifty years have seen the emergence of "the era of witness," the title she gives to her book on trauma in the twentieth century. And in E. Ann Kaplan's book *Trauma Culture*, the author claims that "trauma is often seen as inherently linked to modernity."[19] None of these authors suggests that trauma is unique to the modern era. However, all imply that modernity allows us to attend to trauma in unprecedented ways. Part of this attention is due to the Holocaust. Sadly, the *Shoah* is not the only genocide in human history, but no similar tragedy has received such widespread academic, lay, and media attention. Further, post-Holocaust historians and literary critics have spent much ink wondering whether any language can effectively describe its horrors.[20] Second, returning Vietnam War veterans brought new awareness to the painful emotional and psychological strain that weighs on soldiers as they re-acclimate themselves to their peace-time lives. This strain—previously dismissed as malingering or written off as "shell shock"—was re-evaluated by a new generation of psychiatric specialists, and the suffering of Vietnam veterans led, in part, to the inclusion of post-traumatic stress disorder (PTSD) in the third edition of the *Diagnostic and Statistical Manual of Mental Disorders* (DSM-III)—the definitive diagnostic reference for psychologists and psychiatrists—released in 1980. A third element that contributed to the rise of trauma studies was second-wave feminism's focus on uncovering and decrying both spousal and child abuse. Crucial to this movement is the feminist psychiatrist Judith Herman's pathbreaking book *Trauma and Recovery* (1992), which both helped put trauma studies on the map and called attention to the victimization of women and children.[21] In summary, victimhood is not new to the late twentieth century, but a confluence of factors led academics, medical specialists, and concerned friends and family members to bring new attention to identifying, treating, and witnessing the victims of trauma and abuse. It is not surprising, then, in this "era of witness," that a new wave of authors would use the tools provided by trauma studies to look at the victimhood of Jesus in new ways, to reconceptualize his crucifixion not as atoning sacrifice but instead as a visceral, traumatic wound.

Christian theologians are just coming to learn how trauma studies can lend new insights into religious texts and religious experience. (I will outline some of these insights in chapter 2.) Briefly, trauma theory allows believers to witness—and bear witness to—the death of Jesus as an enduring tragedy, perhaps for the first time since its immediate aftermath. Further, one of the drawbacks of atonement theology is the fact that it hinders any effort to work through the trauma of the cross. Indeed, the very function of atonement is to focus our attention on the *benefits* of the death of Jesus—rather than on the wrenching loss that it represents. Of course, there are traditions in Christianity that focus on the suffering of Jesus both before and on the cross; witness the flagellants of the thirteenth and fourteenth centuries or, more recently, the success of Mel Gibson's devotional bloodbath, *The Passion of the Christ.* Yet there are perhaps fewer who dwell on Jesus's deathful absence, on the span between crucifixion and resurrection during which Jesus is truly *gone*. Thus, in *Spirit and Trauma*, Shelly Rambo warns against another tendency within the faith, a certain desire to hurry past the horror of the cross to the miracles of Easter and atonement; to develop her point, Rambo cites von Balthasar: "We must, in the first place, guard against that theological busyness and religious impatience which insist on anticipating the moment of fruiting of the eternal redemption through the temporal passion—on dragging forward that moment from Easter to Holy Saturday."[22] Holy Saturday is the day on which Jesus is absent, dead and unresurrected, and von Balthasar here writes of the desire to fill the gap it represents. As I argue later, the effort to fill that gap has been an under-acknowledged part of atonement theology as it has developed over the past millennium—and a contributor to the development of a "screen memory" that helps hide the wound of Jesus's absence. Yet when that screen frays—when we are forced to dwell in the doldrums of Holy Saturday—the pain returns, and the cross is transformed from saving miracle to violent injustice that we have yet to work through. For trauma theorists, the process of "working through," of honestly testifying to world-shattering pain, is crucial to convalescence. In part, then, the novels I engage in this project are acts of witness. They are testimonies to both parental and spiritual pain. They help us cope with the traumatic loss of children and, by figural extension, the loss of God's only Son.

I also contend that this wound cuts deeper in the United States, because modern American Christians imagine themselves as having a remarkably— and perhaps uniquely—intimate relationship with Jesus Christ. Some contemporary trauma specialists speculate that later generations may be traumatized by the secondhand experience of trauma, through listening, watching, or reading. And one could argue that American Christians living in arguably the most devout society in history who hear the stories of Jesus's death may be traumatized by those stories. Laub argues that those who hear or read a narrative of trauma are traumatized themselves: "the listener to trauma comes to be a participant and a co-owner of the traumatic event: through his very listening, he comes to partially experience trauma in himself. The relation of the victim to the event of the trauma, therefore, impacts on the relation of the listener to it, and the latter comes to feel the bewilderment, injury, confusion and conflicts that the trauma victim feels."[23] For those who take to the task of earnestly bearing witness to another's trauma, that trauma may be communicable. Marianne Hirsch develops the idea of "postmemory" to explain the process by which trauma is transmitted between generations:

> Postmemory describes the relationship that the generation after those
> who witnessed cultural or collective trauma bears to the experiences
> of those who came before, experiences that they "remember" only by
> means of the stories, images, and behaviors among which they grew

up. But these experiences were transmitted to them so deeply and affectively as to *seem* to constitute memories in their own right . . . To grow up with such overwhelming inherited memories, to be dominated by narratives that preceded one's birth or one's consciousness, is to risk having one's own stories and experiences displaced, even evacuated, by those of a previous generation. It is to be shaped, however, indirectly, by traumatic events that still defy narrative reconstruction and exceed comprehension. These events happened in the past, but their effects continue into the present.[24]

Hirsch's construction allows for the possibility that past traumas—like the crucifixion of Jesus—can negatively affect present believers. But Hirsch is aware of challenges to her theory of transmissible trauma. And we risk watering down the definition of the term if we apply it both to rape and reading about the death of Jesus. Indeed, one hesitates to characterize the passing of a long-dead historical figure as "traumatic." However, I argue that the American Jesus is not such a character; he is a sensed, living presence in the lives of believers.

The United States is the Christian nation par excellence; as Stephen Prothero notes, today it is home to more Christians than any other nation in history.[25] The 2008 American Religious Identity Survey (ARIS) reveals that more than three-quarters of U.S. citizens self-identify as Christian. Further, American Christianity is unique both in its emphasis on the figure of Jesus and on the intimate relationship American Christians share with their Savior. In *American Jesus*, Prothero notes that prerevolutionary American Christians valued an omnipotent God over his human Son: "In their religious training, the Old Testament trumped the New, and Jesus the Son cowered in the shadow of God the Father."[26] He further notes that for Puritan theology, the Son had virtually no role. However, Jesus devotion grew throughout the nineteenth century and exploded in the twentieth. Now, more than two-thirds of U.S. citizens say that they have made a "personal commitment to Jesus," and 75 percent of Americans claim to have sensed his presence.[27] (As I'll mention later, Toni Morrison's mother is one of these Americans.) Given these facts, Prothero suggests that the unofficial motto of modern American evangelical Christianity might as well read, "It isn't a religion, it's a relationship."[28] American Christians imagine themselves to be enmeshed in a close, enduring relationship with a person whose presence is both felt and treasured. Thus, experiencing his loss—whether it be through text, ritual, or prayer—can be understood as traumatic even if reading about the death of Napoleon, or Abraham Lincoln, or even the Buddha cannot. The authors engaged in this study characterize the death of Jesus as a trauma that is not merely historical but has the power to viscerally affect believers today.

Finally, though this project will address crucial pieces of atonement theology, I will spend much of my time engaging novelists' fictional refigurations

of Christ's suffering and death. In doing so, I will heed literary critics—
notably Cathy Caruth and Geoffrey Hartman—who argue that literature has
special power to describe trauma. In *Unclaimed Experience*, Caruth implies
that aesthetic products like screenplays and movies may sometimes represent
trauma more effectively than "objective" language can. As evidence, she cites
Marguerite Duras and Alain Resnais's 1959 film *Hiroshima mon amour*.
Caruth characterizes the film as the result of Resnais's halted effort to make
a documentary about Hiroshima in the wake of the bombing. Shifting away
from total reliance on archival footage, Resnais instead uses a fictional rendering to communicate the "truth" of the event. Writes Caruth, "In his refusal
to make a documentary on Hiroshima, Resnais paradoxically implies that
it is direct archival footage that cannot maintain the very specificity of the
event. And it would appear, equally paradoxically, that it is through the fictional story, not *about* Hiroshima but taking place at its site, that Resnais and
Duras believe that such historical specificity is conveyed."[29] Creative fictions,
then, can testify to trauma even if direct reportage fails. Geoffrey Hartman
extends this argument to include text in a published interview with Caruth.
He claims, "In the non-pathological course of events, the 'unclaimed experience,' as you [Caruth] call it, can only be reclaimed by literary knowledge."[30]
Hartman doubles down on this assertion in his own essay on the relationship between trauma and language, arguing that literature is particularly well
suited to help us "read the wound" of trauma.[31] In this project, I take Hartman's argument seriously; I believe that modern literature can indeed help
us read the wound at the core of Christian faith. I do not accept Caruth's
related claim that trauma is essentially unspeakable—or unrepresentable
in normal discourse.[32] However, I do hold, with the Harvard psychologist
Richard McNally and others, that victims often have real difficulty speaking honestly of their traumas.[33] Literature, then, allows one to approach the
wound obliquely, indirectly—working through pain at the protective remove
that fiction allows.

It is my contention that the six novels addressed in the following chapters
permit readers to begin working through the traumatic nature of the cross.
In each, meditation on the murder of a son or daughter invites reflection
on the crucifixion as a type of infanticide; simply, when a child is killed, the
God who commands his own son to die goes on trial. Sometimes he gets off.
Sometimes he does not.

Chapter 2

Cross as Murder, Cross as Wound

Recent Developments in Atonement
Theology and Trauma Theory

> Insofar as it is a murder, the Crucifixion cannot possibly
> be the means of our justification. The crucified Jesus is not
> suffering retributive punishment at the hands of human agents
> implementing divine justice; he is suffering evil. The issue,
> then, is how can Jesus' death be the divine response to evil if it
> is itself evil—a horrific reality that cries out to heaven.
>
> —Jerome Miller

One of this book's central claims is that the treatment of Christianity in American literature over the past sixty years mirrors its treatment in American theology. More specifically, in recent years, some of the United States' most prominent theologians and creative writers have subjected the cross to sustained scrutiny with an eye to critiquing atonement, the idea that the Jesus's death produces some real benefit for humankind. The five chapters that follow this one are devoted to tracing this trend in six novels, but before we turn to them, we must first review the history of the development of atonement theology in order to answer a few crucial questions: What is atonement, and what are its most prominent versions? What are their origins? And how and why do some modern theologians come to critique—or even reject—these theories? For those who reject atonement outright, the cross is not a salvation but a trauma, a wound that will not heal. Certain theologians, then, turn to the developing field of trauma theory to interpret the post-atonement cross. Thus, the chapter concludes with a review of the pieces of trauma theory relevant to the literary interpretations that play out in the subsequent chapters.

The word "atonement" actually has an English etymology; it is a portmanteau combining the preposition "at" with the arcane noun "onement," which means what it sounds like: union, unity, or oneness. The *Oxford English Dictionary* traces the first recorded use of the word to 1513, and all of its definitions revolve around the notions of reconciliation, togetherness, or reunion. In Christian theology, atonement is the process by which God reconciles himself with the sinful world, almost always with the help of his son, Jesus. In the late second century, Origen and Irenaeus developed the first fully realized theories of Christian atonement, but one can trace related ideas back to Biblical texts. The first references to atonement appear in the classical Judaism of the *Tanakh*. In Leviticus 16, God commands Moses to institute a yearly festival—later referred to as *yom hakipurim*, or the Day of Atonement—during which the sins of the people will be wiped away: "In the seventh month, on the tenth day of the month, you shall deny yourselves, and shall do no work, neither the citizen nor the alien who resides among you. For on this day atonement shall be made for you, to cleanse you; for all your sins you shall be clean before the Lord" (16:29–32). The preceding passages from Leviticus 16 describe a sequence of animal sacrifices that effect the desired reconciliation. And while few Jews continue the sacrificial rituals described in Leviticus, Yom Kippur remains the most important Jewish holiday, and the Jewish portrait of atonement shapes its Christian counterpart.

We can see the clearest link between Christian and Jewish sources in Romans 3, when Paul speaks of the power of Jesus's redemptive sacrifice: "there is no distinction, since all have sinned and fall short of the glory of God; they are now justified by his grace as a gift, through the redemption that is in Christ Jesus, whom God put forward as a sacrifice of atonement by his blood, effective through faith" (3:22–25). Though "sacrifice of atonement" in verse 25 captures some of Paul's meaning, "place of atonement" is actually a closer translation of the Greek original *hilasterion*, which is itself a rendering of the Hebrew *kapporeth*.[1] The *kapporeth* is, roughly, the lid of the ark of the covenant, a piece of furniture remarkable for the fact that God would occasionally manifest himself between the two angel statuettes fastened to it.[2] However, the *kapporeth* gains further importance from its role in the Yom Kippur rituals. As Karl Barth wrote in his exhaustive commentary on Romans, the mercy seat is "the place where, on the great day of Atonement, the people were reconciled to God by the sprinkling of blood."[3] Thus, by calling Jesus the *kapporeth*, *hilasterion*, or mercy seat, Paul suggests that Jesus has taken over some of the responsibilities—and powers—once claimed by the Jewish temple priests. For Paul, Jesus both recalls and ultimately supersedes the temple sacrifices of ritual Judaism, and he takes on the ability to both justify and redeem sinners.

Yet, as Martin Hengel argues in *The Atonement*, Jesus's death on the cross is unique—and ultimately distinct from the atoning work done on Yom Kippur. Jewish atonement rituals are repeated annually, and the expiation they offer is available only to Jews. By contrast, Jesus completes the work of atonement once—on the cross. This sacrifice is understood to be perfectly and permanently efficacious, and available to all people.[4] Thus does Christian atonement, for Hengel, break away from its Jewish forerunner. Hengel further contends that the Christian understanding of atonement dates back to Biblical times—and perhaps even to the teachings of Jesus himself.[5] He identifies a passage from Mark—again, the earliest gospel, likely written approximately thirty years after Christ's death—as an early proof text for Christian atonement.[6] In it, Jesus claims that "the Son of Man came not to be served but to serve, and to give his life a ransom for many" (10:43–45).[7] This idea of death as ransom—that Jesus's demise on the cross might have salvific exchange value—is a seed that will eventually produce fuller-formed atonement theologies in later centuries. Nonetheless, even a few decades after Jesus's death, authors had begun to develop theories regarding the salutary nature of the crucifixion.

While the evangelists interpret the cross in ways that anticipate later Christian atonement theories, the apostle Paul is the early genius of atonement theology. In his epistles, he provides thumbnail sketches of most of the models of atonement to come. Paul is certain that Jesus's death on the cross reconciles God with the sinful world and thus has saving power for the believer; he writes, "In Christ God was reconciling the world to himself, not counting their trespasses against them" (2 Cor. 5:19). However, he offers multiple theories as to how this process of reconciliation actually unfolds. Stephen Finlan reviews the metaphors Paul uses in his *Problems with Atonement*.[8] The most prominent analogies liken Jesus's death to a purification sacrifice, a "mercy seat," a scapegoat ritual, a Passover lamb, a ransom, and a payment for human sin.[9] These last two develop into what we might term "economic" theories of atonement, wherein the death of Jesus takes on fungible value. In Romans 4:25, Paul describes Jesus's death as a currency that pays for the sins of humanity: "It will be reckoned to us who believe in him and who raised Jesus our Lord from the dead, who was handed over to death for our trespasses and was raised for our justification." This passage and others like it lay the foundation for a number of later atonement theories that assert the crucifixion's power to substitute for, satisfy, or compensate God for human sin.

The preceding is not an exhaustive list of the images Paul invents to describe the reconciliation Jesus effects on the cross. However, the list's variety indicates that Paul is not wedded to a single theory. Instead, he chooses to test a variety of models, each of which provides *partial* insight into the nature of Jesus's death. Perhaps taking a cue from Paul, von Balthasar rejects the notion that early interpretations of the cross can ever "be reduced to a 'system'" and instead chooses to characterize the early church's thinking about atonement as "different theologoumena, circling concentrically around a transcendent core."[10] Von Balthasar groups these theologoumena into five categories, or "motifs": "(1) The Son gives himself, through God the Father, for the world's salvation. (2) The Sinless One 'changes places' with sinners . . . (3) Man is thus set free (ransomed, redeemed, released). (4) More than this, however, he is initiated into the divine life of the Trinity.

(5) Consequently, the whole process is shown to be the result of an initiative on the part of divine love."[11] According to von Balthasar, the Christian's understanding of atonement theology must not only take into account all of these motifs but must also give each sufficient weight. "All these elements are involved simultaneously: each has its role, each belongs on stage."[12] What von Balthasar figures as a sort of dramatic balance Finlan calls "interpenetration," and he contends that the Christian Bible—and specifically Paul—"uses many metaphors [to explain atonement . . .] and even uses one metaphor to interpret another. The metaphors interpenetrate, yet they can be discerned as discrete building blocks that are differently combined in different passages. Paul has not invested everything in any one metaphor."[13] Biblical authors' unwillingness to put all their eggs in one basket may inspire later Christian leaders to hedge their bets, too: no major church has ever established a single orthodox theology of atonement.

However, Paul's open-mindedness and von Balthasar's provisos notwithstanding, many Christian thinkers *have* gone ahead to develop single atonement motifs into full-blown theories, or systems. I follow the early twentieth-century theologian Gustaf Aulén in grouping them into three main categories: classic, objective, and subjective.[14] Aulén calls the first the Christus Victor model, which he promotes in his book of the same name. According to Aulén, while the influence of Christus Victor waned in medieval times, it was the predominant interpretation of the cross in the early history of the church. His book is an effort to hasten the church's return to this model for understanding the atoning value of the crucifixion. According to this theory, Jesus's death represents a victory over the forces of evil. Writes Aulén, "This type of view may be described provisionally as the 'dramatic.' Its central theme is the idea of the Atonement as a Divine conflict and victory; Christ—Christus Victor—fights against and triumphs over the evil powers of the world, the 'tyrants' under which mankind is in bondage and suffering, and in Him God reconciles the world to himself."[15] This classic/dramatic model of atonement is, in fact, military, and in it, Jesus is God's secret weapon in the battle against satanic forces. Timothy Gorringe explains the nature of the trap Jesus helps God set: "The devil acquired rights over humankind at the Fall, but when he exercises these rights over a perfectly sinless creature he goes beyond appointed limits and forfeits his due."[16] For proponents of a related atonement theory often called the ransom model, Jesus's death is a payment handed over to Satan in exchange for the rights to humanity.[17] Some theologians—among them Anselm—reject such theories because they assume a dualistic universe in which evil exists and has real power.[18] But Aulén describes one of the model's strengths as its "continuity." In continuous atonement theories, Christ and God stand shoulder to shoulder in the moment of Jesus's death, united in their assault on the forces of evil. In discontinuous theories of atonement, Jesus and God are set apart at the moment of the crucifixion, and a distance opens up between the deity and humanity.[19] Aulén argues that Christus Victor is the dominant model of atonement in the first millennium C.E. and notes that Luther is another of its strong proponents.

A few decades in the eleventh and twelfth centuries give rise to the two other major types of atonement theology, sometimes called "objective" and "subjective." The best-known version of objective atonement theology—often referred to as the "satisfaction" model—is fathered by Saint Anselm, a Benedictine monk, the Archbishop of Canterbury, a Doctor of the Church, and one of the great thinkers of the Christian tradition. In *Cur Deus Homo*, or *Why God Became Man*, Anselm develops the satisfaction model and moves sharply away from the perceived dualism of Christus Victor.[20] Anselm rejects the notion that the devil has any purchase over humanity, and he reconceives atonement as an internal economy of sin and redemption. According to Anselm, sin incurs a debt to God—a debt so heavy that humans are unable to repay it. Though humans try to make up for sin by being righteous, God already expects us to live well, and our righteousness is no fit compensation for our errors. A human who wants a reward for fulfilling basic human duties is as absurd as a convict who expects to be released from prison for paying his taxes. Further, humans cannot offer their deaths as exchange for sin, because those deaths will occur anyway. And while an omnipotent God is capable of forgiving human sin, the unpunished error would be an affront to divine honor—a possibility that Anselm will not consider. However, Jesus's undeserved death on the cross restores divine honor and serves as the punishment that should otherwise fall upon us. Anselm writes, "No member of the human race except Christ ever gave to God, by dying, anything which that person was not at some time going to lose as a matter of necessity. Nor did anyone ever pay a debt to God which he did not owe. But Christ of his own accord gave to his Father what he was never going to lose as a matter of necessity, and he paid, on behalf of sinners, a debt which he did not owe."[21] Essentially, no normal human "owns" anything—neither life, death, nor action. All are owed to the God who creates and provides them. Jesus, on the other hand, owes neither his life nor his death to God. And insofar as Jesus is more than human, his life and death are of infinite worth. Thus, in freely offering himself up to God on the cross, Jesus acts as a supernumerary transaction that restores God's honor by rebalancing the scales that were thrown off kilter by the weight of human sin.[22] For Anselm, only Jesus, who is part divine and part human, can carry off such a transaction. Ironically, the debt of human sin is so onerous that "only God was capable of repaying it, assuming that there should be a man identical with God. Hence it was a necessity that God should take man into the unity of his person, so that one who ought, by virtue of his nature, to make the repayment and was not capable of doing so, should be one who, by virtue of his person, was capable of it."[23] Simply, only a human can "own" the debt of sin, and only a God can repay it; hence, Jesus must be both, and only by his miraculous dual nature is human sin canceled out and reconciliation with God effected. David Bentley Hart clarifies:

> Christ as a man owes God his perfect obedience, which he gladly proffers, but as a sinless man he does not owe God his death; when Christ voluntarily surrenders his infinitely precious life for God's honor, and the Father accepts it, the superabundance of its worth calls forth some gracious recompense from God's justice . . . God's infinite honor being more than infinitely satisfied, humanity's debt before God is remitted and humanity receives the grace of salvation.[24]

Anselm's satisfaction model is similar to another theory often referred to as "penal substitution." Also transactional in nature, the penal substitution model replaces the financial language of Anselm's writing with legal metaphors. John Sanders traces the penal model back to Protestant Reformers like Calvin.[25] Instead of incurring debt, sin deserves punishment from a just God. And while God is merciful, unpunished sin is a stain on divine justice. Nonetheless, rather than afflict humans, God shunts punishment onto Jesus, a loving, perfect man who receives the punishment that we deserve. Though the terms of the penal equation differ from those of Anselm's system, the relationships remain consistent, and the two models are close analogues. Though neither has ever been formally adopted as official Christian doctrine, they are very nearly Christian orthodoxy. In a 2009 edition of *Christian Century*, William C. Placher claims that "a great many Christians would define such a substitutionary view of the atonement as simply part of what orthodox Christians believe."[26] Substitionary, satisfaction, and ransom models of atonement are referred to as objective because in them, humans are the object of atonement: they are its target, its predicate.

Theologians note the ways in which Anselm's model of atonement shows the marks of his historical moment. By the late eleventh century, when Anselm wrote *Cur Deus Homo*, feudalism prevailed as the most popular form of land distribution and social control. Thus, Anselm's God closely resembles a feudal lord. Adolf von Harnack developed this claim in his *History of Dogma*, describing Anselm's deity as a "mighty private person, who is incensed at the injury done to his honour and does not forgo his wrath till he has received an at least adequately great equivalent."[27] Anselm characterizes God as a powerful landowner whose honor is endangered by his serfs' misdeeds. We shall examine some of the defects of this portrait later, but we can begin by noting that the seeming hard-heartedness of Anselm's God—who would rather have bloody punishment inflicted on his son than have his honor slighted—inspires the third major strain of atonement thinking, often called "subjective."[28] Peter Abelard (1079–1142), better known for his ill-fated dalliances with Heloise, offered an alternative to Anselm's objective satisfaction theory in his commentary on Romans.[29] Abelard refuses Anselm's

God, who is only satisfied by the death of an innocent; he exclaims, "How cruel and wicked it seems that anyone should demand the blood of an innocent person as the price of anything, or that it should in any way please him that an innocent man should be slain—still less that God should consider the death of his Son so agreeable that by it he should be reconciled to the whole world."[30] Here, Abelard simply holds Anselm's God to a standard of basic human decency and finds him lacking. Therefore, he develops a "subjective" version of atonement theory that does not require anyone to do penance to an essentially indecent God. Most refer to Abelard's model as the "moral example" theory; in it, Jesus's life and death serve as examples of ideal human behavior, and Jesus reconciles us to God by modeling Christian virtues like self-sacrifice, faithful perseverance, and openness to divine love. That he exemplifies these virtues in his life and on the cross indicates the depth of his devotion to God. Abelard explains:

> Through this unique act of grace manifested to us—in that his Son has taken upon himself our nature and preserved therein in teaching us by word and example even unto death—he has more fully bound us to himself by love; with the result that our hearts should be enkindled by such a gift of divine grace, and true charity should not now shrink from enduring anything for him . . . everyone becomes more righteous—by which we mean a greater lover of the Lord—after the Passion of the Christ than before, since a realized gift inspires greater love than one which is only hoped for.[31]

Though Christ's behavior is a simple act of love, Abelard expects that its effect will be great. Thus, he uses totally inclusive language to explain the change that overcomes people after Jesus: "everyone becomes more righteous . . . after the Passion." Because of its focus on compassion and righteousness, Abelard's is usually understood as a kinder atonement in which Jesus gives up his life because he loves humanity. The moral example theory is often referred to as subjective because it puts the onus on humans to live a life worthy of Jesus's self-sacrifice. (By contrast, Anselmian atonement is "objective" insofar as it requires Jesus to do the work; humans reap the benefits of his death regardless.) Abelard's model is ethical in that it gives us a map for avoiding the sin that keeps us from God. And if we follow in Jesus's footsteps, we are reconciled with the Lord, and Jesus's sacrifice successfully atones. But to focus too heavily on the necessity of a "subjective" human response is to lose sight of the crucial importance of Jesus's example in invoking that response. As Elizabeth Moberly writes, "The fact that reconciliation will include conversion and amendment should not be taken to imply that the change in man is to be detached from what God has done to bring about this change. Change in man is not an *alternative* to the action of God . . . What Abelard does is to speak of both aspects of redemption—what Christ has done, and how this works out in human lives."[32] She prefers to call Jesus's death not merely "exemplarist" but "kenotic," implying that the crucifixion is a self-emptying so dramatic that no one other than Jesus could complete such a feat of virtue.

As the American theologian Paul Tillich notes in his *Systematic Theology*, all of these varied theories of atonement have been approved by the church at some point. Though no one has ever become official doctrine, all speak some unique truth about the nature and power of Jesus's crucifixion. However, Tillich continues, "each of them has a special strength and a special weakness,"[33] and every major strand of atonement thinking is open to critique. We have begun to observe some of the main objections to each theory. Christus Victor grants too much power to the devil. Satisfaction characterizes God as petty—or even cruel. And moral example models downplay the importance of the crucifixion, emphasizing instead the initiative of believers to react to Christ's action. These various critiques have circulated in theological circles for nearly a thousand years. But the murmurs of dissent have occasionally organized themselves into a chorus—first and most vocally during the Enlightenment. As Alister McGrath explains, Enlightenment thinkers who insisted on the importance of reason were loath to accept doctrines derived from revelation, atonement among them.[34] Working in this vein, the nineteenth-century authors Ernest Renan and George Friedrich Strauss wrote critical biographies of Jesus that disavowed his divinity and dismissed atonement theology (and indeed, most theology) as superstition and supernaturalism. However, some argued that these authors and their contemporaries may have done more to strengthen Christianity than damage it. While Renan, as an example, strove to demythologize the gospel accounts of Jesus's life, he also served both to anticipate and to model modern scholarly approaches to Christian scripture. And as C. J. T. Talar remarks, while Catholic critics excoriate Renan for his *Life of Jesus*, the book causes many others to "take religion seriously once more."[35]

However, since the 1960s in the United States, a new group of authors has offered more piercing—and perhaps more persistent—criticisms of atonement theology. James R. A. Merrick, ominously, describes this development as a "dark, thunderous storm, a distant echo of the one during Christ's crucifixion."[36] It boils down to a few crucial points: the crucifixion represents an instance of world-shattering violence that is unjust and undeserved. Christianity is wrong to make violence a condition of salvation. Further, the atonement encourages violent behavior and the dehumanization of the other. Last, prevalent atonement theories bolster systems of oppression like racism and misogyny. These are dramatic claims against one of the core Christian theologies. But most surprising is the fact that many originate from within the Christian tradition, from believers, converts, and professional theologians. Their arguments force Christians to confront difficult questions: does a clear-eyed view of atonement reveal the fact that Christianity is a violent religion? If so, how do Christians revise their faith around this stark revelation? Or if atonement is violent but unnecessary, can believers move on without it? Before grappling with some of these challenges, we should first summarize the most salient modern critiques of atonement.

Many of the authors developing these critiques know Aulén's influential work, and if they do not, they share his contention that subjective and objective versions of atonement are built on what he calls a "discontinuity." Again, Aulén distinguishes between continuous and discontinuous versions of atonement theology. In continuous theories, God and Jesus work *together* in the moment of the crucifixion to enact the process of reconciliation. By contrast, discontinuous models cast Father and Son as standing apart in the moment of the crucifixion; they are notable for the distance that separates them:

> In the Latin [objective] type God seems to stand more at a distance; for the satisfaction is paid by man, in the person of Christ, to God. In the [subjective] type God stands still more at a distance; as far as He is concerned, no atonement is needed, and all the emphasis is on *man's movement to God*, on that which is accomplished in the world of men. That is to say, the essential Christian idea of a way of God to man, which dominates the classic type [Christus Victor], is weakened in the Latin type, and lost in the subjective type.[37]

In other words, discontinuous models of the atonement characterize the suffering of the cross as *inflicted upon* Jesus—rather than shared with him. Perhaps it comes as a surprise that the move to recast the cross as violence the Son must endure is relatively new. Most Christians have evaded or deflected such a characterization for centuries. As Brock and Parker argue in *Saving Paradise*, for the first millennium of its existence, Christianity did not focus on Jesus's pain at the crucifixion. They note that images of Jesus's suffering body do not regularly appear in churches (or in Christian art) until the tenth century.[38] And while Anselm and others refocus Christians' attention on the cross shortly thereafter, they do so in such a way as to emphasize its sacrificial nature. For Anselm, the cross may be a moment of suffering, but that suffering is outrageously productive. Jesus's death is a tragedy that buys the salvation of humanity and the reconciliation of God with a sinful world. And this is the crucial distinction between violence and sacrifice. Violence is destructive; sacrifice is productive—and in the case of the cross, *extremely* productive.[39] In the most recent edition of the *Oxford English Dictionary*, sacrifice is defined as "the destruction or surrender of something valued or desired for the sake of something having, or regarded as having, a higher or a more pressing claim." And what higher claim is there than the salvation of the whole world? Simply, the cross is a harm, but it is a harm of nearly infinite worth. Thus, those who see the cross as a sacrifice tend to ignore the injury it requires. Further, Jesus is resurrected a few days later: what's a few days among the dead as compared with the secure deliverance of all people in all times? This sacrificial reading of the cross persists in the United States well into the twentieth century. Tillich—with Niebuhr, the most important twentieth-century American theologian—takes a distinctly non-Anselmian interpretation of the cross, but he still argues that the crucifixion is a sacrifice whose injury is dwarfed by the fact that it rectifies humanity's estrangement from the deity. Further, Susan Mizruchi argues that sacrifice is a category that underpins not only American theology but American culture. She engages nineteenth- and twentieth-century American authors for whom the category of sacrifice "is not only necessary to modern Western society, it is basic; it makes society what it is."[40] This sacrificial reading of the crucifixion has dominated world Christianity since the time of Anselm and has obscured the competing portrayals of the cross as a moment of destructive violence.

No author is more important to attacking sacrificial readings of the crucifixion than René Girard, the French-born American cultural historian who spent most of his academic career at Johns Hopkins and Stanford. Girard long focused on the powerful bonds that link religion to violence, and in *Things Hidden since the Foundation of the World*, he claims that the crucifixion is not a sacrifice but instead the purest possible representation of human cruelty:

> The Gospels only speak of *sacrifices* in order to reject them and deny them any validity. Jesus counters the ritualism of the Pharisees with an anti-sacrificial quotation from Hosea: 'Go and learn what this means, "I desire mercy, and not sacrifice"' (Matthew 9, 13) . . . There is nothing in the Gospels to suggest that the death of Jesus is a sacrifice, whatever definition (expiation, substitution, etc.) we may give for that sacrifice. At no point in the Gospels is the death of Jesus defined as a sacrifice. The passages that are invoked to justify a sacrificial conception of the Passion both can and should be interpreted with no reference to sacrifice in any of the accepted meanings . . . the sacrificial interpretation of the Passion must be criticized and exposed as a most enormous and paradoxical misunderstanding—and at the same time as something necessary—and as the most revealing indication of mankind's radical incapacity to understand its own violence, even what that violence is conveyed in the most explicit fashion.[41]

For Girard, humanity's penchant for bloodshed is matched only by its inability to recognize violence for what it is, and this stunning failure explains why we are only now coming to realize fully the violent nature of the crucifixion. As the above quote suggests, Girard rejects traditional models of atonement. Jesus does not expiate, he does not substitute, he does not satisfy, and he is not an example of behavior we should emulate. Thus, Girard dismisses all three brands of atonement outlined above. He calls them "absurdities" and singles out Anselmian-style atonement for special disdain: in such theories, "God feels the need to revenge his honour, which has been tainted by the sins of humanity, and so on. Not only does god require a new victim, but he requires the victim who is most precious and dear to him, his very son. No doubt this line of reasoning has done more than anything else to discredit Christianity in the eyes of people of goodwill in the modern world."[42] Girard contends that Christianity would be saved from this "discredit" if only we could acknowledge that the God of the Bible is a "non-violent deity" whose religious *cultus* should primarily involve identifying and ameliorating victimization and violence.[43]

For Girard, however, Jesus's death is not simply one more act of meaningless violence. While Girard claims that it is not a "sacrifice," the crucifixion nonetheless serves an important function: exposing the cycles of retributive violence that underpin all human action. According to Girard, Christ is the prime example of "the scapegoat"—the central figure in his book of the same name.[44] The scapegoat appears first in Leviticus, and for early Jews, it is a ritual animal symbolically loaded with the sin of the community and banished to the wilderness. In Girard's rendering, however, the scapegoat bears not sin but violence. In his anthropology, humans are driven by "mimetic desire": simply, we want things because we see others wanting them, and our shared desire can end only in rivalry. (The reader may hear echoes of Hobbes.) In time, this rivalry will inevitably devolve into violence, retribution, and, if unchecked, conflagration. The scapegoat serves as a pressure-release valve; the violence that would otherwise destroy humanity is redirected onto an innocent individual or group, and the victim's suffering, though undeserved, works to bear away the blood and break the cycle. The contemporary theologian S. Mark Heim sums it up as follows: "Communities solve their internal conflicts by uniting against a chosen victim. This violence staves off more generalized factional or retributive violence."[45] For Girard, Jesus is just such a "chosen" victim, selected to endure and dispel violence; however, as a scapegoat he is too perfect. He is a wholly innocent, pure outsider whose bloody punishment is entirely undeserved and unjust. He does not resist his punishment and death, and his disciples do not seek to avenge his execution. His perfection is a wrench thrown into the system of violence and mimetic desire, and his suffering dramatizes and exposes the injustice of the system that kills him. As Girard's interlocutor Jean-Michel Oughourlian explains, in Christ's crucifixion

the gods of violence are devalued. The machine is broken, and the mechanism of expulsion will not work any more. Christ's murderers have acted in vain. Rather, they have acted in an extremely fruitful way, in so far as they have helped Christ to record the objective truth of violence within the gospel text. This truth—however much it may be understood and travestied—will make its slow way, finally achieving its disruptive effect like an insidious poison.[46]

The systems of violence are entrenched, and this "poison" will take time to do its work. However, Girard—who converted to Roman Catholicism while developing his critical edifice—is the evangelist of his own interpretation of the gospel, and he has faith that with time, a correct understanding of the crucifixion will lead to the slow dissolution of human enmity.

Heim has taken up Girard's call to spread a nonsacrificial reading of the Christian gospel. In *Saved from Sacrifice*, he develops a new theology that builds on Girard's foundation. Though he accepts the bulk of Girardian theory, he presses on in an effort to describe the belief and praxis of what we might call the Girardian Christian. More explicitly than his predecessor, Heim details the ways in which accepting Girard's reading of the cross means denying Anselm's. He contends that Anselm's satisfaction "preserves paradox, but the wrong one. He has made the cross a celebration of the sacrifice it is meant to overcome."[47] Heim also rejects the penal models that build on Anselmian atonement: "Christ did not die as he did to cancel an infinity of deserved punishment for humanity with the infinitely undeserved suffering of innocent divinity. The legal apparatus around the crucifixion is not there because God has a satisfaction case to prosecute . . . but because the machinery of false accusation and political and religious legitimacy are part of the way sacred violence works."[48] For Heim, Jesus dies not to enforce a divine legal system but to show us how human justice—which often involves scapegoating—is actually unjust. So for Heim, when Christ dies on the cross, he doesn't save us from sin; he saves us from ourselves: "Christ died for us, to save us from what killed him. And what killed him was not God's justice but our redemptive violence. He stepped in between our violence and our victims, and has been a haunting presence there ever since."[49] Simply, if Christ did not die, we would kill each other. For Heim, this realization should inspire at least two ethical responses in the believer. First, as the cross teaches us the evil of violence and mimetic desire, the believer has a new responsibility to join and bolster "community without scapegoats."[50] He also argues that believers living under this new dispensation must emphasize nonsacrificial interpretation of texts that have long been read as supporting atonement theologies like Anselm's.

Nonetheless, while both Heim and Girard offer convincing alternative readings of the cross, both preserve the violent death of Jesus as a crucial part of the divine plan. Each is a system in which an act of violence is still the means by which God saves. In brief, any atonement model that maintains that Jesus's violent death has value remains in some sense "sacrificial." Jerome Miller argues that any theory of atonement that preserves the meaningfulness of Jesus's suffering can only perpetuate or encourage others' suffering. He writes, "the wounds inflicted on Jesus and the suffering they entail cannot redeem humanity from historical evil since they are themselves paradigmatic examples of such evil."[51] Heim tries to guard against this critique by arguing that his system is a continuous atonement theory. He writes:

We saw that Anselm's theology requires [God and Jesus] to take up opposing positions in the work of redemption, one inflicting God's wrath and the other bearing it. It is central to Anselm's doctrine that this must be a quite literal opposition, where divine mercy and divine justice settle their differences by violence. The elevation of that opposition is the sign of a mistaken theology. The truth is that God and Jesus together submit themselves to human violence. Both suffer its results. Both reveal and overcome it. God does not require the death of the Son anymore than Jesus requires the helpless bereavement of the father. Jesus' suffering is not required as an offering to satisfy God anymore than one member of a team undertaking a very dangerous rescue mission "requires" another, dearly loved member to be in a place of peril or pain. They are constantly and consistently on the same side.[52]

Here, Heim is channeling the mid-century German theologian Jürgen Moltmann, whose 1973 work *The Crucified God* represents the most influential modern continuous theology of atonement.[53] In it, Moltmann argues not only that God is present in the body of Jesus as he suffers on the cross, but that the very nature of the godhead is altered by that moment of world-rending pain. God, like humanity, is changed by suffering, and the cross allows God both to fully experience and witness to human suffering and grief. Moltmann's theology is revolutionary—and controversial—in that it exchanges God's immutability and omnipotence for his familiarity with the dark side of human existence. Nonetheless, it has struck a chord with believers and theologians alike in a post-Holocaust, postbomb world in which the devastation of human pain has been put so spectacularly on display. Darby Kathleen Ray points out that some American liberation theologians—notably the Peruvian-born Notre Dame professor Gustavo Gutierrez—have incorporated pieces of Moltmann's process theology into their thinking and writing. Liberation theologians, who often focus on the plight of citizens of the developing world, recognize that pain and suffering are a natural part of life, especially for the poor and oppressed. Thus, they characterize Jesus's incarnation, mission, and death as partaking in the full gamut of human experience, both its joys and its sorrows. His death on the cross, then, is simply the logical extension of his participation in humanity. Ray claims that liberation theologians "are keenly aware of massive human suffering and attempt to make theological sense of it. In this effort, they recognize that to exempt God from suffering—to conceptualize God as wholly transcendent and impassible—is to render God irrelevant to human experience."[54] For Moltmann and the liberation theologians, *God* suffers on the cross. And while the crucifixion exemplifies victimization and cruelty, God is their target, not their author. Nonetheless, even this path has its pitfalls. In refiguring suffering as both a human and a divine experience, Moltmann and the rest risk the reification—or even the valorization—of human pain. Suffering is a part of human experience, but it should not be its focus, and while we may want a sympathetic theory of atonement, we do not want a masochistic one. Writes Ray, "The danger of this position is that it tends to eternalize suffering, to offer it a theological back door to acceptability, and that, therefore, it may undermine human resistance to unjust suffering. If *the* locus of redemption is God's suffering and death . . . then suffering and death can be interpreted as salvific *in themselves*."[55] Sensing its danger, Ray distances herself from the liberation theologians' approach to the cross. She also rejects standard interpretations of Anselmian (objective) and Abelardian (subjective) models, noting their "abusive potential," and opts for a reworked version of Aulén's Christus Victor model.[56]

J. Denny Weaver, one of the more vocal contemporary critics of classic atonement theology, follows Ray in taking Aulén's "classic" theory of atonement as a starting point for his efforts to correct our understanding of the cross. However, he offers wholesale criticism of traditional models of atonement, suggesting that all of them are steeped in blood: "all standard images of atonement have problematic violent dimensions that render them unacceptable."[57] His criticism of Anselm unfolds along familiar lines. However, he argues that we should also reject Abelard, whose moral influence theory is intended to avoid some of the cruelties of satisfaction. To review, Abelard changes the motive behind Christ's death; Jesus goes to the cross as a loving exemplar of self-sacrifice and compassion. However, he still goes to the cross—ostensibly at God's request. Writes Weaver, "By directing the death of Jesus toward humanity as an act of love, the result is an atonement motif, in which the Father has one of his children—the divine Son—killed in order to show love to the rest of the Father's children, namely us sinners."[58] Abelard's God is less petty than Anselm's, but he still works salvation through torturous death. Further, for Weaver, traditional Christus Victor models suffer from essentially the same defect. They describe the reasons for Jesus's death differently, but they still cast God the Father as requesting or requiring the death of his son. Whether Christ dies fighting the forces of the devil or as a ransom payment to demonic forces, he still perishes at God's command, and his death is the vehicle of human salvation. Further, Weaver rejects Moltmann's Trinitarian suggestion that God is present in Christ on the cross—subject to the same pain and therefore not "responsible" for Jesus's death. He argues that such continuous versions of the atonement "[camouflage] but [do] not fundamentally deal with the abusive imagery."[59] (He further suggests that a God who would willingly undergo such disgusting torture must be understood as either masochistic or suicidal.) Ultimately, the moral influence and Christus Victor models are as problematic as Anselmian satisfaction, and all three strands of atonement theology boil down to one disturbing truth: "classic atonement doctrines . . . portray an image of God as either divine avenger or punisher and/or as a child abuser, a Father who arranges the death of one child for the benefit of others."[60]

Despite the severity of this claim, Weaver believes that atonement is not beyond rescue; by way of rehabilitation, he develops a new theory called the "Narrative Christus Victor" model.[61] But not all who reject traditional atonement models are so sanguine about the theory's prospects moving forward. Brock and Parker share Weaver's belief that mainstream Christianity portrays God as abusive or, worse, filicidal. Further, they suggest that Christianity loses its power to save and succor—especially for the victimized—if it holds on to such a violent deity: "Christianity could not promise healing for victims of intimate violence as long as its central image was a divine parent who required the death of his child."[62] Incorporating the violence of the cross into a personal belief system is often difficult; for victims of abuse, the task is nearly impossible. Therefore, in developing a deeply personal response to traditional atonement theology, Brock and Parker beat a path away from the cross, imagining it as a tragedy we must live through rather than a victory we should celebrate. Further, they affirm that the presence of Jesus persists to this day not because of the crucifixion, but *in spite of it*. Traditional efforts to turn the suffering of the cross into a symbol of redemption have backfired, leading to the unnecessary valorization of pain and violence while also bolstering systems of oppression. They claim that standard interpretations of the cross strengthen the structures of victimization and, ironically, cut us off from the true message of Christ: "Western Christianity claims that we are saved by the execution, that violence and terror reveal the grace of God. This claim isolates Jesus, as violence isolates its victims. When the victims of violence are made singular, solitary, unprecedented in their pain, the power of violence remains."[63] Unlike mainstream Western Christian theologians who go before, Brock and Parker claim that Jesus's death is neither unique nor special. Instead, the true message of his death is closely related to its depressing unoriginality. Jesus is one of countless millions who have died unjustly at the hands of oppressors. The miracle, then, is not simply that Jesus dies, but that he dies and is remembered—that he dies and we praise him still. The miracle is that his love, and the love of God that he embodies, can be recovered in the wake of the violence done to him. They continue, "Christianity bears the marks of unresolved trauma. Jesus's resurrection and the continuation of his movement are not triumphs, but a glimpse of the power of survival, of the embers that survive the deluge."[64] With the help of Brock and Parker's gorgeous re-visioning, we can curse the powers that bring Jesus low—the violence, the pain, the suffering, and the oppression—while still testifying to the potency of his teaching and the miracle of his survival. Jesus's suffering death is a tragedy to the core, but the love he preaches remains, and it is the responsibility of the believer to carry on in its terrible wake.

There is one more modern response to the atonement that bears mention, and it is the darkest of all. In 1993, Brock wrote an admiring foreword to a "theology of protest" composed by the Jewish theologian David R. Blumenthal. The title of Blumenthal's book, *Facing the Abusing God*, gestures toward the most provocative part of its thesis—that God can be cruel. (I will return to Blumenthal repeatedly in my discussion of Cormac McCarthy in chapter 7.)

In this space, it is impossible to plumb the depths of his complex, multigeneric study. Nonetheless, we may briefly review some of the stark theological questions he poses: Is God at least partially responsible for this world's stunning evils? Can a God that we often paint as loving also be malicious? For Blumenthal, the answer to both questions is yes. His "personalist" theology imagines a God who has various identifiable traits: loving-kindness, fairness, and power, to name a few. But he also asserts, with scriptural backing, that God can be unjust, and that God is not perfect.[65] Recognition of these latter traits leads Blumenthal to develop a sequence of probing commentaries on the Psalms that vent the author's frustration with a deity who often appears arbitrary, stubborn, forgetful, negligent, and, indeed, abusing. In a response to Psalm 109, which Blumenthal calls a song of abuse, the author lays out his accusation: "If I am abused, then He is the Abuser. If I am violated, then He is the Perpetrator. If I must do intimate battle, then He is the Adversary. If I must engage in life-and-death combat in the innermost world of the self, then He is the One Who Threatens. God is the Abuser, and we are the abused. We live and re-live God's abusiveness. We tell the stories, we recall the history, and we do not even know what we are saying."[66] For orthodox theists who often characterize God as omnipotent, omniscient, and omnibenevolent, these are startling statements. For Blumenthal—and other protest theologians—they are not only acceptable but, perhaps, healing. Only by allowing the fact that the mostly good God of the Bible is not totally good can we come to a realistic theology that better explains the pain and suffering in which God simply must have some hand. In her foreword, Brock claims that his "Jewish way of doing theology is rich and breaks new methodological ground. It will, I hope, become more common in Christian theology."[67] To accept the possibility that God can be abusive leads to the simplest but most uncomfortable reading of atonement: the crucifixion is an instance of divine abuse. And it is one that Biblical interpretation and our observation of the world prepare us for. From the vantage Blumenthal provides, God can be cruel, and the cross is an instance of such cruelty.

Thus far, we have focused on theoretical critiques of traditional atonement models. Most deal with the character of God, the portrayal of Jesus, and the nature of the relationship between them. However, in outlining salient modern criticisms of atonement, it is as important to review practical arguments against it. For some contend that atonement theology encourages believers to behave badly. More simply, atonement may be objectionable not only for what it is *but for what it does*. The authors who level practical criticisms of atonement theology come from different backgrounds, but they often return to the following claims: atonement discourages active resistance against injustice and oppression. Atonement encourages passive endurance of unjust suffering and thus encourages victimization. And atonement suggests that guilt—and therefore punishment—is fungible and hence transferable; thus, it lays the groundwork for scapegoating.

James H. Cone, one of the giants of black theology, developed his own critique of atonement in his *God of the Oppressed*. (Cone anchors my reading of Updike's *Rabbit, Run* and *Rabbit Redux* in chapter 4.) He argues that the central meaning of Christianity is liberation from oppression and freedom from unjust persecution. The message of the crucifixion, then, is the same as the message of Jesus's ministry: "This divine event that happened on the cross liberated the oppressed to fight against suffering while not being determined by it."[68] In a move that recalls Moltmann, Cone argues that God is co-present with Jesus in his death, and that in the crucifixion, God both fully experiences and fully identifies with the suffering of the weak, the impoverished, and the abused. Then, in the moment of the resurrection, God defeats the forces that afflict the poor and the lowly, and all may share in this victory. However, for Cone, the crucifixion does not represent the final defeat of evil, an event that will not occur before the end times. The fight against the forces of oppression continues, and the cross ought to rally believers to do as God does—to identify with and share the suffering of victims: "Christians are called to suffer with God in the fight against evil in the present age."[69] However, this "suffering" is decidedly active; it is energetic resistance against injustice. Cone rejects the claim that on the cross, Jesus ennobles suffering, or demonstrates its insignificance when compared to the glory to come. Such a characterization acts as "a sedative that makes the victims of injustice content with servitude."[70] For Cone, active suffering ought always come part and parcel with the struggle against the forces that cause it. He continues, "Without struggle, the negative suffering inflicted by oppressors becomes positive and thus leads to passivity and submission. Without struggle, the idea of redemption becomes a human creation of oppressors designed to numb the pain and forestall challenges to the structures of injustice."[71] Atonement is just such an "idea of redemption" designed to keep reform and revolt at bay, to "[favor] the powerful and [exclude] the interests of the poor."[72] Cone continues, taking aim at Anselmian satisfaction, which "dehistoricizes the work of Christ, separating it from God's liberating act in history."[73] By contrast, Cone argues that the crucifixion is an eminently historical event that represents a real, temporal success over oppressive powers and heralds a new age in which believers are compelled to struggle actively against those powers. History is the stage on which the fight against injustice unfolds, and Anselm errs in removing the cross from history. Returning once again to the terminology of traditional atonement theology, we may note that Cone rejects the "objective" nature of satisfaction theory. Anselm's model is essentially a transaction between God and Jesus in which the believer has no active role. While Jesus's death on the cross erases humanity's debt and preserves divine honor, the individual has no substantial part in the process. Cone's atonement, on the other hand, calls the believer to action. Simply, if Anselm gives the believer a palliative, Cone delivers a call to arms. Cone also takes issue with Abelard's "moral influence" model, claiming that Abelard "failed to grasp the radical quality of evil and oppression."[74] For Cone, to underestimate the objective strength of evil is to risk downplaying the necessity of the struggle against it. Thus, he has kind words for Aulén and his efforts to re-emphasize the power of evil in the Christus Victor model. But Cone even tweaks Aulén, arguing that Christ does not battle abstract, demonic powers, but instead injustice in this world. Cone has no truck with atonement theories that distract the believer from taking up arms against earthly oppressors. Further, Cone believes—contra more radical black theologians like William Jones—that a renewed interpretation of the cross has special resonance for oppressed African-Americans. If traditional atonement models pacify and sedate, Cone's Jesus "died on the cross and was resurrected that we might be free to struggle for the affirmation of black humanity . . . for blacks during slavery and its aftermath, Jesus was not a clever theological device to escape difficulties inherent in suffering. He was the One who lived with them *in* suffering and thereby gave them the courage and strength to 'hold out to the end.' "[75]

Some feminist theologians complain that Cone ignores women's experience in his efforts to rebuild theology.[76] Thus, Delores Williams's *Sisters in the Wilderness* is a valuable complement to Cone's work; in it, she offers a critique of atonement theology from the perspective of African-American women.[77] I will expand on Williams's work at greater length in my reading of Toni Morrison's *Beloved* in chapter 5, but I offer a brief sketch of her argument here. From one perspective, *Sisters in the Wilderness* is a book-length critique of "surrogacy," the slavery-inspired ideology that forces black women to do other people's work. Under surrogacy, African-American women are either compelled or coerced to raise others' children, keep others' households, do others' jobs, and so on. Living as surrogates, these women are hard-pressed to develop or maintain a sense of autonomy and empowerment. Further, Williams argues that traditional atonement models are damaging to African-American women because they feature Jesus in a surrogate role—dying in our place—and thus valorize surrogacy. Therefore, we should discard them.

The pathbreaking feminist theologian Mary Daly takes a similar tack in *Beyond God the Father*. In that work, Daly rejects *imitatio* theologies that, like Abelard's moral example theory, encourage believers to pattern their actions after another—even if that other is Christ. (I invoke Daly in my reading of Joyce Carol Oates's novels in chapter 6.) She argues that the very idea of imitation is a part of the patriarchy, and that those who imitate are always smaller or paler than the models on which they base their behavior. Imitation, then, can be an oppressors' tool, designed to control and anticipate the actions of the oppressed. Further, Daly believes that women especially have been restricted in their behaviors by the influence of "ready-made" models.[78] For instance, when one follows the "ready-made" model Jesus, one is too often forced to live "sacrificially." She writes, "The qualities that Christianity *idealizes*, especially for women, are also those of a victim: sacrificial love, passive acceptance of suffering, humility, meekness, etc."[79] For Daly, this is an incorrect interpretation of the *imitatio* tradition. Those who would follow Jesus, she argues, should mimic his iconoclastic freedom. If believers choose to model their lives after his—and it's not clear to Daly that they must—they ought to reject the very idea of models, opting instead for the vertiginous freedom that allows them to become their "unique selves."[80]

Further, Christians all too often turn the notion of moral example into a weapon used to lacerate the weak. Those who do not or cannot emulate Christian virtue take their frustration out on others by forcing them to imitate another supposedly Christian trait, suffering and persecution: "While the image of the sacrificial victim may inspire saintliness in a few, in the many the effect seems to be to evoke intolerance. That is, rather than being enabled to imitate the sacrifice of Jesus, they feel guilt and transfer this to 'the Other,' thus making the latter 'imitate' Jesus in the role of the scapegoat."[81] For Daly and for us, this is a surprising reversal. However, this "transfer" is made possible by the logics of satisfaction and penal substitution. For these two related theories of atonement allow for the possibility that one person's guilt—or all of humanity's guilt—may be shifted to another human. Daly calls this shift the "scapegoat syndrome," but we encounter something like it in Girard. The atonement theories of Anselm and Calvin allow for punishment transference, and allow the powerful to shift blame onto the weak, the downtrodden, or the oppressed. And as Joanne Carlson Brown and Rebecca Parker note, even the threat of such transference can serve as a potent tool of intimidation: "holding over people's heads the threat that if they do not behave someone will die requires occasional fulfillment of the threat. The threat of death, however, should not be called moral persuasion but should be identified as the most pernicious and evil form of coercion and terror."[82] Thus, the very existence of the scapegoat mechanism is a terrorizing tool for those who would use violence to stifle dissent.

Brown and Parker, also influential feminist theologians, build on Daly's claims in a more explicit critique of atonement theology, "For God So Loved the World?" In it, they argue that the logics of atonement not only disenfranchise and disempower women but justify abuse. If Daly contends that imitating Jesus involves the acceptance of suffering, Brown and Parker remind us—as does Ray—that atonement characterizes suffering as positive, even redemptive. They write, "Christianity has been a primary . . . force in shaping our acceptance of abuse . . . If the best person who ever lived gave his life for others, then, to be of value we should likewise sacrifice ourselves. Any sense that we have a right to care for our own needs is in conflict with being a faithful follower of Jesus."[83] Brown and Parker move forcefully to the most dangerous implication of traditional atonement theology: if Jesus quietly submits to the most unjust punishment ever conceived, and if Christians are called to imitate Christ, then the true believer should be the perfect victim, silently accepting any and all maltreatment. Thus does Christianity hand the patriarchy a Church-sanctioned rationale for domestic abuse of partners and children. Indeed, Brown and Parker fear that the ramifications for our sons and daughters could be even worse. For if we accept a critical reading of the cross as an instance of divine child abuse, the crucifixion then models a heinous instance of parental crime. Brown and Parker continue:

> Children who are abused are forced most keenly to face the conflict between the claims of a parent who professes love and the inner self which protests violation. When a theology identifies love with suffering, what resources will its culture offer to such a child? And when parents have an image of a God righteously demanding the total obedience of "his" son—even obedience to death—what will prevent the parent from engaging in divinely sanctioned child abuse?[84]

Pushing this train of thought to its logical conclusion, the cross may even admit of a rationale for filicide. Oates plays out this grisly thought experiment in *My Sister, My Love.*

Jerome Miller calls traditional atonement models a "cul de sac."[85] He argues that such theologies entrap because they all rely on the logic of retribution; they are founded on the suggestion that violence must be answered with violence. And for Miller, violence is an irredeemable evil from which no good should come—and which God should never dole out. Traditional atonement is flawed, then, because it forces God to respond to the evil of the world with a violence ill-suited to His own justice:

> For Jesus is being murdered, and murder cannot possibly be part of Your justice—or a supplement to it. Insofar as it is a murder, the Crucifixion cannot possibly be the means of our justification. The crucified Jesus is not suffering retributive punishment at the hands of human agents implementing divine justice; he is suffering evil. The issue, then, is how can Jesus' death be the divine response to evil if it is itself evil—a horrific reality that cries out to heaven.[86]

In other words, what do we do with the crucifixion once we wring it of its "atoning" value? How are we to understand the cross if we can find no good in it? Can Christianity survive—can belief persist—if the death of the Son is an ignominious defeat? And we must admit that for many, the road stops with such questions. The violence of the cross is off-putting, and the atonement kills Christianity. Not so for Miller, though. Helping break new theological ground, he suggests that previous commentators on the atonement have mistakenly focused on the *victim* Jesus when they should have instead explored *his wound.* In his reconfiguration of the cross, Miller writes that *"the primary locus of evil is the injury, the harm, the wound, that is inflicted on the creature."*[87] To invoke the notion of the wound is to use the terminology of trauma theory, and here Miller is opening a conversation that others will pick up and develop. For a new generation of theologians, trauma theory offers a means of acknowledging the evil of the crucifixion while still allowing for the possibility that its dark meaning might offer insight.

Among those working in this area is Serene Jones, who argues that the "unending" of the Markan Gospel (which casts the disciples as speechless, confused, and fearful) is testament both to the devastating nature of the crucifixion and the victimhood of Jesus. For Jones, this "unending" is frustrating, but it allows believers to see the gospel violence sometimes obscured by the Christian narratives of resurrection, salvation, and hope: the crucifixion is a trauma. She writes, "traumatic violence often leaves holes in the stories we tell about our lives. There are places in those stories where endings are abrupt and ragged, other places where stories are unfinished; in this way, violence creates open-ended narrative spaces filled with fear, silence, and uncertainty."[88] Mark's fractured narrative records both the trauma of Jesus's execution and the destabilizing effects it has on friends and followers. However, Jones joins Jennifer Erin Beste and Shelly Rambo in arguing that we can wrest new meaning from Christian teaching by considering the crucifixion simply as wrenching loss.[89] All three follow in the footsteps of Cathy Caruth, the scholar most responsible for introducing trauma studies to the humanities, who defines trauma as a "wound of the mind"—an event so painfully disruptive that the individual has trouble assimilating it into normal life narratives."[90] Rambo, whose *Spirit and Trauma* represents the most comprehensive effort to create a theology of trauma, argues that Christians too often hurriedly (and ineffectively) assimilate the trauma of the cross into the story of Easter. By contrast, she channels Hans Urs von Balthasar in dwelling on the dead Jesus. Further, she believes that meditation on Christ's traumatic absence will have salutary effects for Christian theology and devotion. For Rambo as for von Balthasar, theology must not ignore the tragedy of Holy Saturday, a day on which Jesus is a corpse, forsaken and damned.[91] It is only by working through this dark reality that Christians may prepare themselves for the redemptive message of the resurrection: that the traumatic cross painfully but inevitably resolves itself into hope, wonder, and love. Writes Jones, "Where do we find Jesus' glory? Perhaps it is somehow in the form itself, its beauty, the material embodiment of God in his crucifixion; perhaps this is . . . the shape of salvation. Not just any beauty: it is the beauty of love, the form of beatitude."[92] Jones and the theologians mentioned above further hope that their traumatic rendering of the cross will make the Christian message more welcoming to victims of violence. Simply, having recognized the crucifixion as a trauma, Christians may craft a message better suited to reaching the traumatized.

In this book, I hope to contribute in some small way to the growing field of trauma theology. Thus, I will treat authors who characterize Jesus's death first and foremost as a world-shattering loss. However, my project differs from the works of the trauma theologians mentioned above in that it attends to a group of authors for whom the trauma of Jesus's death will not assimilate—and for whom that death is most assuredly not "the form of beatitude." For victims, painful memories of the unassimilated event sometimes return unbidden, and some specialists argue that these memories often take the form of intrusive flashbacks or dreams. In her edited volume on trauma studies, Caruth describes the process by which some traumas force their way back into the lives of victims years after the event itself: "the event is not assimilated or experienced fully at the time, but only belatedly, in a repeated *possession* of the one who experiences it. To be traumatized is precisely to be possessed by an image or event."[93] For victims, trauma haunts. And so it is with the death of Christ; those who see the crucifixion of Jesus as a child murder recognize that death is a trauma we have not yet overcome—a moment of shattering that continues to shatter.

There is a paradoxical sense in which those who are now coming to recognize the traumatic nature of Jesus's death are witnessing to it for the first time. As Rambo notes, the notion of witness has been crucial to devotional Christianity since the religion's founding.[94] The Biblical book of Acts frequently addresses the believer's responsibility to witness to the life, death, and ministry of Christ. In the first chapter, the risen Jesus gives a command to his disciples: "It is not for you to know the times or periods that the Father has set by his own authority. But you will receive power when the Holy Spirit has come upon you; and you will be my witnesses in Jerusalem, in all Judea and Samaria, and to the ends of the earth" (Acts 1:7–8). Early Christians were asked to testify—in what can only be described as a judicial sense—to the truth of Jesus's message, and to spread that message everywhere. However, Christian witness is distinct from traumatic witness. As Rambo argues:

> The language of trauma directs to a different theological territory . . .
> The term "witness" takes on new meaning in this between territory
> and provides a means by which experiences that "fall outside the ordi-
> nary order of things" are brought to light. It takes into account the
> depth to which human persons can be shattered—in Elaine Scarry's
> word, "undone"—and it equally takes into account the important
> work of remaking the world. Witness is the hinge linking the shatter-
> ing and remaking, the undoing and the regeneration. Witness is the
> hinge between death and life, as it is experienced through trauma and
> traumatic survival.[95]

This notion of witness focuses attention not on the believer's responsibility to proselytize, or to offer reliable testimony as to the truth of the Christian message, but instead on the deep suffering of the victimized Jesus and on the ways in which that suffering resembles that of other victims. That this second, traumatic meaning of witness is only coming to light in Christian theology is unsurprising to Rambo given the fact that trauma—as Caruth, Shoshana Felman, Judith Herman, Richard McNally, and most other trauma specialists attest—is devilishly hard to speak of. Rambo suggests that it is the nature of trauma to remain unspoken; she even suggests that perpetrators may have a vested interest in keeping the reality of trauma secret. Drawing on the work of Herman and others, Rambo writes:

> The study of trauma also, [Herman] says, has bouts of recall and forgetting; attention to trauma rises and falls in public consciousness, and this cycle is reflective of the phenomenon itself . . . I am suggesting that this remembering and eclipsing, uncovering and eliding, distinguish witnessing and make it so difficult in respect to radical suffering. This aspect of forgetting (Herman) . . . is akin to what I am referring to as eliding—instances in which certain truths are suppressed, omitted, ignored, or passed over . . . the word "elision" captures the intentionality that is often at play in trauma. It takes into account the fact that, in many cases, certain parties are invested in suppressing the truth of certain events. The effects of trauma may quickly be passed over in order to keep certain persons in positions of power.[96]

Dori Laub, one of the founders of the Fortunoff Video Archive for Holocaust Testimonies at Yale University, offers an example of such suppression in his discussion of the testimonies of *Shoah* victims. He argues that the sad silence surrounding their tragic pain was enhanced by the efforts of a Nazi power structure to reject the traumatic nature of that pain: "Not only, in effect, did the Nazis try to exterminate the physical witnesses of their crime; but the inherently incomprehensible *and* deceptive psychological structure of the event precluded its own witnessing, even by its victims."[97] Both internal and external forces hinder traumatic witness, and these forces increase the possibility that trauma will be elided. In the case of the Holocaust, Laub argues that this combination rendered the historical trauma an "event without a witness."[98] Rambo's characterization of the traumatic nature of Jesus's death suggests that we may understand crucifixion in similar terms, as another event without a witness. Though for centuries, Christians have testified to the message of Jesus, we are only just beginning to witness to the tragedy of his death.

In this book, I contend with Rambo that the cross's trauma has frequently been "omitted, ignored, or passed over." To explain how this omission has persisted, I turn to the Freudian concept of the *Deck-Erinnerung*, or "screen memory." For Freud, the screen memory is a mental formation that stands between the victim and the true memory of an earlier trauma. The screen memory may be an actual reminiscence—an insignificant recollection granted an outsize importance that expands to block out memory of the trauma. Or it may be fantastic in nature—a partially or wholly imaginary memory that may reflect wish more than reality. No matter its content, its function is clear: the screen memory protects the victim from the gut-wrenching recollection of trauma. As Patrick Hutton writes, "Screen memories are defenses employed by the unconscious mind to ward off the recollection of intense, painful, or traumatic experience."[99] In his later work, however, Freud extends the concept of screen memory to cover not only the individual psyche but the collective mind as well. He suggests that a nation, like a person, can fall under the influence of such a mental formation. For Freud, collective screen memories are, in brief, myths. Hutton describes Freudian myth as "screen memories covering earlier events from which humankind wished to shield itself."[100] Richard King argues that Freud's characterization of the Hebrew Bible in his late work *Moses and Monotheism* (which features, not coincidentally, one of the author's most sustained explorations of trauma) is tantamount to a religious screen memory: "It is fair to say that in *Moses* Freud implicitly regarded the Old Testament account of the history of the Jewish people as a screen memory . . . According to Freud the written text existed precisely to repress two truths—Moses' Egyptian origins and his murder by the children of Israel."[101] In Freud's reconstructed history of Jewish origins, the prophet Moses angers the earliest Israelites, and they murder him for it. In the centuries following, the Jews invent a new story of origins that covers and protects them from their true, traumatic history. Freud's reconstruction of Jewish history is unpersuasive (and almost wholly speculative), but his characterization of religious myth as screen memory is promising. In a much more recent work, *The Monstrosity of Christ*, the Slovenian philosopher Slavoj Žižek applies the notion of collective screen memory—a "fantasy-formation intended to cover up a traumatic truth"—first to Hegelian philosophy and then to the book of Job.[102] In the Bible, Job is a righteous man tested by God with a string of increasingly vicious afflictions—the loss of property, the slaughter of servants, the death of his children, and ultimately, an outbreak of painful boils. Though the reader knows that these trials are the result of a wager between God and Satan, Job does not. And when three of Job's friends arrive to comfort him, they attempt to convince Job that his pains are punishment for his sins. Says Eliphaz, the first friend:

> Think now, who that was innocent ever perished?
> Or where were the upright cut off?
> As I have seen, those who plow iniquity
> And sow trouble reap the same.
> By the breath of God they perish,
> And by the blast of his anger they are consumed. (Job 4:7–9)

This is the language of retributive justice, the notion that God visits evil with punishment and good with good fortune. For Eliphaz, Job suffers because Job sins. However, the reader knows that the comforters' logic does not apply to Job, who is just and whose afflictions are a very special case. Their language functions only to cover the deep traumatic reality of Job's existence. Žižek describes the function of the "three theological friends in the story of Job: to obfuscate the impact of the trauma with a symbolic semblance."[103] Retributive justice—the "semblance"—is a screen memory developed to hide a traumatic truth: that God will play violent games with his most devout followers.

It is my contention that traditional atonement theology is potentially just such a screen memory, a narrative Christians use to explain the usefulness—or the "good"—of Jesus's ignominious death on the cross. To those who understand the cross primarily as the site of a trauma—rather than as a symbol of redemption and renewal—atonement theologies shield believers from the truth of the crucifixion and hinder the healing process. For them, there is no clear answer to the question, "What is the good of Jesus's death?" His crucifixion is a tragedy, a shattering crime. We would as soon ponder its "good" as we would speculate on the good of child abuse, or murder, or genocide. And our responsibility is not to explain its usefulness, but instead to explain its gruesome truth honestly—to narrate its reality in simple, direct language. As many trauma specialists now note, the mere act of narrating trauma can give the victim a new sense of control. To speak trauma is to begin to master it; as Susan Brison—herself a trauma survivor—writes, "narrating memories to others . . . enables survivors to gain more control over the traces left by trauma. Narrative memory is not passively endured; rather, it is an act on the part of the narrator, a speech act that defuses traumatic memory, giving shape and a temporal order to the events recalled, establishing more control over their recalling, and helping the survivor to remake a self."[104] Kaplan explains that only by recreating a reliable testimony to trauma—narrative or otherwise—can we create real witness to trauma; by this process, the victim may "[construct] a witness where there was none before."[105] In similar fashion, to get past the screen memory of atonement theology by naming and describing the real trauma of the cross is to create a witness to that event that, perhaps, has gone unwitnessed for all these hundreds of years. By doing so, we may do justice to the real suffering of Jesus while also witnessing to the traumas of those who suffer like him.

The six novels the following chapters engage are part of this recent effort to bear witness to the trauma of the cross and probe the most familiar theories of atonement. In each book, the author's comparison of a murdered child to the Christ forces us to ask whether atonement is truth or screen, sacrifice or trauma, miracle or tragedy. As we will see, the authors' engagement with the cross—and with the theologies that interpret it—vary significantly. Yet all witness with surprising candor to the terrifying shock of the crucifixion, to the ways in which it is the clear image of a father effecting the death of his own, only child. And all force us to dwell—at least for a time—in that gaping space between Good Friday and Easter.

Chapter 3

"Forgotten by God"

✦

Flannery O'Connor and Orthodox Infanticide

> What interests me is simply the mystery, the agony that is given
> in strange ways to children.
>
> —Flannery O'Connor

In July 1960, five nuns from the Our Lady of Perpetual Help Free Cancer
Home paid a visit to Flannery O'Connor, the Catholic author from Milled-
geville, Georgia, whose literary star was near its peak. They came to implore
O'Connor to help them with a book project on Mary Ann Long, a young girl
with a cancerous growth on her face who had recently died in their care at
the age of twelve.[1] Their first request was that the author spin a novel or a
short story out of the life of the girl who, O'Connor reports, "they think . . .
was a saintly child . . . and want it known."[2] O'Connor demurred but eventually agreed to help the nuns edit their own book on Mary Ann, and to
provide an introduction. The nuns, encouraged, produced a manuscript in
a hair under six months, and O'Connor grudgingly sent it (along with her
introduction) to her long-time publisher Robert Giroux in December 1960.
At her friend Caroline Gordon's prompting, she suggested the book be titled
simply *Death of a Child*;[3] the sisters were opposed, however, and the book
was released as *A Memoir of Mary Ann*. It sold so briskly it made the sisters
minor literary celebrities and left O'Connor complaining about an unwieldy
tax bill.[4]

Though O'Connor initially balked at participating in the book project,
she would later claim that her introduction to *Mary Ann* is of crucial—and
perhaps paramount—importance to any later critic who hopes to understand
the rest of her writing: "In the future, anybody who writes anything about me
is going to have to read everything I have written in order to make legitimate
criticism, *even and particularly* the Mary Ann piece."[5] The importance of this
meditation on the death of a child becomes apparent when one reflects on
just how frequently children die in her fiction. As she wrote to Betty Hester (a
frequent correspondent long identified as "A"), "What interests me in [Mary

Ann's story] is simply the mystery, the agony that is given in strange ways
to children."[6] The bodies of agonized and dying children litter the pages of
O'Connor's slim fictional oeuvre, made up of two spare novels and roughly
two dozen short stories. In her first novel, *Wise Blood*, Sabbath Lily tells the
story of a woman who strangles her ugly child and hangs it in a chimney so
she can live in peace with her new lover.[7] In O'Connor's most anthologized
short story, "A Good Man Is Hard to Find," henchmen of the outlaw known
as The Misfit take a young boy and girl out to the woods and shoot them.
In "The River," the young son of negligent parents wanders off to a local
waterway and drowns trying to baptize himself. Stories from her second collection, *Everything That Rises Must Converge*, continue the theme: in "The
Lame Shall Enter First," a young boy ignored by his father hangs himself in
an effort to rejoin his mother in heaven, and "A View of the Woods" culminates with a man named Mr. Fortune bludgeoning his favorite granddaughter
to death. Many readers find it difficult to reconcile these and many other
instances of explicit violence in O'Connor's fiction with her orthodox faith,
and with her admission that "I write the way I do because (not though) I
am a Catholic."[8] However, as the author explains in the concluding pages
of her introduction to *A Memoir of Mary Ann*, she does not share Ivan
Karamazov's conviction that the agony of children is a stain on divine justice.
Nor does she agree with Clamence's suggestion in Camus's *The Fall* that the
slaughter of innocent children negates the redemptive power of the Christ's
sacrifice:

> One of the tendencies of our age is to use the suffering of children
> to discredit the goodness of God, and once you have discredited his
> goodness, you are done with him . . . Ivan Karamazov cannot believe,
> as long as one child is in torment; Camus' hero cannot accept the
> divinity of Christ, because of the massacre of the innocents. In this
> popular pity, we mark our gain in sensibility and our loss in vision.
> If other ages felt less, they saw more, even though they saw with the
> blind, prophetical, unsentimental eye of acceptance, which is to say,
> of faith. In the absence of this faith now, we govern by tenderness. It
> is a tenderness which, long since cut off from the person of Christ, is
> wrapped in theory. When tenderness is detached from the source of
> tenderness, its logical outcome is terror. It ends in forced-labor camps
> and in the fumes of the gas chamber.[9]

For Karamazov and Clamence, the death of the young "discredits" the deity,
for what kind of God fails to protect the vulnerable and the innocent, and
what kind of God allows dozens or scores of infants to be murdered while his
own child Jesus lives? For O'Connor, however, these critiques smack of cheap
sentimentality driven by an easy "tenderness." Further, and for reasons that
remain obscure, this tenderness ends in "terror" and, more startlingly, Stalin's

gulags and Hitler's ovens. By contrast, for O'Connor, acknowledgement of the suffering death of children is not incompatible with religious devotion. Further, she counsels that the appropriate religious response to that suffering is "vision" and a faith tantamount to "acceptance."

It is my contention in this chapter that O'Connor's deep understanding of orthodox Christian scripture and theology—and more specifically, "objective" atonement—allows her to accept the death of children as a mysterious but crucial part of the divine plan. To develop this argument, I bring ideas from the just-quoted long passage from *A Memoir of Mary Ann* into conversation with O'Connor's most sustained fictional treatment of child murder, in her second and last novel *The Violent Bear It Away*. In it, a young "prophet" named Francis kills a boy O'Connor describes as a Christ figure. Yet passages from both the book and the author's commentary on it suggest that O'Connor is unwilling to condemn Francis for his crime, both because the murder is part of a religious quest and because the victim resembles sons from the Catholic tradition who are justly sacrificed (or nearly sacrificed) in God's name. In sum, *The Violent Bear It Away* demonstrates that O'Connor understands that Christian salvation is won at a steep but necessary cost, a cost that sometimes involves the killing of our children, be it on a cross or in a shallow lake.

O'Connor claims that a comprehensive version of Catholic orthodoxy drives her fiction. In a letter to Shirley Abbott, she proclaims, "Let me make no bones about it: I write from the standpoint of Christian orthodoxy . . . I write with a solid belief in *all* the Christian dogmas."[10] Among those dogmas, she identifies three as preeminent: "Fall, Redemption, and Judgment."[11] (In both her fiction and her nonfiction, O'Connor normally capitalizes all of them.) And of these, Redemption is most crucial to O'Connor's own spiritual and fictional vision.[12] In an essay entitled "The Fiction Writer and His Country," she writes, "I see from the standpoint of Christian orthodoxy. This means that for me the meaning of life is centered in our Redemption by Christ and that what I see in the world I see in its relation to that."[13] Redemption is the central truth of both her life and her work, and there is strong evidence that O'Connor's Redemption is what the other authors addressed in this book refer to as atonement—the salvific benefits gained by the death of Jesus on the cross. For an initial definition of O'Connor's Redemption, we may turn to the Baltimore Catechism, the widely used handbook of Catholic belief and practice that Jill Peláez Baumgaertner concludes O'Connor knew well.[14] The Catechism describes Jesus's primary role in terms of his redemptive power: "God did not abandon man after he fell into sin, but promised him a Redeemer, who was to satisfy for man's sin and reopen to him the gates of heaven" ("Lesson Sixth"). This interpretation—in which Christ serves as satisfaction for human sin—echoes Anselmian, or objective, atonement theology. The Catechism later outlines the results of Christ's Redemption in the

Ninth Lesson: "The chief effects of the Redemption are two: The satisfaction of God's justice by Christ's sufferings and death, and the gaining of grace for men." Orthodox Catholic belief of O'Connor's childhood emphasized that Christ's death on the cross pays the debt incurred by human sin and wins our salvation.[15]

O'Connor's remarkable familiarity with Christian theology only deepens her understanding of Redemption and atonement. As evidence of her theological literacy, her friend William Sessions claimed that by the time of her death, O'Connor had amassed "one of the finest private theological libraries in America."[16] To get a better perspective on O'Connor's knowledge of atonement, we may focus on the two theologians with whom she was arguably most conversant: Thomas Aquinas and the contemporary Catholic writer Romano Guardini. Both develop Anselm's argument that Jesus's death on the cross satisfies divine displeasure over human sin. O'Connor's familiarity with Aquinas is well documented. The self-described "hillbilly Thomist" famously wrote that she read his *Summa Theologica* for twenty minutes every night before bed.[17] Further, Brad Gooch cites one of her undergraduate professors, who testified that even in her youth, O'Connor "knew Aquinas in detail" and "was amazingly well read in earlier philosophy."[18] And Helen Andretta notes that O'Connor mentions Aquinas in no fewer than twenty-three of her collected letters.[19] In the *Summa Theologica*, Aquinas describes the atoning power of Christ's death in terms of its capacity to compensate (or even over-compensate) for the weight of human sin: "He atones appropriately for an offense who offers whatever the offended one equally loves, or loves more than he detested the offense. But Christ by suffering out of love and obedience gave to God more than was required to compensate for the offense of the whole human race . . . And so Christ's passion was not merely a sufficient but a superabundant atonement."[20] Briefly, for Aquinas Jesus's suffering not only balances out human error; it outweighs sin. Christ's suffering on the cross is made all the more miraculous by the fact that it is excessive; less, it seems, would have done the trick.[21]

Perhaps only Romano Guardini's book *The Lord* had the same influence on O'Connor's religious vision. Of it, she wrote to Betty Hester, "In my opinion there is nothing like [*The Lord*] anywhere."[22] *The Lord* is best understood as gospel exegesis in the form of a theological biography of Jesus.[23] For Guardini as for other proponents of objective atonement models, Jesus expiates human sin because humans cannot do so themselves. In the midst of a wrenching narrative account of the crucifixion, he describes Christ as

> one who was both human and God. Pure as God; but bowed with responsibility as man. He drank the dregs of that responsibility—down to the bottom of the chalice. Mere man cannot do this. He is so much smaller than his sin against God, that he can neither contain it nor cope with it . . . Though he has committed it, he is incapable of

expiating it. It confuses him, troubles him, leaves him desperate but helpless. God alone can "handle" sin.[24]

In reading both Aquinas and Guardini, we are struck by the enormity of human transgression in the Catholic worldview. Its weight "bows" even the God-man Jesus, and the atonement that "fixes" it is purchased only at a high price. This price is Christ's suffering, and for O'Connor, it is supernaturally heavy. In her copy of Albert Béguin's *Léon Bloy: A Study in Impatience*, she marks the following passage: "*Do you know why Jesus Christ has suffered so much?* I will try to give you a transcendent idea of it in a few words. *It is because in his soul, all his lifetime, the present, the past and the future were absolutely one and the same.*"[25] On the cross, Jesus bears the weight of all error, past, present, and future. Thus, his "superabundant" suffering must be exponentially greater than any pain of which we can conceive. Yet O'Connor often laments that an increasingly secular world likes redemption but forgets its price. In her essay "The Grotesque in Southern Fiction," she writes, "There is something in us, as story-tellers and as listeners to stories, that demands the redemptive act, that demands that what falls at least be offered the chance to be restored. The reader of today looks for this motion, and rightly so, but *what he has forgotten is the cost of it.*"[26]

Demonstrating the cost of individual redemption is a task to which O'Connor repeatedly returns throughout her fiction. And just as in the gospels, so in her writings the price of redemption is often paid in violence. In introductory remarks made at Hollins College before a reading of "A Good Man Is Hard to Find" in 1963, O'Connor noted the frequency with which violence is the cost of her characters' "return to reality"—reality being a true understanding of the work of God in the world:

> In my own stories I have found that violence is strangely capable of returning my characters to reality and preparing them to accept their moments of grace. Their heads are so hard that almost nothing else will work. This idea, that reality is something to which we must be returned at considerable cost, is one which is seldom understood by the casual reader, but it is one which is implicit in the Christian view of the world.[27]

The violence of which O'Connor speaks is sometimes figurative—as with the theft of Hulga's leg in "Good Country People" or Asbury's hallucinatory vision of the water stain in "The Enduring Chill." But elsewhere it is quite literal—as with Sarah Ruth's beating of her husband in "Parker's Back" or the student's attack on Mrs. Turpin in "Revelation." And from time to time, it is the violence of the protagonist's death—as with the grandmother's murder by the Misfit in "Good Man" or Mrs. May's goring in "Greenleaf." As Ralph C. Wood observes, O'Connor's characters often "find Life only in death":

they "violently receive the afflicting truth about themselves only *in articulo mortis*."[28] However, it is an uncomfortable reality in her fiction that the death that brings life is occasionally the violent demise of a child. Such is the case in two stories from *Everything That Rises Must Converge*: "The Lame Shall Enter First" and "A View of the Woods." In the closing moments of the former, the protagonist, Sheppard experiences a moment of religious epiphany at or near the moment the life of his son, Norton, slips from his body: "A rush of agonizing love for the child rushed over him like a transfusion of life. The little boy's face appeared to him transformed; the image of his salvation; all light. He groaned with joy. He would make everything up to him. He would never let him suffer again. He would be mother and father."[29] In death, Norton is "transformed" while Sheppard receives a "transfusion" of life; the prefix before each word indicates that both father and son have crossed over, the latter to "salvation" and "life" even as his son perishes. And in "View," Mr. Fortune, having just murdered his own favorite granddaughter, seems almost drawn up to heaven:

> his heart expanded once more with a convulsive motion. It expanded so fast that the old man felt as if he were being pulled after it through the woods, felt as if he were running as fast as he could with the ugly pines toward the lake. He perceived that there would be a little opening there, a little place where he could escape and leave the woods behind him. He could see it in the distance already, a little opening where the white sky was reflected in the water. It grew as he ran toward it until suddenly the whole lake opened up before him, riding majestically in little corrugated folds toward his feet.[30]

Though some call the experience a stroke or a heart attack, O'Connor's description of it recalls the language of prophetic transport used in the Biblical book of Habakkuk, whose main character God lifts by his head and whisks away through the skies.[31] O'Connor knows the story and makes explicit reference to it in *The Violent Bear It Away*: "His whole body felt hollow as if he had been lifted like Habakkuk by the hair of his head, borne swiftly through the night and set down in the place of his mission."[32] Though Fortune's fatal beating of the young girl may coincide with his own death, it also results in spiritual gain.[33] We see a similar series of events in *Violent*, in which an infanticide effects religious transformation—the start of a new prophetic mission.

O'Connor's second and final novel features four main characters. Mason Tarwater is a solitary preacher who, Richard Giannone argues, resembles the fourth-century Christian desert fathers who remove themselves to the wilderness to seek God.[34] Fourteen years before the novel opens, Mason, "who said he was a prophet," kidnaps his great nephew Francis Tarwater and brings him to Powderhead, his backwoods home, to "raise him up to justify his Redemption."[35] Mason hopes to bring Francis into the family business, to make him a prophet, too. Decades before, Mason had tried to do the same thing to his nephew Rayber: "He had kidnapped him when the child was seven and had taken him to the backwoods and baptized him and instructed him in the facts of his Redemption."[36] But Rayber's parents rescue him, and Mason's influence persists "only for a few years; in time the child had set himself a different course" (333).[37] (By contrast, Francis is orphaned by a car crash, so he has no parents to extricate him; and though Rayber once tries, Mason scares Rayber off with shotgun blasts to the leg and ear.) Last is Rayber's young son Bishop, afflicted with Down syndrome and speechless. According to Joseph Zornado, "for Rayber, Bishop is the result of divine indifference."[38] And though he loves his son, he suffers from what Desmond identifies as a profound "sense of guilt over having fathered a retarded child."[39]

At the novel's start, Mason has died, leaving Francis with two tasks: bury Mason's body, and return to town to baptize Bishop. In both, Francis is torn between carrying out Mason's requests and fighting the religious call they represent. His resistance is fueled by a mysterious—some say diabolical— "voice" tempting him. Thus, rather than burying Mason, Francis gets drunk and burns down his great uncle's house. Yet even after this initial rebellion, he nonetheless hitches a ride into the city, where he finds his uncle Rayber and his cousin Bishop. Francis's first glimpse of his cousin hits him with the force of a "revelation . . . silent, implacable, direct as a bullet. He did not look into the eyes of any fiery beast or see a burning bush. He only knew, with a certainty sunk in despair, that he was expected to baptize the child he saw and begin the life his great-uncle had prepared for him."[40] The burning bush marks the beginning of Moses's divine work in Exodus, and the vision of the fiery beasts initiates Ezekiel's. These allusions suggest that Bishop is the signal that Francis's religious quest has begun. However, Rayber sees Francis not as a new prophet but as the son he wants, and he immediately takes upon himself to educate the teenager and break him from his religious upbringing. These efforts fail, for Francis resents Rayber for his inability to bring him away from Powderhead. But neither can Francis leave Rayber's home, because Mason's command that Francis baptize Bishop holds a mysterious sway over him. All comes to a head when Rayber takes the boys to a lakeside lodge. Late one evening, Francis brings his cousin out in a boat and drowns him by the swampy shore, thinking the murder of the boy he would baptize the most forceful denunciation of his prophetic call. But in a twist, the words of baptism slip out as he holds his cousin down. Francis initially feels that the drowning outweighs the baptismal words, but he's wrong; the baptism—though darkly inflected by the murder—has the effect Mason intended, initiating the prophetic "life his great-uncle had prepared for him." In the novel's closing pages, Francis receives a vision of Mason in an ethereal crowd preparing to receive the bread of life from Jesus, and then he hears the voice of God[41]:

a red-gold tree of fire ascended as if it would consume the darkness in
one tremendous burst of flame . . . He knew that this was the fire that
had encircled Daniel, that had raised Elijah from the earth, that had
spoken to Moses and would in the instant speak to him. He threw
himself to the ground and with his face against the dirt of the grave,
he heard the command. GO WARN THE CHILDREN OF GOD OF THE TER-
RIBLE SPEED OF MERCY.[42]

Francis has been drafted into a line of prophets that extends back to the
Torah, and the fiery tree again recalls Moses's burning bush. In the last lines
of the book, Francis stalks back toward the city, "where the children of God
lay sleeping."[43]

The climax of the story, in which O'Connor juxtaposes an infanticide and
a baptism, forces readers to confront an unsettling question: what is the relationship between the religious ritual and the child murder? Her language
makes answering the question difficult. Though orthodox interpretations
of baptism vary, most Christians characterize the ritual as the individual's
official entrance into the Christian community—and the moment at which
the baptized gains access to the forgiveness of sins effected by Jesus's life
and death on the cross. Yet clearly Bishop's is not an "orthodox" baptism,
and its nature remains mysterious. From the text itself, it is unclear whether
Bishop's drowning is a baptism despite a murder, a murder despite a baptism,
a murder that invalidates a baptism, a baptism that overshadows a murder,
or some other sundry combination.[44] Her language indicates only that it is a
baptism *and* a murder. When Rayber first realizes what Francis has done, he
knows his nephew "had baptized the child even as he drowned him."[45] The
subordinating "as" indicates only that the two events merely coincide; and
"even" has the effect of emphasizing the coincidence. Later, when Francis
tells the story, he says, "I drowned a boy . . . Yes. . . . I baptized him."[46] The
"Yes," which serves as an idiosyncratic conjunction, only affirms that both
events occur without describing the connection between them. Francis's next
utterance—"It was an accident. I didn't mean to"[47]—opens with the vague
pronoun "it," which may refer back to either act. And while Francis later
tries to emphasize the drowning over above the baptism—"in the order of
things, a drowning was a more important act than a few words spilled in the
water"[48]—he immediately backtracks: "Even if by some chance [the baptism]
had not been an accident, what was of no consequence in the first place was
of no consequence in the second; and he had succeeded in drowning the
child."[49] And yet, that the end of the novel marks the beginning of Francis's life as a prophet seems to indicate that the baptism is "successful," too.
O'Connor's ambiguous language helps her preserve the sense of mystery that
is central to her religious and fictional vision.

Nonetheless, critics have tried a number of tacks in explaining both the
relationship and the slaughter itself. Giannone, who calls it the "sheerest

butchery," attributes the murder to the diabolical voice that haunts Francis throughout the novel: "the demon gets Tarwater to drown in cold blood the very child that Mason ordered Tarwater to save."[50] Gary M. Ciuba takes a psychological approach when describing the killing, noting that "psychologist James Garbarino explains that boys kill when they seek to redress what is perceived as an intolerable sense of injustice. Taking another's life thus becomes not random and meaningless but perversely moral in their eyes."[51] Susan Srigley argues that O'Connor would surely think of the murder as "intolerable" but suggests that readers should focus not on the crime but on its "meaning."[52] And Joyce Carol Oates provocatively likens Tarwater to Abraham, ready to slaughter his own son: "Thus Tarwater rows the child out to drown him, but in drowning him he cries out the words of baptism. Here we have the paradox, which Kierkegaard probes, of the sacred operating simultaneously with the ethically evil."[53]

Here, I would suggest a simpler explanation. Though others condemn the crime, O'Connor reacts to it nonchalantly because she faithfully accepts child murder as part of Christianity and, occasionally, as part of the religious experience. In her letters, O'Connor frequently defends Francis and explains that his actions are unobjectionable. She thinks that readers who see him as pitiable or tragic misunderstand him; for O'Connor, Francis acts appropriately throughout: "People are depressed by the ending of *The Violent Bear It Away* because they think: poor Tarwater, his mind has been warped by that old man and he's off to make a fool or a martyr of himself. They forget that the old man has taught him the truth and that now *he's doing what is right*, however crazy."[54] In a separate letter to Hester, she even argues that she'd do the same thing in similar circumstances: "I don't feel Tarwater is such a monster. I feel that in his place I would have done everything he did. Tarwater is made up out of my saying: what would I do here? I don't think he's a caricature."[55] Elsewhere, she writes of her aspirations to write a sequel to *Violent* that follows Francis into the city, but she pauses to note that in the second book, the boy would not be punished for the murder: "There would be no reformatory I assure you. *The murder is forgotten by God* and of no interest to society."[56] Let's repeat for emphasis: Bishop's murder is *forgotten by God*. This is a striking statement, but less striking if considered in the context of other of O'Connor's statements.

First, O'Connor notes that violence is occasionally a useful tool for making spiritual gains. As evidence, we may turn to her title, *The Violent Bear It Away*, which is taken from the Douay-Rheims translation of Matthew 11:12: "From the days of John the Baptist until now, the kingdom of heaven suffereth violence, and the violent bear it away."[57] This is a famously thorny passage whose meaning remains either unclear or troubling. Is Jesus indicating that suffering will still exist in the kingdom of heaven? Is he arguing that "the violent"—violent people—have borne off the kingdom of God? In trying to understand the title, many critics resort to one of O'Connor's own interpretations of Matthew 11, in which she characterizes the "borne" violence as self-sacrifice, asceticism, or exceeding love: "That this is the violence of love, of giving more than the law demands, of an asceticism like John the Baptist's . . . all this is overlooked."[58] However, other quotes indicate that O'Connor also accepts a more troubling but straightforward reading of the passage as referring to actual, physical violence. In a discussion of the bloody culmination of "A Good Man Is Hard to Find," in which the Misfit shoots the grandmother, O'Connor quotes Matthew 11 again, writing, "Violence is a force which can be used for good or evil, and among other things taken by it is the kingdom of heaven."[59] Given the context—an examination of homicide—it seems likely that this "violence" is neither ascetic nor loving; it is physical and fatal. And here O'Connor indicates that it too can be useful in "taking" the kingdom of heaven. As she and many critics note, the grandmother in "Good Man" experiences true grace directly before her death.[60]

Further, from her reading of the Bible and Catholic theology, O'Connor knows that child murder is one variety of violence that sometimes "takes" the kingdom of heaven. Though it seems unreasonable to nonbelievers, she admits that her paragon of Christian virtue is Abraham in the moment the knife hovers over Isaac's throat: "[My understanding of the reasonable man] is certainly something else—God's reasonable man, the prototype of whom must be Abraham, willing to sacrifice his son and thereby show that he is in the image of God Who sacrifices His Son."[61] Unlike subjective atonement theologians who see the suffering Jesus as a model for Christian praxis, O'Connor takes the God who kills him as the pattern for virtue. Willingness to sacrifice our innocent sons, O'Connor admits, is part of the Christian tradition, and to ignore this grisly truth is to engage in a pick-and-choose theology that O'Connor would have found abhorrent.[62] Thus, when the young Tarwater puts Bishop down in advancing his own religious mission, he is somehow both Abraham and indeed God, sacrificing a child for the furtherance of the faith.

One might raise a variety of objections to the suggestion that O'Connor's theological training—and her understanding of atonement specifically— prepares her to accept the murder of Bishop. As I bring this chapter to a close, allow me to address a handful of them.

First, though O'Connor takes Abraham, "willing to sacrifice his son," as a model human, one might argue that willingness and actual sacrifice are different things. More bluntly, Abraham does not kill Isaac, whereas Francis does kill Bishop. However, O'Connor's reading of the *Summa Theologica* may have taught her that for Aquinas, Abraham would have been justified even if he had slaughtered the boy. In the *Summa* and elsewhere, Aquinas famously developed the idea of the "natural law." In simplest terms, natural law is the imprint of the divine law on every human soul; the existence of the natural law means that everyone has innate access to religious morality. O'Connor accepts the natural law as valid and valuable; she writes, "The

Catholic has *the natural law* and the teachings of the Church to guide him."[63] Yet in developing this idea, Aquinas seems to leave himself open to criticism if and when the natural law conflicts with the "teachings of the Church." Jack Mulder summarizes this line of thinking in *Kierkegaard and the Catholic Tradition*. The natural law would seem to forbid the murder of innocents. Yet in Genesis, God commands Abraham to kill his innocent son, Isaac. Thus, the objection goes, the natural law is fallible if the teachings of God occasionally contradict it. But in the *Summa*, Aquinas both anticipates and tries to silence this critique. Aquinas argues that death, whenever it arrives, is just compensation for original sin; thus, whether God requires one's death early or late, that death is justified:

> God regulates the length of a person's earthly life, and so, should God determine that this life will be shorter than one might ordinarily expect, God may do so. Notice also that this is not a violation of the natural law at all, for Aquinas. This is because it is written into the very nature of the natural law that the eternal law, from which the natural law is derived, can overrule some, though not all, things that would otherwise be violations of the natural law.[64]

In suggesting that the eternal law (or the divine will) can sometimes override the natural law, Aquinas—via Mulder—argues that *an untimely death is never unjust if God commands it.* The ramifications of this conclusion on Abraham's case are as striking as they are straightforward: "in insisting that Abraham's deed (were the knife to come down and slay Isaac) would not be a violation of the natural law, Aquinas is also insisting *that it would not, for that reason, count as murder.*"[65] O'Connor's Thomism, then, can help us understand why she would suggest that God "forgets" Bishop's death. Elsewhere in the Hollins College speech cited above, O'Connor implies that the divine will drives Francis's actions throughout *The Violent Bear It Away*: "if [Francis] appears to have a compulsion to be a prophet, I can only insist that in this compulsion there is the mystery of God's will for him."[66] And insofar as God seemingly commands Bishop's death, O'Connor refrains from calling that death unjust. This is not to say that she doesn't find it disgusting or horrifying. In another context, she admits that "There are long periods in the lives of all of us . . . when the truth as revealed by faith is hideous, emotionally disturbing, downright repulsive."[67] But even if the will of God sometimes appears to us as "hideous," O'Connor is not compelled to defend it: "The Catholic fiction writer . . . *feels no need to apologize for the ways of God to man.*"[68]

One might offer a second objection, however, by suggesting that Bishop's death is not apparently related to Francis's mission. It is only in fighting that mission that he kills the young boy. And yet in her letters O'Connor characterizes Bishop as both "redemptive" and Christlike; she calls him "a kind of Christ image, though a better way to think of it is probably just as a kind of redemptive figure."[69] Christ redeems most perfectly in the moment of his death; therefore, in likening Bishop to Jesus, O'Connor implies that his murder produces spiritual merit. While Karl E. Martin rejects O'Connor's own description of Bishop as Christlike, many textual cues confirm the similarity.[70] O'Connor describes Bishop as "the lowest form of innocence," and the child, like Christ, seems unblemished and unblemishable; Mason describes him as "one [Rayber] couldn't corrupt."[71] Further, Jesus—even more than humans—is a mirror reflection of God, and Rayber "did not believe that he himself was formed in the image and likeness of God but that Bishop was he had no doubt."[72] Other characters in the novel detect an aura of sacredness around the boy and seek to protect him; a worker at the lakeside lodge defends Bishop against one of his cousin's taunts, "looking at [Francis] fiercely as if he had profaned the holy."[73] Other descriptions of Bishop recall stories from Matthew, the gospel that gives O'Connor her title. In one of Francis's early attempts to baptize Bishop, the disabled child falls in a fountain; O'Connor writes that Francis's "eyes were on the child in the pool but they burned as if he beheld some terrible compelling vision. The sun shone brightly on Bishop's white head and the little boy stood there with a look of attention."[74] The divine light that sets a halo ablaze on Bishop's brow recalls the opening of the skies at the time of John's baptism of Jesus: "and lo, the heavens were opened to him: and he saw the Spirit of God descending as a dove, and coming upon him" (Matt. 3:16, Douay-Rheims translation). Bishop's dying cry also reminds us of the gospel narrative. In Matthew, a wordless scream is the last sound Jesus makes before perishing: "And Jesus again crying with a loud voice, yielded up the ghost" (27:50). Likewise at the moment of his death, Bishop screams so loudly that his father can hear it across the lake: "The bellow rose and fell, then it blared out one last time, rising out of its own momentum as if it were escaping finally, after centuries of waiting, into silence."[75] As it is unlikely that a child whose head is being held under water would emit a cry audible so far away, O'Connor inserts this "bellow" against nature and sense—a fact that strengthens my own conviction that it is an intentional Biblical allusion.[76] Further, that the cry escapes "after centuries of waiting" harks back to the crucifixion, which occurs long before. The scream's origins in the distant past recall Béguin's contention, cited previously, that Jesus's suffering on the cross outweighs all the sins committed through eternity—past, present, and future. Last, and more playfully, the gospel of Matthew provides an interpretation for one of the more inscrutable symbols in *The Violent Bear It Away*. In an early mention of Bishop, O'Connor writes, "The child had on a black cowboy hat and he was gaping over the top of a trashbasket that he clasped to his stomach. He kept a rock in it."[77] Is the rock this little Jesus's Peter, right-hand man and church founder? Perhaps. Says Christ in Matthew 16:18: "thou art Peter; and upon this rock I will build my church, and the gates of hell shall not prevail against it." Simply, there is ample evidence that Bishop is a Christ, and according to the atonement theologies O'Connor knows well, only his death makes him the "redemptive figure" who can save us. Thus, when Francis kills Bishop, the boy is not collateral damage; instead, his death is a part of a divine plan.

In developing a third objection, one might note that *Violent* features not one but two potential child killers: why does O'Connor praise Francis and "forget" his crime while describing Rayber as demonic? In her letters, O'Connor paints Francis and Rayber as two sides of the same coin. Both are "educated" by Mason, but one (Rayber) resists his spiritual vocation while the other (Francis) eventually submits. In a letter to Alfred Corn, she writes, "[Francis] Tarwater wrestles with the Lord and Rayber wins";[78] Rayber conquers his spiritual urges and flees them. Yet for O'Connor, the academic secularism that drives Rayber from God is diabolical.[79] In a separate letter, O'Connor—who identifies the disembodied voice of Francis's "friend" as the Devil's—explains that in early drafts of the novel, Rayber is totally evil: "When I first set out I had in mind that Rayber would echo all his friend's [the Devil's] sentiments." And while in revisions, Rayber is not "pure evil," he remains menacing.[80] He terrifies because his godless compassion for children masks a deadly streak; I contend that it exemplifies the "tenderness" O'Connor describes in the quote above that leads to "the fumes of the gas chamber."[81] Near the center of the novel, Rayber hears a child preacher sermonizing about Herod's slaughter of children. The child proclaims, "The world hoped old Herod would slay the right child, the world hoped old Herod wouldn't waste those children, but he wasted them. He didn't get the right one. Jesus grew up and raised the dead."[82] The child rejoices with Christians everywhere that Herod fails in his attempt to kill Jesus, leaving the Christ alive to save the rest of us. But Rayber is aghast; forgetting Jesus, he focuses on the children Herod *does* kill and all the other innocents God's mercy does not cover: "Rayber felt his spirit borne aloft. But not those dead! he cried, not the innocent children, not you, not me when I was a child, not Bishop, not Frank [Francis]! and he had a vision of himself moving like an avenging angel through the world, gathering up all the children that the Lord, not Herod, had slain."[83] As with Ivan Karamazov and Camus's Clamence, Rayber implies that the blood of children who die (or suffer) is on God's hands, and he dreams of himself as their savior and avenger. As Desmond writes, "Rayber [is] a caricature of the suffering savior; he would displace Christ and appropriate the role of victim-savior for himself."[84] But as the rest of the novel reveals, Rayber's tenderness is hypocritical, or at least purely theoretical; it is a clever response to a child preacher's sermon and nothing more. For when he is faced with an actual suffering child he turns murderous. Swimming with Bishop one day, Rayber decides to end him:

> He had taken him out on his shoulders and when he was chest deep
> in the water, had lifted him off, swung the delighted child high in the
> air and then plunged him swiftly below the surface on his back and

held him there, not looking down at what he was doing but up, at an imperturbable witnessing sky, not quite blue, not quite white. A fierce surging pressure had begun upward beneath his hands and grimly he had exerted more and more force downward. In a second, he felt he was trying to hold a giant under. Astonished, he let himself look. The face under the water was wrathfully contorted, twisted by some primeval rage to save itself. Automatically he released his pressure. Then when he realized what he had done, he pushed down again angrily with all his force until the struggle ceased under his hands.[85]

Though Bishop survives, one cannot miss the father's firm resolve in the moment of his attempted filicide. In this passage, O'Connor makes it clear that Rayber must struggle to kill his child and redouble his efforts midway through. The only reason Bishop lives is because "The beach which [Rayber] had thought empty before had become peopled with strangers," one of whom performs artificial respiration on the boy.[86] Further, if the father initially fails in murdering Bishop, many critics note that he is complicit in the boy's eventual death. Gentry argues that he "allows" his son to die;[87] Giannone suggests that Rayber "rejects [Bishop] as an ugly burden created by a brutish deity";[88] and Desmond claims that "Rayber's manipulation of his son Bishop leads inexorably to the child's death."[89] In other words, Rayber's concern for children is the "tenderness" "wrapped in theory" that O'Connor rejects. Cut off from Christian mercy, the father's love is an abstraction with no real-world value. Further, this abstraction hides a distinct eugenic urge. Shortly before his son's death, Rayber admits to Francis, "Nothing ever happens to that kind of child . . . In a hundred years people may have learned enough to put them to sleep when they're born."[90] Rayber yearns for a more "enlightened" future in which the state will kill his handicapped son for him. This move illuminates O'Connor's link between theoretical tenderness and the gas chambers, because the Nazis' first targets—before the Jews—were the mentally and physically handicapped.[91] All this is not to say that Rayber doesn't feel real love—the tenderness founded in Christian faith that O'Connor distinguishes from mere sentiment. Rayber has compassion for his son but fails to comprehend that emotion because it is, in Martin's language, "non-utilitarian."[92] Its overflowing energy terrifies Rayber. Writes O'Connor, "Rayber's love for Bishop is the purest love I have ever dealt with. It is because of its terrifying purity that Rayber has to destroy it."[93]

Of course, Francis's drive toward prophecy is destructive too, and Bishop is destined to play the victim no matter which relative, Rayber or Francis, snatches him up. But it is Francis who ends the boy's life, and O'Connor keeps her peace as he holds Bishop under. In discussing Abraham's near-murder of Isaac, Mulder complains that the saint's position "is not as difficult to discern as it is to swallow."[94] The same might be said of O'Connor's claim that Bishop's murder is forgotten by God. Statements like these compel

Srigley to call O'Connor's a "dark faith" and cause Gooch to mention the author's "extreme theology" in his excellent 2009 biography. With respect to both of these skilled readers of O'Connor's writing, I beg to differ. Indeed, O'Connor's faith is not dark; it is merely honest. And her theology isn't extreme; it is remarkably orthodox. She is just more willing than most devout Catholics to approach the most startling aspects of her tradition with a spirit of acceptance—or with a respect for mystery.

Chapter 4

"God Descended to Suffer with Us"

John Updike's Search for a Sensitive Atonement

Well, I drowned the baby.
> —John Updike, Interview with Charlie Reilly

Abraham's willingness to sacrifice his son Isaac . . . and God's willingness to let His son, Jesus, be crucified echo the sinister familial murders of Greek legend.
> —John Updike, *More Matter*

John Updike never liked killing off his own characters; thus, unlike Flannery O'Connor, he seldom did. In an interview with Charles Samuels, he spoke of the affection that kept him from such brutality: "I feel a tenderness toward my characters that forbids making violent use of them."[1] In his many novels and short stories, that tenderness works in tandem with the author's desire to avoid cheap drama to produce a collection largely free of violence; Updike says elsewhere, "I detect in myself a wish not to have *false* violence. It's terribly easy when you're sitting at a typewriter, of course, to kill and maim and produce explosions."[2] Hence, when Updike does end a character's life, the work of killing exhausts him. Perhaps it's unsurprising, then, to hear that no death weighed on Updike so heavily as the drowning of the infant Rebecca Angstrom at the climax of his most famous novel, *Rabbit, Run*. In it, Harry "Rabbit" Angstrom, fed up with the drudgery of his rust-belt, middle-class home, leaves his pregnant wife, Janice, and toddler son, Nelson, for the better part of a summer, taking up with another woman. Guilt and boredom send him scurrying back on the birth of his second child, Rebecca, but he slips away again just a few weeks later after a fight with his wife. The next morning, Janice copes by turning to the bottle, and shortly thereafter, an ill-fated attempt by the drunken woman to bathe her newborn ends with the baby's death. The usually sure-handed Updike describes his own difficulties writing the episode:

A part of me didn't really want to write the *Rabbit* scene at all. *I knew the infanticide had to happen* and I had been building up to it for some time. As matters worked out, I wound up writing it during one long afternoon. This was back in the days when I smoked, and by the time I finished I had composed about seventeen pages and had smoked so many cigarettes that I was dizzy. When I finally came down the stairs, I remember telling my family, "Well, I drowned the baby."[3]

Updike's dizzy exhaustion notwithstanding, a pressing question remains: why does baby Becky's death *have to* happen? For an author who resists depictions of violence, there are less spectacular ways to demonstrate the steep costs of breaking up a family. So why must this child perish?

I argue that the answer has everything to do with theology, especially given that Updike has described *Rabbit, Run* as an "attempt to examine the human predicament from a theological standpoint."[4] Further, that *Rabbit* culminates in the killing of a child suggests that for Updike as for O'Connor before him, the death of an infant provokes theological reflection. But if O'Connor uses faith, scripture, and theology to see infanticide as part of the divine plan, Updike cannot. Simply, his religious response to child murder is not acceptance; it is skepticism. In a 1996 *New Yorker* essay on evil, Updike observes that the modern mass media pushes the suffering of children into our consciousness in unprecedented ways; he further notes that contemporary theology may not equip believers to explain that suffering satisfactorily:

> Distant famines that would have received a paragraph or two in the Victorian press now engender televised closeups of skeletal, moribund children . . . child abuse that used to be hushed up is publicized and prosecuted, even decades after the event . . . We are more sensitive, it may be, and less willing to forgive the heavens than were our ancestors, who accepted fate's blows as part of God's inscrutable plan or as shortcuts to a blissful afterlife.[5]

Updike, it seems, counts himself among those who are "less willing to forgive the heavens" when the most vulnerable among us are abused or killed. Yet "less willing" is not "unwilling," and in both his nonfiction and in his novels, there is ample evidence that while Updike cannot simply "forgive" God for the abuse of innocents, he still pursues more satisfying theological responses to it. And indeed, such a pursuit fuels the "theological" novels of the *Rabbit* tetralogy. For Rabbit, too, is a skeptical believer and a surprising seeker after new answers to the oldest, hardest religious questions.

In this chapter, I claim that Becky's death speeds Rabbit's search for a new theology that is more "sensitive" to the suffering and death of innocents. More specifically, I argue that her drowning is the gravitational center of a religious discussion that spans both *Rabbit, Run* and its sequel—and that sees the waning of older atonement models and the rise of a new Christology that affirms God's willingness to both witness and share the suffering of victims. Updike dramatizes this movement by depicting Rabbit's drift away from traditional religious figures—the Revs. Kruppenbach and Eccles of *Rabbit, Run*—and his unexpected attraction to Skeeter, the black prophet and revolutionary of *Rabbit Redux* whose thinking echoes that of the great African-American theologian James H. Cone.

Perhaps no author is better prepared to moderate such a nuanced discussion of religion as John Updike, along with O'Connor the most theologically literate American author addressed in this project (and perhaps in the twentieth century). As Larry Woiwode says of his fiction, "the alert reader recognizes the inclusion of Christian iconography and symbols and apologetics, even doctrine, in nearly every book."[6] Updike's grandfather was a minister, and his father was extremely active in the local Lutheran parish. This upbringing gave the young Updike what would now be considered a remarkable familiarity with Christian scripture: "In my childhood home, which was of average Protestant piety, Biblical characters were as familiar, and as frequently mentioned, as relatives on a distant farm."[7] His own churchgoing continued regularly even after he left home, and he frequently attended services through college and even during his early stint as a staff writer for the *New Yorker*: "I felt lost and lonely without it," he wrote.[8] (He would remain an active member of various parishes throughout his life.) Nonetheless, his early twenties were a period of religious crisis, and it was during this decade that he gave himself a master class in theology in order to rebuild and sustain his flagging faith. Though he tested liberal theologians like Tillich and Rudolf Bultmann, he found them insubstantial and instead took refuge in the writings of the conservative Karl Barth, whose thinking was as seminal to Updike as Aquinas's was to O'Connor.[9] (Jack DeBellis notes that Updike also read widely in Aquinas during this period.[10]) He also found valuable insights in the works of other Christian writers, among them G. K. Chesterton, T. S. Eliot, Miguel de Unamuno, and Søren Kierkegaard;[11] in his memoir-like collection of essays, *Self-Consciousness*, Updike writes that this handful "helped me believe."[12] Nonetheless, later writings prove his familiarity not only with the moderns but also with Tertullian, Anselm, Aquinas, Luther, Calvin, and other classic thinkers of the Christian tradition. And while Updike admits that his personal beliefs changed little after this period of religious crisis,[13] he continued to read theology throughout his career, as evidenced by his later reviews of new work by (or on) Barth, Tillich, and Kierkegaard.

In his mature writings, both fictional and nonfictional, Updike repeatedly indicates his rejection of traditional atonement. Ralph Wood argues that many of Updike's heroes are "version[s] of [their] creator,"[14] and nearly all of his religious protagonists are uncomfortable with atonement. In *Roger's Version*, a 1986 novel in which Updike stages a theological debate between a middle-aged divinity school professor and a young evangelical computer programmer, the jaded academic finds the cross earrings his niece wears "repulsive," in part "because of the *barbaric* religion of blood atonement they symbolized."[15] In the first movement of *In the Beauty of the Lilies* (1996), the Reverend Clarence Wilmot—his faith in decay—writes off atonement theology as a "bloody tit-for-tat."[16] And in *A Month of Sundays*, the pastor-protagonist Tom Marshfield mocks the comic-book version of the mystery of the cross peddled by a bedraggled Jesus freak: "Under odious purple illustrations, and in a coarse printing aimed at the puerile, we find this travesty of the epic mystery of the Atonement: 'God is our great father in Heaven and we are his children on Earth. We've all been naughty and deserve a spanking, haven't we? *But Jesus, our big brother*, loved us and the Father so much that he knew the spanking would hurt us both, so he offered to take it for us!' "[17] That the monstrous weight of the crucifixion might be shrunk to a bruised bottom is the type of reductive theology Updike himself rejects; elsewhere, he writes, "I try . . . not subject the world to a kind of cartoon theology which gives predictable answers."[18] And for Updike, there is something "cartoonish" about atonement. Indeed, the notion that God might require expiation—be it a "spanking" or a crucifixion—in exchange for our naughtiness smacks of an outmoded interpretation of the Christian message. In *Self-Consciousness*, Updike writes, "An age of anxiety all too suitably takes God as a tranquillizer, just as feudal times took Him as Lord or King, leaving us a language of piety loaded with obsolete obeisances, and other eras took him as a magical incantation, *or an insatiable repository of blood sacrifice and self-mutilation*."[19] Only "other eras" roll out a God who needs either sacrifice—which objective atonement theologies entail—or self-mutilation—the radical end of subjective atonement. He puts a finer point on it earlier in the same work, noting that "Our brains are no longer conditioned for reverence and awe . . . *we feel morally superior to the Biblical notions of atonement* and damnation."[20]

Though Rabbit is no theologian, he too feels morally superior to the religious logics that drive both subjective (Abelardian) and objective (Anselmian) atonement models.[21] That the character shares such thinking with his creator is no surprise given Updike's own admission that he is quite like Rabbit: "Intellectually, I'm not essentially advanced over Harry Angstrom. I went to Harvard, it's true, and wasn't much good at basketball; other than that we're rather similar."[22] He says much the same thing of the Rabbit of *Redux*, arguing that the latter is "a receptacle for my disquiet and resentments, which would sit more becomingly on him than on me."[23] Such statements lend credence to the idea that Rabbit is the most prominent of Updike's religious avatars.[24]

In *Rabbit, Run*, institutional Christianity is represented by two figures, the Reverends Kruppenbach and Eccles. The former is Rabbit's own Lutheran pastor (though Updike indicates that Rabbit hasn't been to church in years).

The second is Janice's family pastor, who repeatedly tries to coax Rabbit back into his wife's arms. That Rabbit never actually speaks with Kruppenbach—and that he seemingly hasn't in years—indicates that the stalwart Lutheran's message holds little value for him.[25] And Kruppenbach's message, at least as delivered in the booming monologue to which he subjects Eccles, suggests that he cleaves to the Abelardian or "subjective" atonement model. As a reminder, Abelard's theory of atonement—often referred to as "moral influence"—suggests that Jesus dies on the cross to set an ethical example for humanity. Jesus's selfless suffering and death serve as a model for human behavior. More briefly, if Christ sacrifices himself, so may we. Here is Kruppenbach's understanding: "There is your role: to make yourself an exemplar of faith. *There* is where comfort comes from: faith, not what little finagling a body can do here and there; stirring the bucket. In running back and forth you run from the duty given you by God, to make your faith powerful, so that when the call comes you can go out and tell them, 'Yes, he is dead, but you will see him again in Heaven. Yes, you suffer, but you must *love* your pain, because it is *Christ's* pain.' "[26] For Kruppenbach, believers are called to emulate Christ, both in faith and in suffering. But Rabbit, it seems, has given up on Kruppenbach long ago. Further, the Lutheran pastor's message of self-sacrifice—of suffering freely accepted in mimicry of Jesus—is anathema to Harry, who, as his lover, Ruth, puts it, "got the idea he's Jesus Christ out to save the world just by doing whatever comes into his head."[27] Rabbit will model himself after no one but himself. Or, as Wood puts it, he will live by "the only divinity he knows—his own egoistic energy."[28]

Eccles, on the other hand, may be understood as preaching some version of the Anselmian atonement. And while the theologian's name does not appear in *Rabbit*, we can confirm that even early on, Updike knew Anselm well; in 1962, Updike published a review of Barth's monograph on Anselm.[29] Eccles, Updike writes, is not theologically hyperliterate, but he speaks in Anselmian language: at Becky's funeral, he says to Rabbit, "Harry, it's not for me to forgive you. You've done nothing to forgive. I'm equal with you in guilt . . . Harry, I *know* that people are brought to Christ. I've seen it with my eyes and tasted it with my mouth."[30] Here, Updike gives us a fragmentary sketch of objective atonement. Humans are equal in guilt and incapable of forgiving one another. Hence, we need Christ to salve the wound we cannot. But in another frequently quoted passage, we learn that such thinking is not to Rabbit's "taste." After listening to one of Eccles sermons, Rabbit is unmoved: "Harry has no taste for the dark, tangled, visceral aspect of Christianity, the *going through* quality of it, the passage *into* death and suffering that redeems and inverts these things, like an umbrella blowing inside out. He lacks the mindful will to walk the straight line of a paradox."[31] A suffering that inverts and redeems—this is satisfaction talk. Further, Updike cheapens Christianity's crucial paradox with his choice of metaphor: redemptive suffering is an "umbrella blowing inside out"—a useless item to be discarded. Statements like these lead Lewis A. Lawson to contend that Harry "will not believe that God entered history as Christ, then died to redeem mankind . . . [and] will not hear of a religion where acknowledgement of sin and the necessity of a Redeemer become apparent."[32] Or, more concisely, there is evidence that Rabbit rejects the logics of objective atonement.

All of which is not to say that Rabbit, raised a relatively orthodox Christian, doesn't occasionally fall into the thought patterns of objective atonement. Most crucial among these are the closely related notions of vicarious suffering—the idea that one person might suffer for another's sin—and penal substitution—that one might bear another's deserved punishment. As a simple but instructive example of these related notions, William Placher identifies *The Whipping Boy*, the Newberry award–winning children's book by Sid Fleischman (later made into a television movie). In the story, the family of a prince employs a peasant boy to receive the young royal's punishment when the latter misbehaves, "because punishment had to be apportioned, but it was unfitting to punish the prince."[33] Objective atonement theologies feature a similar transfer as Jesus suffers then punishment humans ought to receive for their own sins. Rabbit, waiting in the hospital while Janice labors to deliver Becky, fears the same thing might happen to his wife or his newborn daughter—that either might die for his mistakes: "A damp warm cloth seems wrapped around his heart. He is certain that as a consequence of his sin Janice or the baby will die. His sin a conglomerate of flight, cruelty, obscenity, and conceit; a black clot embodied in the entrails of the birth."[34] In explaining Rabbit's sense that his daughter's life is threatened by his own sin, Updike completes a metaphor he introduces earlier in the novel when he compares Harry and Janice to "David and Michal."[35] David is the great king of Israel, Michal his first wife. When David sleeps with Bathsheba, God, in another key instance of Biblical penal substitution, kills not David but the child his paramour bears. Thus, Rabbit's philandering recalls the old Israelite king's, and he fears that his punishment will be the same. However, when Rabbit is given the chance to seek forgiveness for his sin from a priest sitting next to him in the hospital waiting room, he demurs: "Though his bowels twist with the will to dismiss this clot, to turn back and undo, he does not turn to the priest beside him, but instead reads the same sentence about delicious fried trout again and again."[36] The priest beside him might offer Rabbit expiation. But Harry quite consciously keeps his attention on the "delicious fried trout," spurning the promise the priest represents.

Yet the baby dies just a few pages later, after Rabbit flees his home once more and Janice accidentally drowns the child. In the aftermath, Rabbit might take solace in the promises of atonement—that his sins are great but that Christ's death outweighs them. But Rabbit's truest urge in the final pages of the book is not to avoid blame for his daughter's death but to assign it, either to himself or to others. Shortly after the drowning, Rabbit is relieved to find that guilt has settled on his shoulders: "The house again fills with the thought that he is a murderer. He accepts the thought gratefully; it's true, he is, he is, and hate suits him better than forgiveness."[37] Rabbit would rather be guilty than the recipient of an ersatz pardon. He's not a masochist; he just prefers the simpler math of retributive justice: sin brings blame. Indeed, throughout the novel, he ably bears the social scorn that is punishment for fleeing his wife, whether that scorn comes from Mrs. Eccles, his mother-in-law, or his lover, Ruth. Thus, Rabbit is disappointed to hear that no charges will be filed in his daughter's death, and that his in-laws will accept him grudgingly back into the family: "It disgusts him to feel the net of law slither from him. They just won't do it for you, they just won't take you off the hook."[38] Ironically, the hook here is either forgiveness or forgetfulness. His child is dead, and he wants blame apportioned. This drive to identify a culprit helps explain his disgusting outburst at Becky's funeral, over which Eccles presides. As the family huddles round the infant's grave, Janice looks up to her husband for comfort, and he bursts out, "'Don't look at me,' he says. 'I didn't kill her . . . You all keep acting as if I did it. I wasn't anywhere near. She's the one . . . Hey it's O.K. . . . . You didn't mean to.'"[39] For Rabbit, this is the "simplest factual truth."[40] A baby dies. Someone is at fault. If it's not him, it must be his wife. For Harry, blame is a burden to bear, not a commodity to be passed from buyer to seller. As Placher notes—and as Harry would agree—such a transfer "makes no moral sense"; "The young whipping boy found the whole idea ludicrously unfair, and so, I suspect, do most of us."[41] David Lewis further notes that even Christians who believe in penal substitution reject it when applied to this-worldly situations: what court would allow a convicted burglar's friend to serve his jail time?[42]

So Rabbit runs once more, away from his daughter's corpse, away from the family who weakly forgives, and away from Reverend Eccles, Updike's standard-bearer for objective atonement. But where is he running? For Bailey, Stephen H. Webb, Suzanne Henning Uphaus, and others, he runs away from the faith;[43] these critics see in the sequel to *Rabbit, Run* Harry's "rejection of religion."[44] To the contrary, however, I argue that *Rabbit Redux* stages Harry's surprising acceptance of an unorthodox new religion, the theology of the revolutionary Skeeter, whom Rabbit surprisingly welcomes into his home. Among other things, Skeeter echoes the promises of a theology of black power just gaining traction when the novel was published. This new theology, espoused most famously by James H. Cone, offers a unique understanding of the atonement that is both attractive to Rabbit and quite close to Updike's own.

Rabbit Redux opens roughly ten years after Becky's death. At the outset, we find that Harry returned to Janice after the funeral and that the couple remains together. However, in this book it is Janice's turn to stray from the marital bed, and she spends most of the novel living with a coworker named Charlie Stavros. In her absence, Rabbit becomes unmoored and invites two unexpected guests into the family home—first Jill, a young hippie in hiding from her rich parents in Connecticut, and later Skeeter. The latter brings with him a small library with which he educates Rabbit and Nelson on black history from the victims' perspective. In it are works by Frederick Douglass, W. E. B. DuBois, Frantz Fanon, and Eldridge Cleaver, and Skeeter has the Angstroms read aloud from these and other works as part of a series of nightly "seminars." However, as Updike notes, Skeeter's message isn't only historical: "There seems to be not only a history but a theology behind his anger."[45] Because critics can trace the history not only through Skeeter's words but through an identifiable corpus, it has received more attention. In the following, I flesh out Skeeter's theology while arguing that certain of its elements are especially attractive to Rabbit as he continues to cope with his daughter's death so many years before.

Skeeter has long made professional readers of *Redux* nervous. Wood calls him an "angel of wrath" and a "black prophet of destruction."[46] Bailey claims that he advocates a "grotesque, self-serving, and murderous theology."[47] Kyle A. Pasewark dubs him an "insane demoniac";[48] and Vargo names him the "anti-Christ."[49] (By contrast, Toni Morrison argues in *Playing in the Dark* that Skeeter is Updike's most convincing character.) And there's no denying the man has a mean streak. He's vulgar and sexually manipulative. Local police suspect him (erroneously) of inciting violence. He's a drug user and a drug dealer. And he enables Jill's heroin use despite the fact that she's a recovering addict. Thus, few take him at his word when he calls himself "the real Jesus . . . *the* black Jesus, right?"[50] But one who most certainly does is Updike himself: "no one's given serious consideration to the idea that Skeeter, the angry black, might *be* Jesus. He *says* he is. I think probably he might be. And if that's so, then people *ought* to be very nice to him."[51] Here, Updike echoes Rabbit, who says of Skeeter early in their idiosyncratic friendship, "If he is the next Jesus, we got to keep on His good side."[52] And despite Rabbit's ignorance, racism, and occasional repulsion, he does just this, taking Skeeter into his home, keeping him there despite eventual protests by Jill and Nelson, and later abetting Skeeter's escape from town.

I believe that Rabbit sustains the relationship in part because of Skeeter's religion, and I strongly suspect that the unnamed theology "behind" Skeeter's anger is the black theology of James H. Cone, who introduced many of his most influential ideas in *Black Theology and Black Power*, released in 1969 just two years before *Rabbit Redux*. Today, Cone is lauded as the father of black theology and one of the great American religious thinkers of the last half-century. But the power of Cone's ideas was apparent from the outset. The religious historian Patrick Allitt notes that upon its publication, *Black Theology* "caused a sensation."[53] In a 1969 review published in *Christian Century*, then the voice of mainstream Protestantism, Will Herzfeld called Cone's first book "authentically revolutionary."[54] And in a glowing *Theology Today* review, Glenn R. Bucher called Cone a "major theological voice" and argued that *Black Theology and Black Power* "introduced the notion of black theology, and Cone as its first spokesman."[55] That a Christian author as theologically literate as Updike would not know of Cone is unlikely. But the most convincing evidence of Cone's influence on *Redux* is the fact that in Skeeter's language, Updike imports Cone's central image, that of the black Jesus. Here is Cone, in one of the most frequently quoted passages from *Black Theology*: "Whether whites want to hear it or not, *Christ is black, baby*, with all of the features which are so detestable to white society."[56] Yet Cone is less interested in blackness as a racial category than as a contemporary marker of oppression. In simplest form, his argument is as follows: throughout history, God has sided with the incarcerated, the downtrodden, and the abused. Thus, in ancient Egypt, God champions the enslaved Jews. But in the middle of the twentieth century, the oppressed are poor blacks, and God's wish for them is liberation. Cone argues that God not only identifies with blacks but *empowers* them. Thus, his message is not only theological; it is political and ethical: "Through Christ the poor man is offered freedom now to rebel against that which makes him other than human."[57] For Christians living during the civil-rights era, this "rebellion" involved fighting the particular methods used to oppress blacks: thus, Cone "refuses to embrace any concept of God which makes black suffering the will of God. Black people should not accept slavery, lynching, or any form of injustice as tending to good."[58] Simply put, Cone advocates nothing less than a religious revolution that has as its primary goal the freedom of oppressed blacks, here, now. Further, if white Christianity stands in the way, it becomes the enemy: "In America, God's revelation on earth has always been black, red, or some other shocking shade, but never white. Whiteness, as revealed in the history of America, is the expression of what is wrong with man. It is a symbol of man's depravity. God cannot be white, even though white churches have portrayed him as white . . . Reconciliation to God means that white people are prepared to deny themselves (whiteness), take up the cross (blackness) and follow Christ (black ghetto)."[59]

Frequently, the black Jesus Skeeter channels Cone. Like Cone, Skeeter rejects the "white" God as merely a prop the powers that be use to uphold the status quo and ignore the violence it promotes. He opens, "I got news for you. Your God's a pansy. Your white God's queerer than the Queen of Spades."[60] He later decries the white "Puritan" Jesus as preaching a convenient blindness to others' pain: "All these people around here are walking around inside their own *heads*, they don't even know if you kick somebody else it *hurts*, Jesus won't even tell 'em because the Jesus they brought over on the boats was the meanest most de-balled Jesus the good Lord ever let run around scaring people."[61] For Skeeter, the white Jesus of mainline American Christianity fails to promote the most basic human compassion. A real Jesus would enliven us to the other's pain; the white Jesus hides it from us, even when we are its cause—even when we are doing the kicking. In the American South, the "white Jesus" even tacitly condones the worst crimes of Jim Crow:

"So what did the South do? They said baboon and lynched and whipped and cheated the black man of what pennies he had and thanked their white Jesus they didn't have to feed him anymore."[62] By contrast, Skeeter's black theology—like Cone's—promotes empowerment for the oppressed. Frederick Douglass's famous aphorism on the relationship between strength and integrity—"A man without force . . . is without the essential dignity of humanity"[63]—brings Skeeter near-sexual ecstasy. Further, he preaches a message of love that liberates and a chaos that breaks the status quo. If white Christianity bolsters the structure that promulgates racial injustice, Skeeter preaches a vertiginous freedom devoted to breaking oppressive power: "I am full of love . . . Love strikes and liberates. Right? Jesus liberated the moneychangers from the temple. The new Jesus will liberate the new moneychangers. The old Jesus brought a sword, right? The new Jesus will also bring a sword. He will be a living flame of love. Chaos is God's body. Order is the Devil's chains."[64] Strength, sympathy, liberation, and rebellion are the watchwords of Skeeter's theology—as they are of Cone's.

That Skeeter echoes the father of black theology is unsurprising. On the other hand, Harry's attraction to Skeeter is quite unexpected. How can we describe the friendship that flowers between these two dissimilar characters? And further, how can we explain Updike's investment in black theology?[65] To answer these questions, we must examine Cone's Christology—and his understanding of atonement. Though Cone—like both Harry and Updike— explicitly rejects both objective and subjective atonement theologies in his 1975 volume *God of the Oppressed*, one can detect his preference for an alternate theory in *Black Theology and Black Power*.[66] For Cone, Christ's death on the cross neither saves us from sin nor sets a moral example. Instead, it indicates in spectacular fashion that God enters the world in Christ to share our suffering with us. In the crucifixion, God proves that he partakes of our pain and that he too experiences the anguish that sometimes defines human existence. On the cross, says Cone, God takes on the suffering of the oppressed: "Their suffering becomes his; their despair, divine despair."[67] Later, Cone speaks in the voice of the God of black theology, writing, "Remember, I know the meaning of rejection because in Christ I was rejected; the meaning of physical pain because I was crucified; the meaning of death because I died."[68] In coming to earth in Jesus, God demonstrates that he knows and shares humans' physical pain, mental anguish, and social rejection.[69]

Updike has a similar understanding of the cross. In a review of Mailer's *Gospel According to the Son*, Updike writes of the meaning of *kenosis*, the Christian notion that Jesus empties himself of his divinity when he becomes incarnate: "Without such an emptying [kenosis], the suffering would not be real, nor the Christian answer to the theological problem of suffering—*that God descended to suffer with us*—persuasive."[70] This brief passage lends insight into Updike's own interpretation of Jesus's incarnation and death. Jesus empties himself of his godhood so that he might truly suffer.[71] Further, his suffering with us is apparently *the* purpose of his descent. In Aulén's theological vocabulary, Updike and Cone both preach a "continuous" version of atonement. In the figure of Christ on the cross, Jesus and God are both present, here to experience human suffering and thus bear its burden with us.

Such a continuous version of atonement, which forcefully affirms God's presence—in Jesus, on the cross, on earth—is appealing for both Updike and Rabbit. Indeed, it responds to basic questions about God's existence that fuel Updike's early-adult spiritual crises. In describing the way these crises manifest in the author's prose, Thomas M. Dicken writes, "Like a tongue returning to a rough filling, Updike goes back to basic existential issues. In the last analysis, is there God or just Nothing?"[72] Updike articulates this seminal Christian doubt in *Assorted Prose*: "I doubted perhaps abnormally little. And when they came, they never roosted on the branches of the tree, but attacked the roots; if the first article of the Creed stands, the rest follows as water flows downhill. That God, at a remote place and time, took upon Himself the form of a Syrian carpenter and walked the earth willfully healing and abusing and affirming and grieving, appeared to me quite in the character of the Author of the grass."[73] The first article of the creed states that one believes in God the Father, and Updike's doubts about this claim and its most important corollary—that God takes human form in Jesus—are briefly expressed: Is there a God? Is Jesus God? Continuous theories of atonement answer both these questions with an emphatic yes. Thus, the God crucified is a comforting image for Updike. He writes, "It was a scandalous act [for God] to send His Son to earth to suffer a humiliating and agonizing death . . . Yet it answered, as it were, to the facts, to something deep within men. God crucified formed a bridge between our human perception of a cruelly imperfect and indifferent world and our human need for God, our human sense that *God is present*."[74] God is present, and God is present in our suffering. This is the simple, potent message of Cone, Skeeter, and Updike.

Rabbit seeks signs of such a divine presence as he quests through *Rabbit, Run*. As he says to Eccles in one of their first conversations, "Well I don't know all this about theology, but I'll tell you, I *do* feel, I guess, that somewhere behind all this . . . there's something that wants me to find it."[75] And after the death of his daughter and through his long grieving, the allure of this presence for Harry becomes more pointed even as his sense of it dulls in *Rabbit Redux*. Thus, if Skeeter is this "it" incarnate, Harry's attraction to him makes all the sense in the world. Skeeter both preaches and *is* God present in a deeply flawed world, and he claims that the deity participates in and testifies to human suffering. If Skeeter is Jesus—as both Updike and Rabbit sense—then God is present for the tragedies Harry endures: his wife's departure, his mother's declining health, his lost job, Jill's passing, and, most pressingly, the persistent trauma of his daughter's death. Updike admits that the last of these is ultimately the central theme of Harry's four-book-long development, and the tetralogy is driven by "Harry's search for the daughter he lost, and

his attempt to right, somehow, the wrong of her death: life becomes a long
attempt to heal a central trauma."[76] And in that lifelong effort, a God who
witnesses to our traumas is more valuable than a God who forgives our sins
or exemplifies self-sacrifice.

Yet Skeeter/Jesus isn't the only spiritual presence to witness tragedy in
Rabbit and *Redux*. Best known among these is the "other person" whose
presence Janice senses in the apartment as she stumbles toward killing her
own child.[77] This mysterious force haunts the edges of the page while baby
Rebecca is in the Angstrom home but expands to bursting when the child
dies: Janice's "sense of the third person with them widens enormously, and
she knows, knows, while knocks sound at the door, that the worst thing
that has ever happened to any woman in the world has happened to her."[78]
Boswell posits that this "person"—whom Janice names "Father, Father"—is
God.[79] (That it is a "third" person recalls the language of the Christian trinity.) And in a phrase that recalls O'Connor's *Violent Bear It Away*, John
Stephen Martin goes a step further, contending that "if the infant's death
was watched over by God, her drowning was also her baptism."[80] The "third
person" seemingly appears again when Skeeter stages exploitative sex acts
with Jill shortly before her death in a house fire and once more when Charlie Stavros nearly dies of a heart attack.[81] Updike's attraction to continuous
atonement theologies—which affirm God's presence in times of trial—makes
such interpretations more plausible. Perhaps this is the God whose praises
Cone and Moltmann sing; perhaps this is the deity who witnesses to our suffering and shares our pain.[82]

Of course, in all three instances, the mysterious third person is potentially
menacing. For Janice, it towers over her as Becky slips under the surface of the
water: "under her clenched lids great scarlet prayers arise, wordless, monoto-
nous, and she seems to be clasping the knees of a vast third person whose
name, Father, Father, beats against her head like physical blows."[83] Likewise,
the figure who presides over Jill's abasement and Charlie's near-death experience is disturbing. But even this threatening "god" finds a home in Updike's
own theology. For Updike's divinity is not omnibenevolent. Indeed, God creates and loves, but God also oversees death and destruction. Like Moses's
Yahweh, Updike's will be what he will be. As Updike explains elsewhere, "I've
never really understood theologies which would absolve God of earthquakes
and typhoons, of children starving. A god who is not God the Creator is not
very real to me, so that, yes, it certainly *is* God who throws the lightning bolt
and this God is above the nice god, above the god we can worship and empa-
thize with."[84] Accordingly, Ralph Wood notes that Updike shares his by turns
kind and killing God with his mentor Kierkegaard: "Like Updike, Kierkegaard has a dialectical view of God as both monstrous and merciful."[85] And
in an interview with Jeff Campbell, Updike confirms that it is this God who
presides over the *Rabbit* books, describing Him as "[hardhearted . . .] He's
God of the earthquake, of the volcano, as much as of the flowers."[86]

Yet for Updike, Jesus has that same obstinacy, that same moral ambiguity. Simply, Updike's Jesus isn't nice: "I was struck as a child, and continue to be struck, by the hardness of heart that Jesus shows now and then in the New Testament, advising people to leave their families, driving the money-lenders out of the temple in quite a fierce way."[87] So it is unsurprising that Updike's black Jesus is rough-hewn, not smoothly polished. Skeeter enables Jill's return to addiction and manipulates her sexually. And like Jesus, Skeeter will rage if rage is called for, and he will not necessarily conform to our own standards of moral behavior. Nonetheless, like those who condemn Jesus for killing a fig tree while ignoring that he cures the blind and the lame, Skeeter's harshest critics always overemphasize his negative qualities. They miss the simple fact that he's a remarkably polite house-guest, a patient teacher, and a mentor-figure to Nelson. And while his sermons are angry, they're also true. Finally, though Skeeter flees a conflagration that kills Jill, it's clear that Rabbit's bigoted neighbors start the fire. Further, for Rabbit, Skeeter's moral rectitude is beside the point; his presence is what matters. He stays when everyone else has gone. And like Jesus, his spirit lives on after his departure and eventual death in a shootout. Near the end of *Rabbit Is Rich*, Harry sees the phrase "SKEETER LIVES" spray-painted on various walls around his home-town, and Harry intones the same phrase one last time just pages before his death in *Rabbit at Rest*.[88] Skeeter abides.

I say in closing that this reading of Updike's God—as present in and witnessing to our traumas—meshes with previous theological readings of his novels, most of which focus on the influence of Barth and Kierkegaard. From Barth, Updike learns that God is *totaliter aliter*—totally other, in the theologian's famous phrase. This "Other" God is particularly congenial to Updike as he writes his early novels, among them *Rabbit, Run*; that God is Other means, for Updike, that his ways are "totally inscrutable."[89] Indeed, for both men, we may only know God through what he reveals to us, and no human mind, no matter how clever its devices, may comprehend the divine. To this effect, Lambert quotes Barth in *Roger's Version*: "There is no way from us to God— not even a *via negativa*—not even a *via dialectica* nor *paradoxa*—The god who stood at the end of some human way—even of this way—would not be God."[90] For Barth, at no place is our understanding of God so deficient as on the cross, which Barth describes in *The Word of God and the Word of Man*, the work that influenced Updike most, as a "crisis that denies all human thought."[91] For Barth, perhaps the only thing we can say with any certainty about the cross is that God is *present* there—which is the forceful message of continuous atonement.

Updike also learns from Barth that God's ways may not conform with our standards of morality. Simply, he may stand by as a child dies, whether that child is the son of the king of Israel or of a peeler salesman from Pennsylvania. As Barth writes, again in *Word of God*, "At certain crucial points the Bible amazes us by its remarkable indifference to our conception of good and evil. Abraham, for instance, as the highest proof of his faith desires to sacrifice his son to God; Jacob wins the birthright by a refined deception of his blind father; Elijah slays the four hundred and fifty priests of Baal by the brook of Kishon."[92] Kierkegaard presses this line of thinking further, probing the vexed relationship between revelation and human ethics in *Fear and Trembling*, whose reworkings of the story of Abraham and Isaac Updike calls "splendid."[93] For Kierkegaard, from the perspective of human ethics, when Abraham lifts the knife over Isaac's bound form, he is a murderer; it is only from the god's-eye—or "ultimate"—view that he is a saint.[94] That the Lord commands the sacrifice—and that Abraham trusts God to see him through— lifts Isaac's father into an amoral realm Kierkegaard memorably describes as a "teleological suspension of the ethical."[95] Though the theologian's variations on this theme are complex and multiple, they boil down to one simple truth: the divine is not the ethical, and God's will does not always conform with human morality. For Ralph Wood, this tension is one of the lasting messages of *Rabbit, Run*, which he calls "Updike's most persuasive fictional demonstration of his Kierkegaardian conviction that faith cannot be reduced to morality but may have, on the contrary, a strange kinship with immorality."[96] That God is a witnessing presence to acts we must call immoral is a "strange" mystery whose depths we cannot plumb—or, if we so choose, that we must accept as we strive to become Kierkegaard's "knights of faith."

Updike knows that such faithful acceptance is difficult, and that his God is hard to love. It is difficult to rejoice in the crucifixion or the *akedah* because each resembles a child murder. As Updike writes in his essay "Religion and Literature," "At the heart of the Judaic and Christian religions respectively, Abraham's willingness to sacrifice his son Isaac at God's behest and God's willingness to let His son, Jesus, be crucified echo the *sinister familial murders* of Greek legend."[97] And while Updike admits that "redemptive intercession" softens the likeness (at least in Abraham's case), the resemblances are not easily denied: God is Zeus and Jesus Sarpedon, cut down on the field of battle while his father in heaven watches on. Abraham is Agamemnon and Isaac Iphigenia, slaughtered at Artemis's command. In the preface to a new edition of *Rabbit Redux*, Updike again calls upon the language of Greek family murder to describe the deaths of Becky and Jill: "America and Harry suffered, marveled, listened, and endured. Not without cost, of course. The cost of the disruption in the social fabric was paid, as in the earlier novel, by a girl. Iphigenia is sacrificed and the fleet sails on, with its quarrelling crew."[98] Becky and Jill are thus both Iphigenia figures and Christ figures, killed while God watches on—and perhaps because the gods desire it. And the meaning of the cross does not explain why. Rather, the cross only tells us that God knows our pain because he has shared our pain—and is present witness to it.

Chapter 5

"People Who Die Bad Don't Stay in the Ground"

✦

Surrogacy and Atonement in *Beloved*

> The game of who suffered most? I'm not playing that game.
> That's a media argument. It's almost about quantity. One dead
> child is enough for me.
>
> —Toni Morrison

On October 2, 2006, Charles Roberts walked into a schoolhouse in Pennsylvania's Amish country, lined ten female students up against the blackboard, and began firing. Five of the girls died, as did Roberts, who shot himself before local authorities closed in. Though Roberts's motives remain unclear to this day, the *New York Times* cites the Pennsylvania state police commissioner as saying that Roberts "was angry with life; he was angry with God."[1] Toni Morrison invoked the massacre in her Ingersoll Lecture on Immortality, delivered at Harvard in 2012. In her talk, entitled "Goodness: Altruism and the Literary Imagination," she admits that the evil of the act itself does not grab her: "I've never been interested in or impressed by evil itself."[2] What intrigues her—as it has intrigued many others—is the community's response, which was characterized by both silence and, in Morrison's words, "the shock of forgiveness." In the wake of the tragedy, the Amish community reached out to Roberts's family, consoling them and including them in their circle of mourning. Further, they said almost nothing to the local media, instead choosing to keep their pain to themselves. Says Morrison, they "refused to be lionized, televised." For Morrison, the community's reaction is "characteristic of genuine goodness."

That Morrison is drawn to a story about forgiving a child murderer is no surprise, given the fact that her Pulitzer Prize–winning novel *Beloved* turns on another community's faltering efforts to forgive—or at least understand—a filicide. In that book, the escaped slave Sethe kills her daughter Beloved in an effort to save the baby from a master returned to claim his lost property. And yet it seems as if for Morrison—who, like O'Connor before her, identifies as Catholic—our efforts to pardon or comprehend such heinous crimes may be hindered by our faith. Indeed, a close reading of other writings and interviews suggests that for Morrison—as for Updike—infanticide does not easily give way to forgiveness; instead, it provokes religious skepticism and raises difficult questions about the nature of a God whom we expect will protect the innocent and defend the vulnerable. We begin to see explicit traces of the author's skepticism in *Paradise*, the novel Morrison calls her most comprehensive exploration of religion. The book—which focuses on the lives of the residents of an all-black town called Ruby—features a character named Reverend Misner, who can be understood as Morrison's spiritual alter ego. Of him, she writes, "I suppose the one that is closest to my own sensibility about moral problems would be the young minister, Rev. Misner. He's struggling mightily with the tenets of his religion."[3] We learn more of the nature of that struggle in a sermon Misner delivers following the death of a child named Save-Marie:

> This is why we are here: in this single moment of aching sadness—in contemplating the short life and the unacceptable, incomprehensible death of a child—we confirm, defer or lose our faith. Here in the tick tock of this moment, in this place all our questions, all our fear, our outrage, confusion, desolation seem to merge, snatch away the earth and we feel as though we are falling. Here, we might say, it is time to halt, to linger this one time and reject platitudes about sparrows falling under His eye; about the good dying young (this child didn't have a choice about being good); or about death being the only democracy. This is the time to ask the questions that are really on our minds. Who could do this to a child? Who could permit this for a child? And why?[4]

The child's death is "unacceptable" to a Christian because it contradicts the gospel message to which Misner alludes; the "sparrows falling" come from the tenth chapter of Matthew, when Jesus asks, "Are not two sparrows sold for a penny? Yet not one of them will fall to the ground unperceived by your Father. And even the hairs of your head are all counted. So do not be afraid; you are of more value than many sparrows" (10:29–31). The verses promise that the God who "perceives" the insignificant sparrow will not fail to protect us. And yet the Father does not save Save-Marie. That this failure is also the culmination of Morrison's "religious" novel is both telling and predictable, given Morrison's other statements about God. In a 2004 interview with Antonio Monda, she refuses paternal imagery for the Lord and, like Misner, rejects the "platitudes" that depict the deity as a father who guards and keeps us: "I don't believe in a God the father . . . And I challenge the image of God as a protective father."[5] As for Ivan Karamazov, so for Morrison and Misner, the father god who cannot protect vulnerable children may be no father at all. In the same interview, Morrison expresses admiration for Ivan's creator Dostoevsky, an author who "never left the Heavenly Father in peace."[6]

In this chapter, I argue that Morrison disrupts the peace of the "Heavenly Father" in her earlier, more sustained treatment of child murder, *Beloved*. In that book, a filicide confronts us with a theological challenge that endangers Christian faith—and more specifically, the customary understanding of the atonement. To explain that challenge, I use the work of Delores Williams to argue that *Beloved* illustrates the dangers of traditional atonement theology to the black community—and to black women in particular. For Williams, African-American women are trapped in a system of surrogacy that frequently demands they play others' roles. Further, they can only gain some measure of independence and health if they remove themselves from this system. However, Williams continues, traditional atonement models depict Christ as a surrogate—and thus as a poor model for black women. In *Beloved*, Morrison gives us Sethe, a protagonist caught between surrogacy and self-ownership after the murder of her child—whom the author explicitly likens to Christ. And it is only by moving past the logics of atonement that Sethe can accept the difficult message of self-ownership the novel promotes.

Flannery O'Connor and John Updike wore their faith on their sleeves. In interviews, speeches, and essays, they freely and frequently shared their reflections on spirituality, theology, and belief. The same cannot be said for Morrison, a Nobel Prize winner who has written some of the best-respected novels of the past four decades. Interviewers seldom ask Morrison about her religious background, and when they do, she often directs the conversation towards ethical themes.[7] Yet there is ample evidence that religion plays a crucial role in shaping both her thought and her prose. Morrison, who was born Chloe Wofford, joined the Catholic church at the age of twelve, and—according to one version of the story—adapted her nom de plume from her baptismal name, Anthony.[8] Describing her religious formation, she says, "I had a Catholic education, even though my mother, who was very religious, was Protestant. As a child I was fascinated by the rituals of Catholicism, and I was strongly influenced by a cousin who was a fervent Catholic."[9] While she notes that her faith faltered after Vatican II,[10] she still identifies as Catholic[11] and even suggests that her religion affects her writing as much as her race; asked by Elissa Schappell about her frequent identification as an African-American author, Morrison responds, "It just happens that that space for me is African American; it could be Catholic, it could be Midwestern. I'm those things too, and they are all important."[12] A deep familiarity with the Bible bolsters her Catholicism. In an interview with Charles Ruas, Morrison claims that especially in her youth, "The Bible wasn't part of my reading, it was part of my life."[13] Her grandfather was famous in his day for having read the Bible straight through three times. His influence apparently rubbed off, and Morrison describes her parents as moving "easily into the language of the King James Bible."[14] Of them, her mother sustained the deeper faith; a talented singer who anchored the local church choir, she thought of Christ as a living presence. Says Morrison,

"My mother is one of those deeply spiritual people who had a personal relationship with Jesus. She would have long talks with him regularly."[15] If the rest of her family did not share the depth of her mother's faith, they did partake of her religious devotion, and that devotion marked Morrison; as she puts it, "I have a family of people who were highly religious—that was part of their language. Their sources were biblical. They expressed themselves in that fashion. They took it all very, very seriously, so it would be difficult for me not to."[16] It is unsurprising, then, that Morrison has since developed an interest in theology, which she describes as "totally compelling and interesting."[17]

Though she doesn't elaborate on her exploration of theology, it might make sense that Morrison would turn to someone like James Cone, whose writing on Christianity is a powerful tool for both civil-rights-era and contemporary African Americans. However, a variety of authors have characterized his message as male-centered, or even sexist.[18] Thus, in the waning years of the twentieth century, a new wave of African-American authors published new theologies designed to address the spiritual concerns of black women. Among the most influential is Delores Williams's *Sisters in the Wilderness* (1993), an effort to refigure Christian theology from the perspective of black women. And it is her voice—and her critique of atonement—that is most helpful in mapping the racial and religious landscape of *Beloved*.

Williams identifies "surrogacy" as the defining characteristic of African-American women's experience both during slavery and after. Surrogacy is simply playing a role or completing a task that should be carried out by another. According to Williams, black women are too often compelled to serve as surrogates. For enslaved black women, surrogacy

> was a condition in which people and systems more powerful than black people forced black women to function in roles that ordinarily would have been filled by someone else. For example, black female slaves were forced to substitute for the slave-owner's wife in nurturing roles involving white children. Black women were forced to take the place of men in work roles that, according to the larger society's understanding of male and female roles, belonged to men . . . Sometimes black women were even forced to substitute for the slave owner and his wife in governing roles connected directly with the slave-owner's household.[19]

While emancipation brought a formal end to coerced surrogacy, Williams argues that the social system survived through the Jim Crow period and even into the late twentieth century as voluntary or "pressured" surrogacy, in which the insidious powers of poverty, racism, and sexism continued to force black women to serve inappropriate functions.[20] The challenge for black women both then and now is to reject surrogate roles they do not choose while striving for autonomy and self-ownership.

For Williams, traditional models of atonement theology bolster the institution of surrogacy and hinder black women from reclaiming themselves. She writes, "Ransom, satisfaction, substitution and moral theories of atonement may not be serviceable for providing an acceptable response to African American women's question about redemption and surrogacy."[21] All are suspect because they potentially cast Jesus as being either pressured or forced to take on roles he wouldn't otherwise choose; briefly, each makes Jesus a surrogate. Williams singles out the objective, or satisfaction, atonement model as particularly damaging to black women because it renders surrogacy holy; in objective atonement, "Jesus represents the ultimate surrogate figure; he stands in the place of someone else: sinful humankind. Surrogacy, attached to this divine personage, thus takes on an aura of the sacred. It is therefore fitting and proper for black women to ask whether the image of a surrogate-God has salvific power for black women or whether this image supports and reinforces the exploitation that has accompanied their experience with surrogacy."[22] In the language of objective atonement theology, surrogacy often has other names; satisfaction theorists write of vicariousness or substitution. But no matter the name, the action is the same: Jesus plays a part he isn't rightly supposed to play. Thus, he is a poor model for black women whose exploitation is based on this process of re-placement.[23] Theologians interested in speaking to the experience of black women must then develop new interpretations of the cross or shift the focus away from Golgotha.

Morrison characterizes black womanhood in terms similar to those Williams uses. In an interview with Robert Stepto, she notes, "Black women have had some enormous responsibilities, which in these days people call freedoms—in those days, they were called responsibilities—they lived, you know, working *in other people's, white people's, houses* and taking care of that and working in their own houses and so on and they have been on the labor market."[24] In Morrison's understanding, black women not only manage their own households; they too often take on the added burden of tending to "other people's" houses as well, serving as surrogates for white homeowners. They were and are surrogates.

In what follows, I argue that *Beloved* is first and foremost the story of one black woman's efforts to reject surrogacy even after she escapes slavery. Further, I contend that just as Williams would predict, her efforts are hampered by the patterns of atonement theology that are seminal to black Christianity. And it is only by moving past the most prominent themes of that theology that Sethe can complete her journey out of slavery and surrogacy and into true freedom.

As Susan Bowers and many others note, *Beloved* is based on a true story drawn from *The Black Book*, a collection of primary-source African-American historical documents Morrison worked on during her time as an editor at Random House.[25] In the run-up to the Civil War, Morrison's protagonist,

Sethe, and six men are slaves on a Kentucky farm owned by the Garners. When Mr. Garner dies, a relative simply referred to as "Schoolteacher" comes to run Sweet Home. Schoolteacher is a harsher master, and worsening conditions compel the men, Sethe, and Sethe's children to attempt an escape to Ohio. Only Sethe and her four children make it; they are taken in by Sethe's mother-in-law, Baby Suggs, a free Northern black and a self-styled preacher. Yet four weeks after Sethe's arrival, Schoolteacher comes to reclaim her and her children; immediately upon seeing Schoolteacher, Sethe rushes her children to the woodshed with the intent of killing them all. Caught before she can complete the bloody task, she kills just one, a baby who will come to be known as Beloved. Though Sethe serves jail time, she remains free, and she eventually comes to settle with the rest of her children in Baby Suggs's home at 124 Bluestone Road. The opening of the novel is set roughly two decades after the murder and years after Baby Suggs's passing. In its first pages, Paul D, one of the surviving Sweet Home men, unexpectedly shows up at Sethe's door and moves in. Shortly thereafter, a mysterious woman arrives, and it becomes clear over the course of the novel that she is Beloved, the slaughtered daughter raised from the dead. After a months-long stay that comes to resemble a demonic possession, Beloved is exorcised by members of the community who are able to cast the woman from Sethe's home.

Beloved takes place over a twenty-year period that spans the American Civil War. Thus it features slaves, ex-slaves, and freed slaves, many of whom are women. And the novel is replete with examples of black women either forced or pressured to be surrogates. Of course, the whole institution of slavery is designed to produce surrogate labor; every black character in the novel's antebellum South therefore has experience doing another person's job. Some women, like Baby Suggs, do domestic work while others, like Sethe and her mother, work in the fields. But women fall into other forms of surrogacy unique to their gender. Some women are required to be surrogate mothers, both nursing and caring for the children of their masters and of other slaves. As an example, Sethe can barely recall her own mother; instead, her most vibrant childhood memories involve Nan, a one-armed woman "whose job it was" to suckle abler slaves' children.[26] Unsurprisingly, white offspring get milk first; black children get what's left.[27] Nan also cooks and tends to other women's young children.[28] Sometimes slave women serve as sexual surrogates for their masters, as is the case with another woman named Vashti, the wife of another slave named Stamp Paid but also her master's concubine.[29] Such arrangements mean that slaves are effectively denied sexual satisfaction; as Denver puts it, "Slaves not supposed to have pleasurable feelings on their own; their bodies not supposed to be like that."[30] They must, however, have children, whether they want them or not, and while Mr. Garner doesn't countenance such practices, most other owners do, either forcing slaves to impregnate one another—producing new, valuable property—or "[renting] their sex out on other farms."[31]

Such conditions continue both in the free North and after emancipation. Many women remain domestics or kitchen hands. Others do the work "men don't want to do" at the local slaughterhouse.[32] And we see a reflection of antebellum sexual surrogacy in Sethe's trading of sex for a tombstone carving of her daughter's not-quite-name, Beloved.[33] When characters in *Beloved* realize the ubiquity of surrogacy, the insight can be crippling, or even lethal; this revelation is "what Baby Suggs died of, what Ella knew, what Stamp saw and what made Paul D tremble. That anybody white could take your whole self for anything that came to mind."[34] Black people—and black women especially—are used and disposed of at the prerogative of the powerful. However, both in *Beloved* and elsewhere in her fiction, Morrison elaborates on why constant, coerced surrogacy is so damaging to the human psyche. For when one is so frequently used, repeatedly forced to play parts one normally wouldn't play, one comes to realize that for whites, one has no value as a human but only as an object, a thing. This revelation arrives with harrowing force for at least three of Morrison's main characters. Baby Suggs comes to feel like a chip on a game board: "in all of Baby's life, as well as Sethe's own, men and women were moved around like checkers. Anybody Baby Suggs knew, let alone loved, who hadn't run off or been hanged, got rented out, loaned out, bought up, brought back, stored up, mortgaged, won, stolen or seized."[35] The verbs in the second half of the quotation indicate that Baby, her family, and friends are not so much checkers as poker chips, commodities with exchange value. A similar revelation rocks Paul D when he learns for the first time his actual price as a slave: "He had always known, or believed he did, his value—as a hand, a laborer who could make profit on a farm—but now he discovers his worth, which is to say he learns his price. The dollar value of his weight, his strength, his heart, his brain, his penis, and his future."[36] Sethe's lesson is different but no less painful. She nearly breaks when she realizes that Schoolteacher has been taking physical measurements of herself and the Sweet Home men as part of his "research" into the pseudo-science of race. She overhears Schoolteacher, during lessons, ask his nephews to arrange her characteristics into a human column and an animal column. It is this knowledge that leads her to try her escape: "Ha ha. No notebook for my babies and no measuring string neither."[37] She is unwilling to submit her children to scientific objectification just as Baby and Paul D bridle at the thought of their commoditization.

This insight helps us expand on Williams's argument as to why traditional atonement models—and objective atonement specifically—would be unsuitable for pre- and postwar blacks. In the instances listed here, slavery dehumanizes because it objectifies and commoditizes. And according to ransom theorists, Jesus's death has exchange value. Depending on the angle from which one views the cross, Christ is either a surrogate, dying in our place, or a payment, exchanged to buy humans freedom from the debt of sin. That on the cross and in *Beloved* debts might be paid not with money but with lives—black lives—explains why multiple characters in the novel have a nagging fear of debt. First among them is Sethe's husband, Halle; under Mr. Garner, he is able to work during his free time to earn money to buy his mother Baby Suggs's freedom. Schoolteacher takes over the farm, however, before the debt is paid off, and he menacingly cancels it while demanding that Halle do all his extra work at Sweet Home. Sethe asks him:

> "Is he going to pay you for the extra?"
> "Nope."
> "Then how you going to pay it off? How much is it?"
> "$123.70."
> "Don't he want it back?"
> "He want something."
> "What?"
> "I don't know. But he don't want me off Sweet Home no more."[38]

The labor Halle may use—and sell—is a measure of self-ownership that threatens both Schoolteacher and the institution of slavery itself. Halle's daughter has a similar distaste for indebtedness. Denver loves to hear the story of how the girl Amy saves Sethe's life and helps her deliver the newborn Denver; however, there is something about the story that makes her feel uncomfortable nonetheless: "She loved it because it was all about herself; but she hated it too because it made her feel like a bill was owing somewhere and she, Denver, had to pay it."[39] That Amy is white likely serves unconsciously to enhance Denver's discomfort. One character in the novel, Stamp Paid, even changes his name to escape the sense of his own indebtedness. He does so after he is forced to let his wife serve as a sexual surrogate for his white master's son. Morrison writes, "he renamed himself when he handed over his wife to his master's son . . . With that gift, he decided that he didn't owe anybody anything. Whatever his obligations were, that act paid them off."[40] Whether the renaming works is another matter, however. Stamp "thought it would make him rambunctious, renegade—a drunkard even, the debtlessness, and in a way it did."[41] But in a way it did not, and years later, Stamp wonders if "after all these years of clarity, he had misnamed himself and there was yet another debt he owed."[42] Of crucial importance is Stamp's original name, Joshua, which is actually a closer translation of the Hebrew word for Jesus. Thus in taking a new name, Stamp actively flees the name of the man who purportedly dies on the cross to erase human indebtedness.

Other characters in the novel seek to evade the symbols that most clearly evoke Jesus's death: the cross and the tree. Though Sethe never learns her mother's name, she does remember an identifying mark on her mother's body. That mark is a cross Sethe's mother shows her one day behind the smokehouse: "she opened up her dress front and lifted her breast and pointed under it. Right on her rib was a circle and a cross burnt right in the skin. She said,

'This is your ma'am. This,' and she pointed. 'I am the only one got this mark now. The rest dead. If something happens to me and you can't tell me by my face, you can know me by this mark.' "[43] Sethe, unsure of how to respond, asks if she might have one too. Her mother replies in a rage:

> "Did she?" asked Denver.
> "She slapped my face."
> "What for?"
> "I didn't understand it then. Not till I had a mark of my own."[44]

In the Stepto interview, Morrison notes that often "Black women have held, have been given, you know, the cross."[45] Sethe's mother is given one quite literally, and she refuses to pass on a mark that signifies Christian sacrifice. But Sethe will get a "mark of [her] own" when she is mercilessly whipped by Schoolteacher's nephews. The result is a huge network of scars on her back that many call a "tree." Christians have often referred to the cross on which Jesus dies as a "tree," and the tradition goes all the way back to the biblical book of Acts, which uses the word repeatedly to refer to the wood structure on which Christ is hung.[46] Critics frequently note that Sethe's tree is her own cross.[47] But Paul D, for one, rejects the likeness. For him, the scar is neither cross nor tree; it's just a disgusting reminder of a slavemaster's cruelty. It's "not a tree, as she said. Maybe shaped like one, but nothing like any tree he knew because trees were inviting; things you could trust and be near; talk to if you wanted to as he frequently did since way back when he took the mid-day meal in the fields of Sweet Home."[48] Paul D rejects the scar-as-tree trope, instead opting to think of his favorite tree, a living thing so near to him he gives it a name, "Brother." Abed with Sethe, he thinks, "*that* was a tree. Himself lying in the bed and the 'tree' lying next to him didn't compare."[49] Even for Sethe herself, there is something unnatural—perhaps even *un*holy—about trees as vehicles of sacrifice. Remembering Sweet Home, where she sees the lynched bodies of her friends hanging from sycamores as she escapes, she nonetheless cannot put the two images together; she cannot remember the trees and the bodies: "Boys hanging from the most beautiful sycamores in the world. It shamed her—remembering the wonderful soughing trees rather than the boys. Try as she might to make it otherwise, the sycamores beat out the children every time and she could not forgive her memory for that."[50] Sethe's mother, Paul D, and Sethe herself all reject both cross imagery and imagery that equates trees with suffering, sacrifice, or execution. Morrison's implicit message is Williams's explicit one: "black women [and black men, for that matter] cannot forget the cross, but neither can they glorify it. To do so is to glorify suffering and to render their exploitation sacred. To do so is to glorify the sin of defilement."[51]

It makes sense, then, that the black residents of Cincinnati are drawn to the cross-less sermons of the "unchurched preacher" Baby Suggs, who delivers her message from a rock in "the Clearing—a wide-open place cut deep in the woods nobody knew for what."[52] In an essay on Baby's theology, Emily Griesinger argues that Suggs's message is "genuinely"—if not "typically"—Christian,[53] noting that her sermons maintain crucial parts of Jesus's teachings while avoiding all talk of the crucifixion: "Suggs' sermons omit key aspects of Christian doctrine—she says nothing about Christ's death on the cross."[54] In isolating the pieces of Christian teaching she finds useful, Baby implements an interpretive strategy nineteenth-century African-Americans developed in tailoring the Christian experience to their own lives. As Williams describes it, citing Lawrence Levine, "African Americans (especially during slavery) did not accommodate themselves to the Bible. Rather, they accommodated the Bible to the urgent necessities of their lives."[55] Morrison notes that her grandfather—who was a young child at the time of emancipation—and his generation did the same thing: "they selected out of Christianity all the things they felt applicable to their situation."[56] Baby leaves aside both the cross and the potentially damaging atonement theologies that serve to interpret it. Instead, her teaching promotes a message of self-ownership that serves explicitly to combat the patterns of surrogacy and human commoditization:

> We flesh; flesh that weeps, laughs; flesh that dance on bare feet in grass. Love it. Love it hard. Yonder they do not love your flesh. They despise it. They don't love your eyes; they'd just as soon pick em out. No more do they love the skin on your back. Yonder they flay it. And O my people they do not love your hands. Those they only use, tie, bind, chop off and leave empty. Love your hands! Love them. Raise them up and kiss them. Touch others with them, pat them together, stroke them on your face 'cause they don't love that either. *You* got to love it, *you*! And no, they ain't in love with your mouth. . . . *you* got to love it. . . . More than life-holding womb and your life-giving private parts, hear me now, love your heart. For this is the prize.[57]

The pronouns in this brief passage are as important as the message of self-love it promotes. In the extended paragraph from which this excerpt comes, Baby uses second-person pronouns and possessives no fewer than twenty-three times, and the moral of her speech is simple: *you own you now.* Self-ownership is the opposite of surrogacy, the pattern that underpins the atonement reading of Christian theology. Baby's message is an antidote to surrogacy; it counteracts the forces that turn ex-slaves into "checkers" or require that they do other people's work. And it's a message that recently freed slaves desperately need, for as Morrison writes, "Freeing yourself was one thing; claiming ownership of that freed self was another."[58] Or as Bowers puts it, the escape from slavery has to happen twice: "first to leave physical enslavement by whites and the second time to escape the psychological trauma created by their brutality."[59] Though the process by which one moves past that trauma and arrives at self-ownership is difficult, Sethe makes great strides in the twenty-eight days she spends with Baby Suggs before School-teacher's return: "Bit by bit, at 124 and in the Clearing, along with the others, she had claimed herself."[60] We can see evidence of that "claiming" in the language an older Sethe uses to describe her escape from Sweet Home: "I did it. I got us all out. Without Halle too. Up till then it was the only thing I ever did on my own."[61] In the long paragraph from which these brief sentences derive, Sethe uses first-person pronouns and possessives at least twenty-seven times. In the departure from Sweet Home, Sethe for the first time invents jobs for herself and carries them out. This self-employment is the opposite of sur-rogacy, and a step on an ex-slave's road to self-reclamation.

However, Beloved's death brings Baby's preaching career to an end and sends her to bed for the short remainder of her life. When Stamp presses her to explain why the tragedy ends her religious vocation, Baby is evasive. And while she rejects his suggestion that she's "blaming God,"[62] the filicide none-theless provokes a religious crisis: "God puzzled her and she was too ashamed of Him to say so."[63] While Morrison never clearly explains this puzzlement, I contend that the murder devastates Baby because it represents the intrusion of the cross and atonement into a community she tries to protect from such forces. Indeed, as Morrison depicts her, Beloved is a Christ figure, and Sethe's interpretation of her death is an atonement theology in miniature. Deborah Guth lists similarities between Beloved returned and the risen Christ:

> Sethe's first view of her sitting on a stump, shining like the angel next to Jesus' empty grave (Luke 24:4), her otherworldly strangeness; Sethe's folding of linen reminiscent of the folded linen graveclothes found next to Jesus' empty tomb as she remembers the mark of the cross on her mother's side, and her subsequent exclamation 'Oh, my Jesus' (76); the three scratches on her forehead, the focus on her hands on feet, and the fact that like Mary, Sethe does not at first rec-ognize her resurrected child (John 20:14)—all these hints frame the return of Beloved in a clearly Christological light.[64]

To these we might add others. Beloved's extreme thirst upon arriving at Sethe's house recalls Christ's own thirst on the cross (John 19:28). And the bridal imagery Morrison uses in evoking Beloved—both in her name and her attire (notably the lacy white dress that embraces Sethe early in the novel)—reminds us of the nuptial language New Testament authors use when describing the resurrected Christ's relationship with the church.[65] But I would argue that the most important similarity between Jesus and Beloved is also the only one that Morrison makes explicit. After Beloved's appearance, Ella and Stamp Paid argue about her identity, and Ella implies that the girl is Sethe's dead baby resurrected. Stamp initially balks, chastising Ella, "Your mind is loaded with spirits. Everywhere you look you see one." She replies,

"You know as well as I do that people who die bad don't stay in the ground." Stamp demurs, "He couldn't deny it. Jesus Christ didn't."[66]

It is important here to note not only the similarity between Beloved and Christ—both "die bad" and "don't stay in the ground"—but the unique reading of the cross it entails. Christian atonement theology is built on the simple but powerful premise that Jesus "dies good"—that his death is not merely un-tragic but miraculous. Depending on the version of atonement one selects, Jesus's death either defeats the devil, sets a universal moral example, or saves all humanity from damnation. It's hard to imagine a better death. Yet for Stamp, it's simply "bad." His pithy characterization of the cross dovetails with the arguments of contemporary theologians who see the crucifixion as a trauma. It also fits with Baby Suggs's message, which ignores sin and "bad" death while affirming life, love, and self-ownership. Only through the logics of atonement can one come to see filicide as good, and I would argue that Baby Suggs's abandonment of her mission derives in part from Sethe's erroneous interpretation of Beloved's death as good. In adopting such a reading of her daughter's murder, Sethe falls into the patterns of thinking Baby hopes to counteract and fails her mother-in-law as a student and disciple.

Morrison makes sure to open up some distance between the filicide itself and the interpretation of it. In a chapter Denver narrates, Sethe's daughter describes why she remains afraid of her mother nearly two decades after Beloved's death: "there sure is something in her that makes it all right to kill her own. All the time, I'm afraid the thing that happened that made it alright for my mother to kill my sister could happen again. I don't know what it is, I don't know who it is, but maybe there is something else terrible enough to make her do it again. I need to know what that thing might be, but I don't want to."[67] The "thing" Denver fears is not so much her mother's crime; the "thing" is what *makes the crime "all right."* Here, Denver makes a distinction between an act and the interpretation of that act and identifies the latter as frightening. Ella makes a similar distinction; when explaining her scorn for Sethe, she thinks that she "understood Sethe's rage in the shed twenty years ago, but not her reaction to it."[68] Here again we see distance between action and reaction. And there is ample evidence in the text that the community, frequently represented by Ella, condemns Sethe for the reaction, not the action. Indeed, Ella can understand the murder because she's a filicide herself. Raped by a white man, she bears a pale child, "a hairy white thing" she refuses to nurse, and the baby dies from her neglect. Both Nan and Sethe's mother do the same on the slave boat that carries them across the Atlantic. Sexually assaulted by members of the crew, both women throw the babies they bear into the sea. Nan tells Sethe that she is the lone exception: "She threw them all away but you. The one from the crew she threw away on the island. The others from more whites she also threw away. Without names, she threw them."[69] Such passages make it seem as if in antebellum times, the child who lives is the exception—not the child who dies. Bouson supports this claim, citing Morton in noting that filicide was one of the "resistance tactics" that enslaved American blacks would use to fight back against those who use them as sexual surrogates.[70] All of which is not to contravene the unnamed character who says, "You can't just up and kill your children."[71] But whether or not one "can," enslaved black women pushed to the brink by white oppression repeatedly did. Simply put, filicide as depicted in *Beloved* and elsewhere is a weapon of the weak. Thus in context, Sethe's act is less objectionable than it is to modern eyes. Her interpretation of it, however, is quite problematic.

It's worth noting here that the novel offers a number of possible interpretations of Sethe's crime. As just one example, Stamp Paid argues that in killing her child, Sethe "was trying to outhurt the hurter."[72] Bystanders' perspectives aside, Sethe herself has at least two takes on why she does the bloody deed. In the first, she characterizes the murder as a protective act. According to this reading, she "Collected every bit of life she had made, all the parts of her that were precious and fine and beautiful, and carried, pushed, dragged them through the veil, out, away, over there where no one could hurt them."[73] This is the first argument she tries in explaining the murder to Paul D: "I took and put my babies where they'd be safe."[74] Here, death is a form of safety, a bad place that's still better than a return to slavery. But Paul D doesn't buy this reading, and he forces what I believe to be Sethe's real interpretation, a justification of her murder as shocking as it is pithy: "It worked."[75] And how does it "work"? It keeps her offspring and herself from Schoolteacher's clutches. "They ain't at Sweet home. Schoolteacher ain't got em."[76] In this reading, Sethe gives her infant daughter a job—dying—that she completes successfully. She redeems the value of her baby's life and buys freedom with it.

However, as we've seen above, these are dangerous hermeneutics for a former slave because they enforce the patterns of surrogacy and human commoditization on which slavery stands. Just as Sethe works for Mr. Garner and Schoolteacher—against her will and for her masters' gain—so does she make Beloved "work" for her and for her other children. Further, if the death "works," it does so either because Sethe puts her child in a surrogate role, forced to die in the place of others, or because Beloved's life has exchange value that Sethe realizes in killing her. Such thoughts will serve to keep a free woman enslaved, if not in body then in mind. In thinking them, Sethe turns her daughter into a baby Christ and creates a miniature atonement theology to justify her death in a woodshed.

But such an interpretation is not only damaging; it's false. Or it's only paradoxically true, because it "works" only insofar as it proves to Schoolteacher that Sethe can't "work" any longer. Morrison describes Schoolteacher's response to the carnage: "Right off it was clear, to schoolteacher especially, that there was nothing here to claim . . . the woman schoolteacher bragged about . . . [had] gone wild."[77] As Yvette Christiansë insightfully notes, Sethe's murder of Beloved makes her "aneconomic": Schoolteacher "can no longer 'appropriate' her value, even symbolically. She is a 'nothing' now, not even a slave. Her capture will not convert itself into any currency."[78] The murder has worth because it makes Sethe worthless; it removes her from the economy of slavery. Yet even this characterization of Sethe's act is only partially correct, for Schoolteacher notes that the murder is not the act that renders her aneconomic; rather, the relevant event is Sethe's brutal beating by School-teacher's nephews: "she'd gone wild, due to the mishandling of the nephew who'd overbeat her and made her cut and run. Schoolteacher had chastised that nephew, telling him to think—just think—what would his own horse do if you beat it beyond the point of education."[79] Though Beloved's slaughter reveals Sethe's "wildness," the nephew's abuse initiates it. And the fact that Schoolteacher chastises the nephews before chasing down Sethe suggests that he's suspected as much from the start.

But no matter how false or damaging it is, Sethe is tied to her reading of the filicide, her own personal theory of atonement. Indeed, she is so sure of her interpretation that she tries to press it upon Beloved. Shortly after she learns the revenant's true identity, Sethe obsesses over the need to justify herself to her resurrected daughter, and Morrison uses the word "explain" four times in writing Sethe's justification: "I don't have to explain a thing. I didn't have time to explain before because it had to be done quick . . . I'll explain to her, even though I don't have to. Why I did it. . . . When I explain it she'll understand, because she understands everything already."[80] Denver later describes these efforts: "This and much more Denver heard her say from her corner chair, trying to persuade Beloved, the one and only person she felt she had to convince, that what she had done was right."[81] Yet Sethe's explanations fail, Beloved doesn't understand, and the dead daughter's presence becomes a full-blown possession that also represents Sethe's inability to move past the trauma of her daughter's murder. As Beloved's stay at 124 stretches on, her relationship with her mother turns into a cycle of failed explanation and recrimination that threatens to drown Sethe: "Denver thought she understood the connection between her mother and Beloved: Sethe was trying to make up for the handsaw; Beloved was making her pay for that. But there would never be an end to that."[82] And as the unhealthy connection deepens, Sethe comes to serve as *Beloved's* surrogate, feeding her, consoling her, and scraping before her. Denver senses that this process will kill her mother; thus, she reaches out to the community in her search for aid, and the neighborhood women who respond to her pleas bring about the exorcism of Beloved.

When the women arrive, encircling the house, Sethe and Beloved come out to stand on the porch. And it is the women's wordless, collective prayer that drives Beloved away. (Whether she vanishes or simply runs off is a mystery the novel doesn't solve.) Yet I argue that this exorcism works because it represents the return of Baby Suggs and the triumph of her message of self-ownership. As Morrison describes the women's arrival, "For Sethe it was as though the Clearing had come to her with all its heat and simmering leaves."[83]

In the Clearing, Baby Suggs once preached a message of self-reclamation that is at odds with the surrogacy-inspired "explanations" around which Sethe has built her life in Baby's absence. The force of thirty women bearing Baby's message overwhelms its alternative—incarnate in Beloved—and defeats it. Further, the arrival of Mr. Bodwin, the white abolitionist from whom Sethe rents 124 Bluestone, gives Sethe a chance to replay the events near the wood-shed nearly twenty years ago. But this time, with Beloved at her side and a potentially threatening white man riding up to the front gate, Sethe reacts as she should have reacted before. She grabs an ice pick and rushes Bodwin. Though the women wrestle her to the ground before she can do any dam-age, this act represents a healthier, more appropriate response to a perceived threat. Sethe, on the road to self-reclamation, sees that there is a job to be done: protect her family and her home. And she does it herself.

The combination of the Clearing's return and Sethe's rush toward Bodwin runs Beloved off and sends Sethe where she should have gone originally in the wake of her daughter's death—to bed, to cry. When Paul D arrives, he fears he has seen this before: "This reminds him of something."[84] Morrison contin-ues, "now he knows what he is reminded of and he shouts at her, 'Don't you die on me! This is Baby Suggs' bed! Is that what you planning?'"[85] I would argue, however, that Sethe is weeping not because she's dying but because she's finally begun the process of mourning for Beloved:

> "Paul D?"
> "What, baby?"
> "She left me."
> "Aw, girl. Don't cry."
> "She was my best thing."[86]

In the closing pages of the novel, Beloved's death has finally been trans-formed from atoning sacrifice back to tragedy. And Sethe reacts as she ought: she begins to grieve. Indeed, that response has been there, buried, from the moment Schoolteacher arrives in the yard. Morrison writes of the scene movingly: "Simple: she was squatting in the garden and when she saw them coming and recognized schoolteacher's hat, she heard wings. Little humming-birds stuck their needle beaks right through her headcloth into her hair and beat their wings. *And if she thought anything*, it was No. No. Nono. Non-ono. Simple. She just flew."[87] In the moments leading up to her daughter's murder, Sethe's only thought is simple, repeated negation. Any other ratio-nalization comes later. According to Richard McNally, finding the words to describe trauma is not impossible, but it is both difficult and painful.[88] And Sethe's barely verbal response here is also as appropriate an interpretation of a child's death as I can think of: "No. No. Nono. Nonono. Simple." On the bed, after Beloved's second departure, Sethe can finally begin the wrenching process of moving past that "no." And the best response to trauma—even the trauma of a "bad death"—is mourning and working through.[89] Sethe starts the hard task of working through when she begins to speak honestly of her loss for the first time to Paul D.

But it is Baby Suggs who gets the last word in *Beloved*. When Paul D hears Sethe's last complaint—"She was my best thing"—he re-teaches her the lesson that is so difficult for ex-slave women raised in surrogacy to remember: "You your best thing, Sethe. You are."[90] This is Baby's message, and Paul D is keeping it alive at the end of the novel. If Sethe can remember it, she will finally discard her "bad" readings of her daughter's death, mourn her loss, and heal.

Chapter 6

"You Are Crucified Too"

✦

Joyce Carol Oates, Atonement, and Human Behavior

> Whoever had taken her would not harm a six-year-old child.
> There was no logic in harming a six-year-old child. These were
> Christian people, obviously.
>
> —Joyce Carol Oates, *My Sister, My Love*

It is either surprising or predictable that the prolific, perennial near-Nobel-nominee Joyce Carol Oates has taken to Twitter, composing (at the time of this writing) no fewer than 20,000 tweets. By turns funny, political, superficial, and serious, her feed is as eclectic and entertaining as her ever-growing oeuvre. Further, she occasionally uses Twitter as a platform to comment on religious faith, often sounding like the spunky devil's advocate in the back row of Religion 101.[1] In a pair of posts from September 17, 2013, she points out the supposed "failure" of religion to make humans more generous, sympathetic creatures: "It is said that over all science has 'failed'—human beings are as superstitious & anti-rational as ever; yet, religion too has 'failed'—human beings are as lacking in spiritual generosity & sentiment as ever. Belief in God doesn't seem to make a difference in human behavior." I haven't room in this narrow space to debate her first claim, that religion does not augment generosity. But her second—that faith "doesn't make a difference in human behavior"—is belied by her own novels, which repeatedly depict believers whose religion *does* affect their actions in often startling ways. In this chapter, I address one of Oates's late novels, *My Sister, My Love*, and argue that one of its functions is to demonstrate the potentially toxic effects of belief in atonement theology on human behavior. More specifically, in *Sister*, the logic of atonement encourages scapegoating, victimization, and the passive acceptance of unjust suffering. It also serves to justify murder.

As with the other works addressed in this book, Oates's engagement with atonement theology takes place in a book about infanticide, a topic the author tackles with surprising frequency throughout her work, often with an eye to its relevance to religion. One particularly telling discussion of child murder comes in her comments on Job and Dostoevsky in her early essay collection, *The Edge of Impossibility*. Perhaps the most disturbing message of the book of Job is that dead children are replaceable. In the opening chapters, God tests his righteous servant by taking Job's property, his health, and eventually his ten children (seven sons and three daughters), who are killed when a great wind destroys the house in which they are dining. At the end of the book, God rewards Job for (ostensibly) passing the test by healing him, returning twice his past wealth, and giving him ten new children—again seven sons and three daughters. In *The Brothers Karamazov*, Father Zossima defends God's macabre gift—new children!—by proclaiming the miracle that human grief naturally gives way to tender joy as "mild, serene old age" replaces the "ebullient blood" of youth.[2] That Job mellows later in life, coming to find peace and love his replacement children, is one of God's gifts. And for Zossima, even this succor is subsumed by "God's truth, moving, reconciling, all-forgiving!"[3] In her essay on Dostoevsky, Oates offers a critique of Zossima's interpretation of Job, writing that "the children who suffer and die clearly do not exist for Father Zossima as existing individuals, but only as objects in a continuous evolution that brings us closer to God and 'truth.'"[4] For Zossima, as Oates characterizes him, Job's original children are nonexistent "objects" whose sole purpose is to help us gain revelatory knowledge. Oates, by contrast, would seem to side with Ivan Karamazov, who—as mentioned previously—claims that "Divine Truth" is worthless if it requires a child's death: "And if the suffering of children goes to make up the sum of suffering needed to buy truth, then I assert beforehand that the whole of truth is not worth such a price."[5]

For Oates, the suffering death of children not only "exists" but is an object of sustained attention in both her fiction and her nonfiction. One of her earliest short stories, "Where Are You Going, Where Have You Been?" (1966) is based on the true account of an Arizona serial killer who murders three young girls. Her 1984 novel *The Mysteries of Winterthurn*, which features an infant whose head is eaten off, is inspired by the true story of mummified baby corpses found in the attic of a Pennsylvania woman. A 1994 essay on the literature of serial killers opens with a meditation on "The Babysitter," a Detroit-area murderer who left "nude, violated corpses of abducted boys and girls . . . like nightmare art works, by roadsides or in parking lots or snowy fields" while Oates was living in Michigan in the mid-1970s.[6] In *Zombie*, a fictionalized version of Jeffrey Dahmer stalks, tortures, and kills a young boy. And in "Dear Husband," a short story from a 2009 collection of the same name, Oates inhabits the mind of Andrea Yates, the Texas mother who drowned her five children in 2001.

Oates's frequent literary depictions of murdered children are in keeping with a long-standing interest in victimhood. She characterizes her writerly project as an ongoing effort to sympathize with the plight of the suffering, and she argues that her ability to do so springs from her own early victimization: "It was extremely important for me, retrospectively, to have these early experiences of being a helpless victim, because it allows me to sympathize—or compels me to sympathize—with victims . . . I was part of a world in which almost everybody who was weak was victimized. This seems to be the human condition: to be picked on, to be a victim."[7] Her willingness to address this part of the human condition places her in a long tradition of authors who "read the wound" (again, Hartman's phrase) of traumatic victimization.[8] In a 2008 talk entitled "The Writer's 'Secret Life': Woundedness, Rejection, and Inspiration," Oates names Beckett, Dickinson, Hemingway, Twain, and O'Neill as other great authors who ably testify to traumatic victimhood in their fictions and plays: these "are brilliant examples of individuals who rendered *woundedness* into art; they are not writers of genius because they were *wounded* but because, being *wounded*, they were capable of transmuting their experience into something rich and strange and new and wonderful."[9] That new "something" is healing, and Oates echoes trauma theorists in claiming that literature has therapeutic powers. In another essay from *The Edge of Impossibility*, Oates writes, "Suffering is articulated in tragic literature, and so this literature is irresistible, a therapy of the soul."[10] Oates claims that conducting such "therapy" is a pressing responsibility for creative writers; she herself feels the compulsion to "bear witness—in an almost religious sense—to certain things . . . the experience of suffering, the humiliation of any forms of persecution."[11] Like Rambo, Jones, and the trauma theologians mentioned previously, Oates hears the double valence of the word "witness"; one testifies to religious truth as one testifies to pain and loss. Thus, Oates sees herself as having a duty to give voice to great suffering, and perhaps especially to the suffering of those who lose a child.

Throughout her expansive collection, Oates testifies most energetically to the tragic death of JonBenét Ramsey, the six-year-old beauty pageant princess murdered in her Colorado home in 1996. (To this day, the case remains unsolved.) Oates began bearing witness to her death in an energetic review essay in a 1999 issue of the *New York Review of Books*; the charged piece engages some half-dozen book-length studies of Ramsey's death and at least as many related true-crime volumes. Her research for the essay culminated in the 2008 publication of *My Sister, My Love: The Intimate Story of Skyler Rampike*, a novel that is asymptotically based on the story of Ramsey's murder.[12] That *Sister* appears a dozen years after the death of the child suggests its staying power in Oates's mind. But as for Zossima, Ivan, Job, and Dostoevsky, so for Oates the murder of this child is a matter of religious importance: the killing of the main character by her devout mother allows Oates to develop the suggestion that pieces of Christian theology can potentially justify infanticide.

To understand how this theme unfolds, we must first review the complex spirituality of an author who is too often caricatured as anti-Christian. Oates's religious background is a patchwork quilt of influences, and one simplifies it at one's peril. Early in her youth, her family was not very religious, attending church only infrequently—that is, until the death of her grandfather, an event that "traumatized" them and spurred her parents to convert to Catholicism.[13] In her adolescence, then, she attended "numberless" masses—though she found them "fatiguing" and "unrewarding."[14] Nonetheless, she picked up enough material to enter and win a Bible-verse-memorization contest that got her a free trip to summer camp. (She didn't enjoy it.)[15] After moving away from home, she went to mass infrequently, citing her frustration with the Church's anti-intellectualism, misogyny, and political conservatism.[16] But despite her aggravation, she married her husband Ray Smith—himself a "lapsed" believer—at a Catholic chapel. Indeed, this phrase—"lapsed Catholic"—remains the best way of describing Oates's religiosity; though she doesn't "believe" in the truths of Catholicism, its forms still permeate her life and her fiction. She explains, "You're born a Catholic and you're baptized, then you become a lapsed Catholic for the next 90 years. It's like an alcoholic—you're never not an alcoholic"; and though she's sometimes identified as an atheist, she continues, "I'm a person who feels very friendly toward organized religion."[17] Her vexed relationship with Catholicism notwithstanding, Oates has had genuine religious experiences. Through a friend, she once got involved with a Methodist congregation in which she was "more active and engaged; for a while, she even played the organ . . . while the congregation sang. She was impressed by the 'raw, unmediated emotion' she felt in the church, 'the sense that people really believed God, or Jesus Christ, was present."[18] And in December 1971, Oates had what she still describes a moment of mystical transport. Johnson quotes Oates in describing it: "The primary feature of the experience, which lasted for several minutes, was the sensation that her individuality, her 'ego,' had surrendered to a larger, transcendent reality . . . no single word could adequately describe this 'wildly transcendent' experience: 'Transformation. Conversion. Can these things really happen so quickly . . . ? Indeed they can, indeed they can.' "[19] This "transforming" religious experience came part and parcel with a new-found interest in mystical writing. In 1974, Oates published *New Heaven, New Earth*, a long critical study of "the visionary experience in literature" that addresses the works of O'Connor, Beckett, Plath, Mailer, and others. In it, Oates examines a Western literary-mystical tradition that reaches into the twentieth century.[20] But even given such heterodox religious yearnings, she has never quite shaken her Catholic upbringing. When her husband died in 2008, Oates took unexpected comfort from the figurine of Saint Theresa given to her by a close friend: "How can I explain this statue of St. Theresa in our home, I can't explain. Except that the statue is facing me, in my nest, across a distance of less than six feet . . . The St. Theresa statue is astonishing in our bedroom. It exudes an air of antique calm and beauty."[21] She continues, later on, "I love the beautiful St. Theresa figure, it suggests such calm and seems to rise above time. I think, It will outlive us all. This is only right. Today is Easter, and I am hoping to see 'newness' in things."[22] In the wake of her husband's death, Oates was once again open to the hopeful message of the Easter promise and respectful of the persistence of her slumbering Catholic faith. Her enduring attachment to the abandoned beliefs of her youth partially explains Oates's continuing identification with her own Christian characters, notably Nathan Vickery, the evangelical preacher in *Son of the Morning*: "In many respects I am closest in temperament to certain of my male characters—Nathan Vickery of *Son of the Morning*, for instance— and feel an absolute kinship with them."[23] At the very least, such statements undermine Timothy Schilling's claim that Oates "seems not merely indifferent to Christianity, but emphatically averse."[24] Indeed, she is not.

But whatever the definition of her evolving spiritual stance, one thing is certain: Oates's frequent proximity to religious texts, traditions, and rituals has given her a thorough religious literacy. After her adolescent upbringing in the Catholic Church, Oates attended Syracuse University, where an early (and enduring) interest in philosophy led her to take courses in religion and philosophy. Two decades later, after joining the faculty at Princeton, she audited similar courses taught by her friend Walter Kaufmann.[25] In *New Heaven, New Earth*, she engaged the works of some of the great spiritual thinkers of the Western tradition, among them Paul, Tertullian, Augustine, Duns Scotus, Aquinas, and Kierkegaard. And perhaps most crucially, Oates threw herself into religious research when preparing to write *Son of the Morning* (1978), her sublime, troubling exploration of American fundamentalism. Judith Applebaum writes that "While working on *Son of the Morning*, Oates devoted hours each day to reading the Bible. 'I wanted to put myself in the place of a fundamentalist Protestant who could go to the Bible every day for guidance and would not have any critical or historical preconceptions,' she said, adding that 'getting into that frame of mind was a very shattering experience.'"[26] Her Catholic upbringing and her engagement with spiritual material in her research and writing have caused her to define her fiction in religious terms. In an interview with Leif Sjoberg, Oates describes her creative work as "a kind of homage or *worship*, very difficult to explain."[27] And in *New Heaven, New Earth*, Oates writes that "the novelist's obligation is to do no less than attempt the sanctification of the world!"[28] In such quotes, Oates seems to suggest, as Matthew Arnold did more than a century before, that literature can fulfill some of the functions usually reserved for organized religion.

Though Oates characterizes all of her novels as fulfilling a spiritual function, and though many of them feature religious characters, three books in particular address Christianity in sustained ways: *With Shuddering Fall* (1964), *Son of the Morning*, and *My Sister, My Love*. Oates claims that *With Shuddering Fall*, her first published novel, "was conceived as a religious work."[29] Oates's most explicit treatment of American religion comes in *Son of the Morning*, a novel she describes as "trying to create in words a 'religious consciousness' set in a recognizable United States, in the era of Born-Again politicians and other hazards to one's mental health."[30] Shortly after completing *Son*, Oates claimed that she would not return to writing about spiritual matters for a time, though she added, "I probably will write some more about religious experience, because I haven't fully explored it yet."[31] She would wait until the presidency of another born-again politician—George W. Bush—to produce *My Sister, My Love*, a piece of crime fiction that serves as a similarly thorough exploration of the effects of American Christianity in the new millennium. Five churches uphold the spiritual canopy flung over *My Sister, My Love*: early American Puritanism, Methodism, Episcopalianism, the Assembly of God, and the nondenominational social ministry of a man known simply as Pastor Bob. The novel's main characters engage all of these traditions, and all have deep if divergent beliefs on Christian faith and practice. But in *Sister*, religious content dovetails with Oates's understanding of the moral function of literature.[32] In interviews, the author claims that the ethical value of fiction is apparent when "sometimes, . . . we glean from it a sort of obverse instruction in how *not* to live."[33] For Oates, fiction may map the path that we should avoid. And indeed, *My Sister, My Love* is an ethico-religious project that is also a map of how *not* to apply the lessons of atonement theology—or, more specifically, how the lessons of atonement theology may be warped in such a way as to justify violence and murder.

Oates's reading in religion, philosophy, and theology makes her familiar with Christian atonement, and she refers to the doctrine repeatedly in her critical essays. In an early piece on *Dracula*, she describes a system of salvation that is roughly the same as Anselm's satisfaction theory, a "benign Christian model [wherein] . . . the individual is all: Christ died for each of us, as individuals, and we are redeemed by his sacrifice."[34] This "benign" promise features the language of substitution: Christ dies in our place and humans are saved by his death. Her other references to atonement, however, are less sanguine. In *New Heaven, New Earth*, Oates comments on the spiritual landscape of Flannery O'Connor's novel *The Violent Bear It Away* (considered in chapter 3 of this volume), calling it a world "in which the Atonement does not seem to have worked; it is the atmosphere of the Old Testament, haunted by senseless violence."[35] And then again in her essay on Dostoevsky, she comments on Ivan Karamazov's imagined conversation with "the devil," writing, "Of the Atonement nothing is said; this too is perhaps no more than an 'emanation' from the mind of man."[36] A full explication of either of these interpretive statements would take us too far afield; suffice it to say that Oates's tone in describing Christian atonement is by turns skeptical and dismissive. In O'Connor, atonement doesn't work. In Dostoevsky, it's illusory, a mere human invention. We might also add that the appearance of these theological comments in her critical essays on *Dracula*, *The Violent Bear It Away*, and *The Brothers Karamazov* suggests that for Oates, atonement is a subject proper for literary consideration. It is in this spirit, then, that we may turn to her treatment of the logics of atonement in *My Sister, My Love*.

My Sister, My Love fits into a group of Oates novels—among them Black Water (1992), Zombie (1995), and Blonde (2000)—that are fictionalized versions of real (and often sensational) historical events.[37] Cleaving closely to the investigative record of the JonBenét Ramsey murder, Sister tells the story of Edna Louise Rampike—later simply "Bliss"—an elementary-age ice skater whose fast rise through the sport's junior circuit is cut short when she is found dead in the basement of her family home. Bliss's father is Bix, a philandering, hard-charging business executive whose own rise propels the Rampikes into the upper class of a New Jersey exurb.[38] Her mother/manager is Betsey, a plump former skater—and evangelical Christian—who thrusts Bliss through a sickening regimen of training, drugs, therapy, modeling, and public relations events in the benighted hopes of living out her own dream through her daughter's too-hard-won successes. One morning, after one of Bliss's skating setbacks, the girl's body is found behind the furnace. As in the Ramsey case, suspicion quickly falls upon the family; Bliss's older brother Skyler is a prime suspect, and Oates narrates the story from his perspective. His sister's slaying throws Skyler into ten years of drug-riddled emotional turmoil, during which he must not only grieve for Bliss but cope with the suggestion—implanted by his parents—that he is her killer. In the wake of the murder, the family explodes: Bix divorces Betsey and continues his ascent up the corporate ladder. Betsey capitalizes on her daughter's death by releasing a string of best-selling memoirs that land her numerous television appearances. And Skyler suffers through a string of prep schools, psych wards, and halfway houses on his way to rock bottom. Ten years after Bliss's passing, Skyler finds himself at his mother's funeral (the result of a botched cosmetic surgery), where his father delivers him Betsey's hand-written confession. Bliss's death, it turns out, was part of a staged kidnapping gone terribly wrong. Betsey planned the ill-fated caper as a pathetic ploy to punish her wandering husband, and she bludgeoned her daughter to death when she resisted.

From the opening pages, Oates hints that this ripped-from-the-headlines novel is also a piece of serious religious speculation. She takes her title from the King James translation of the Song of Songs: "I sleep, but my heart waketh: it is the voice of my beloved that knocketh, saying, Open to me, my sister, my love, my dove, my undefiled: for my head is filled with dew, and my locks with the drops of the night" (5:2). The Song is an extended dialogue between two lovers, and the passage from which Oates pulls her title is of a piece with the romantic conversation that fills the rest of the book. For Oates, these lines from the fifth chapter prefigure Skyler's impossible wish, repeated throughout the book, that his voice might awaken his sister. However, the title may hide a second layer of meaning. Jews and Christians have long read the Song of Songs as an allegory for the relationship between God and his people: the lovers are then either Yahweh and Israel or Jesus and his Church. Thus, in naming her book after a line from this scripture, Oates opens up the possibility that Sister might be read as an unlikely examination of the deity's connection to humanity.

Further evidence for the theological importance of her book comes in the first epigraph, a full quote of the first line of Søren Kierkegaard's *The Sickness unto Death*, an exploration of the nuanced intermingling of despair and Christian belief. In the text of the novel, both Betsey and Skyler make oblique references to the work, which references suggest—somewhat unbelievably—that both have at least a passing familiarity with the Danish philosopher/theologian. Whether or not the Rampikes are conversant with Kierkegaard, we know from frequent references in Oates's essays and journals that she is, and some of his thinking seeps into her novel. In *The Sickness unto Death*, Kierkegaard addresses Christian atonement, describing it as a paradox: why God would mire humans in sin and then—through atonement—alleviate it is a mystery whose truth transcends human speculation.[39] But more important for our purposes is the fact that, according to David Gouwens, Kierkegaard accepts both the Anselmian and the Abelardian versions of atonement theology. He acknowledges that Jesus's death on the cross can *both* model perfect human behavior *and* satisfy the divine displeasure that results from the creep of human sin: Gouwens writes, "Neither is it that Kierkegaard uses Abelardian images alone . . . he can also employ the Anselmian language of satisfaction and substitution with clear reference not to the believer's experience, but to Christ's life and death."[40] Though other theologians feel the need to pick between subjective and objective atonement models, Kierkegaard does not; thus, both interpretations of the cross survive in his writing. And the same can be said of atonement in *My Sister, My Love*, a novel written under Kierkegaard's banner.

It is Skyler, the novel's narrator, who introduces crucial elements of objective and subjective atonement theology to the story. Though an unbeliever, Skyler is nonetheless the well-read product of expensive prep schools, and he even plays with the idea of going to seminary at one point. Ideas central to both major atonement theories appear in Skyler's thinking. First, the boy announces in the opening pages that his narrative engages susbstitutionary death, the central trope of objective atonement. Skyler is haunted by the ghostly voice of his dead sister, which Oates often renders in irregularly spaced, italicized lines that resemble poetry. We hear it for one of the first times in the second chapter, in which Bliss's words arrive as "a vision of God":

> *Skyler it's so dark in here*
> *Skyler don't leave me alone here*
> *Skyler would you die in my place?*[41]

Bliss's brother replies, "And that is the crucial question, isn't it? *Would you die in my place?*"[42] Dying in another's place is the pith of Anselm's atonement, in which Jesus is killed for us. That Skyler's reference comes in the midst of a discussion of sin, evil, and redemption further emphasizes the fact that his query—Would you die in my place?—is patently theological. Here, Skyler wishes he could play the role of Christ for his sister, substituting his death for hers. Having grown up in the church, he may also recall Jesus's words in the gospel of John: "No one has greater love than this, to lay down one's life for one's friends" (15:13). Of course, Bliss is long dead, and Skyler could as soon die in her place as he could in President Lincoln's.

Near the end of the novel, Skyler also toys with the idea of Christian *imitatio*, the central theme of subjective atonement. Struggling to deal with the suffering brought on by his mother's death and the revelation of her guilt, Skyler asks his mentor, Pastor Bob, what he should do: "Pastor Bob! Should I t-try to think what J-J-Jesus would do? In my place?"[43] Abelard would say yes, but Bob, a refreshingly candid spiritual guide, replies, "Why bring Jesus into it, Skyler? D'you think Jesus is a crutch?"[44] Bob discourages Skyler from engaging in the imitative logic of subjective atonement, later counseling the troubled teen to rely on himself in making difficult choices in the wake of personal tragedy: "Whatever decision you make, Skyler, it must be yours. It must come from a place in your heart, that is purely you."[45] Skyler obliges. But if the child seems familiar with the themes of Christian atonement, he hesitates to act on them. Indeed, necessity and good counsel keep him from implementing the substitutionary and imitative practices he draws from his understanding of Jesus and the cross. Further, the fact that his toying with atonement theology comes in the form of questions—"Would you die in my place?" "Should I think what Jesus would do?"—suggests that his engagement is not active but speculative. Though he plays with atonement, he does not accept it, remaining—perhaps like Oates—one who reflects seriously on religious themes without embracing them.

The same cannot be said of Skyler's mother, Betsey, who flaunts a personal but unreflective faith in Jesus. Skyler explains, "Mummy and Daddy were Christians of the most American kind: unquestioning, and adamant."[46] The Rampikes' Christianity also partakes of the kind of prosperity gospel described by Max Weber in *The Protestant Ethic and the Spirit of Capitalism*: those who have earned God's favor are blessed with wealth and achievement. Describing his parents' faith, Skyler writes, "Worldly success is certainly a sign of divine grace in the eyes of most Christians—no matter what priggish old theologians . . . preached."[47] Such thinking leads the Rampikes—and Betsey especially—to interpret her daughter's skating victories as signs of divine favor; after a gratifying win, Betsey proclaims, "Now everything is perfect again, Jesus has taken our pain from us and replaced it with His grace and you saw the fruits of that grace tonight: our daughter is Little Miss Jersey Ice Princess 1996."[48] Here, a skating title is the "fruit of grace," but elsewhere, Betsey describes Bliss's victories in more explicitly transactional terms, as deserved payment for her own devotion: "my daughter will be the way God will reward me for my faith in Him and God will elevate my daughter above all rivals."[49] This is Christianity as quid pro quo: Betsey will have faith in

God, and God will make her (and her daughter) a winner. As the novel pro-
gresses, however, it becomes clear that Betsey believes that Bliss is not merely
a reward, but a special gift reserved only for her: "Possessed by the certitude
of her Christian faith, Betsey never wavered, or doubted that God had desig-
nated her, as well as her daughter, for a special destiny."[50] Elsewhere, Oates
intensifies the language of special designation, until finally Bliss is not merely
a unique gift from God, but a kind of Christ figure. That Bliss is, for Betsey,
a sort of second coming becomes clear when Betsey explains the dream that
inspires her to rename her daughter:

> It was as if my eyes were open, there was blinding light in the room,
> at first I was terrified it must be the Angel Gabriel who comes in
> blinding light but more wondrous yet it was my own daughter who
> came to me transfigured in light in the guise of a blond angel touching
> my face with both her gentle hands saying Mummy I am not Edna
> Louise, you must not call me by that wrongful name I am BLISS, I am
> your daughter BLISS bearing a vision from God that you are blessed
> as I am blessed, with God's blessing we will realize our destiny on the
> ice in the face of all our enemies, we will not be defeated.[51]

Oates laces the passage with Biblical allusions, first and foremost to the story
of Abram, whose name God changes to Abraham to mark his inclusion in the
covenant (Gen. 17:5). But the references to the gospels are even more striking. First, that Bliss appears "transfigured"—divinely revealed in a "blinding
light"—recalls the story of Jesus's own transfiguration, told in all three syn-
optic gospels. In one version of the story, Peter, James, and John accompany
Jesus to a mountain, where he "was transfigured before them, and his face
shone like the sun, and his clothes became dazzling white" (Matt. 17:2). After,
Jesus converses with the shades of Elijah and Moses and is lauded by the
voice of God as "my son, the Beloved" (17:5). Betsey's revelation also echoes
the annunciation, when God informs Mary that she will bear the Christ child
(Luke 1). As in the Luke gospel, in *Sister* an angel called Gabriel appears
to Betsey to call her blessed, name her child, and assure here that the girl
will reign over her enemies. These allusions make clear what other passages
imply: for Betsey, Bliss is a kind of Jesus; further, her death only confirms the
resemblance, and the murdered child is even more Christlike in and after her
passing. In the wake of that tragedy, Betsey gives a series of ghoulish interviews in which she testifies to Bliss's continuing spiritual influence. In one, she
speaks of her dead daughter in the same terms the evangelist uses to describe
Jesus in John 1:5; when Bliss is born, it is "as if a light had shone upon me out
of the darkness. And a light is shining within me, where there had been but
darkness."[52] In a later television interview, Betsey, asked how she copes with
Bliss's absence, claims, "My faith sustains me. Knowing that Bliss is with me
always, and that her spirit abides with all who love her."[53] Here, she uses the

language of the author of 1 John, who summarizes Jesus's teaching in the call that we "love one another, just as he has commanded us. All who obey his commandments abide in him, and he abides in them. And by this we know that he abides in us, by the Spirit that he has given us" (3:23–24). Like Jesus, Bliss is a holy spirit who abides with those who love her.

How, then, can a Christian mother who sees her daughter as a second coming kill that same small girl? Her husband unknowingly articulates the dark irony of his wife's deadly love when he explains his hope, upon learning of his daughter's disappearance, that her supposed "kidnappers" will not hurt her: "Whoever had taken her would have mercy on him. Whoever had taken her would not harm a six-year-old child. There was no logic in harming a six-year-old child. These were Christian people, obviously."[54] Bix assumes that the logic of Christianity and the logic that drives one to harm a child are opposed. Sadly, he is wrong, and the faith that allows Betsey to see her daughter as a Messiah also allows her to justify murder. Indeed, Betsey takes the tropes of Christian atonement that her son tests and discards and instead presses them to some logical but deeply disturbing conclusions.

Recall for a moment the reasons that critics like James Cone, Mary Daly, Rebecca Parker, and Rita Nakashima Brock object to both objective and subjective atonement theologies. Objective atonement is dangerous because it seems to suggest that sin and punishment are transferable commodities. The commoditization of sin is part of Daly's "scapegoat syndrome," which she describes in some depth in *Beyond God the Father*:

> While the image of the sacrificial victim may inspire saintliness in a few, in the many the effect seems to be to evoke intolerance. That is, rather than being enabled to imitate the sacrifice of Jesus, they feel guilt and transfer this to 'the other,' thus making the latter imitate Jesus in the role of scapegoat. It appears that what happens is that those under the yoke of Christian imagery often are driven to a kind of reversal of what this imagery ostensibly means. Unable to shoulder the blame for others, they can affirm themselves as 'good' by blaming others.[55]

In objective atonement, neither sin nor punishment necessarily attach to those who earn them; instead, they float and eventually stick to another (Jesus), causing his death. (As suggested in chapter 4, Updike's Rabbit resists such transferability.) Though according to atonement theology this process is the miraculous vehicle of our salvation, the unscrupulous exploit its underlying logic: simply, if one's own sin and punishment can attach to the Christ, why not to another? Or, if one can't bear to suffer for one's own misdeeds, why not shift that suffering to someone else? God accomplishes just such a transaction on the cross. By this shift, the Christian miracle of redemption becomes a tool of oppression and persecution. Subjective atonement theories can be distorted in similar ways. As Daly explains elsewhere in the same volume, in calling Jesus on the cross a model for human behavior, such theologies glorify the passive acceptance of suffering. The salutary reading of subjective atonement is simple: instead of responding to injustice with injustice—or even violence—Jesus instead turns the other cheek. It is this Jesus who inspires Gandhi and King. For Daly, however, oppressors might also exploit this system, using it to reinforce patterns of victimization—especially for those who are already being victimized. Simply, we may be inspired when strong leaders refuse to exchange blows, but we should be aghast when a battered woman sees in Christ the rationale for her suffering silence. For Daly, victims—too often, women—should not seek to emulate the crucified Jesus: "Given the victimized situation of the female in sexist society, these 'virtues' [e.g., passive acceptance of suffering] are hardly the qualities that women should be encouraged to have."[56]

As Betsey's confession letter reveals, she uses these exploitative interpretations of both objective and subjective atonement to justify her actions. Betsey is able to avoid suspicion in the death of her daughter because an obsessed fan (and convicted child molester) named Gunther Ruscha steps forward to confess to the crime. Though Betsey knows—and Bix suspects—that his confession is false, she nonetheless allows him to be convicted and imprisoned for Bliss's murder. Ruscha later commits suicide in jail. In her garbled note to Skyler, Betsey explains her reasons for allowing his unjust incarceration: "it came to seem—& so your father thought too that Ruscha was a 'gift from God' to the Rampikes in their Hour of Need & many came to believe that it was so—that man had hurt Bliss there was the wish to believe for in truth G. R. was a sex prevert by his own admission." She continues, explaining that Bix goes along because he believes it will spare his son further suspicion, "& your father said—'This will save Skyler.' "[57] Ruscha is the Rampikes' own personal scapegoat. He will accept both guilt and punishment—erroneously for Skyler but in reality for Betsey. Betsey's religious language—her claim that Ruscha is a "gift from God"—suggests that she has adopted the skewed interpretation of objective atonement whose ramifications Daly fears, whereby the divine plan allows that others may bear the burden for the misdeeds of God's chosen. From Betsey's perspective, God offers the family a substitionary victim onto which they might transfer both sin and death. And just like Jesus, Ruscha dies for the Rampikes' sin.

Betsey feels guilty about this transaction—and about killing Bliss—but the logics of subjective atonement again help assuage her pain. In the same letter to Skyler, she writes, "I prayed to Jesus to forgive me I would allow an 'innocent man' to be maligned in my place—& Jesus said 'So it was with me Betsey—an innocent man to be crucified' & at a latter time Jesus said 'And now you know Betsey—you are crucified too—you have lost your darling angel until you are joined in Heaven.' "[58] We hope that the guilt Betsey feels at causing two deaths is sufficient motivation to make her come clean, but her understanding of the cross allows her to cope—and even thrive. The tropes of subjective atonement theology teach Betsey that pain—either Jesus's innocent suffering or her chafing guilt—is not an injustice to fight but a burden to bear. And the American Jesus, who speaks to believers in prayer and dream, tells her that her guilt is also her cross. Atonement makes Betsey feel Christlike while conveniently justifying her decision to keep quiet.

Moving past these subtler distinctions between objective and subjective atonement theologies, we may remember that all models of atonement make the suffering death of another person valuable. Whether Jesus's crucifixion saves us from our sins, defeats the devil, or provides a model for just behavior, it nonetheless has positive, redemptive worth. And perhaps the most tragic piece of *My Sister, My Love* is the fact that Betsey uses the language of Christian salvation to characterize the infanticide she commits as similarly valuable—even redemptive. Oates provides a fleeting hint that Betsey has come to interpret the murder in such a fashion when she refers to it as a "sacrifice"[59]—a giving-up that nonetheless entails a getting-back. How can the death of a child be anything but loss and wrenching absence? With time, Betsey comes to see it as a productive exchange. In another of the interviews she gives in the wake of the murder, quoted in part above, Betsey explains her daughter's continuing effect on her life: Bliss remains "a light . . . shone upon me out of the darkness. And a light is shining within me, where there had been but darkness. And wherever I go whether I am recognized as the mother of Bliss Rampike or whether I am but anonymous, I am bathed in this radiance which is the gift of God. I am redeemed!"[60] Her daughter's death is redeeming; it brings her radiance and, crassly, fame. And the language of atonement allows her to continue characterizing it as such, both to herself and others. Further, the sick truth of the novel (and Oates's unsubtle critique of the Ramseys) is that Bliss's death makes Betsey rich and famous. Simply, atonement makes death profitable.

Earlier in this project, I argued that atonement is a sort of collective screen memory, a mental formation that hinders the process of mourning necessary to one's recovery from trauma. Atonement theology and its related themes obstruct healing by screening us from the stark truths of death, pain, and loss, and it is only by dispelling these themes that we may begin the journey back to health. In closing, I suggest that *My Sister, My Love* dramatizes the ways in which screen memories keep victims—in this case, Skyler—from working through death and painful loss. Further, I suggest that in Oates's novel, this process is tied up with the language and logic of atonement. Indeed, Betsey's repeated exploitation of one crucial piece of atonement theory—substitionary sacrifice—keeps Skyler from properly mourning for his sister's death. As he admits near the end of the book, Betsey, who has already sacrificed both Ruscha and her own daughter, has done the same to him: "She had sacrificed him, to save herself: his mother."[61] For nearly ten years, Betsey lets her son remain a suspect in Bliss's murder while cultivating in the boy's mind the possibility that he is the killer. Thus, just as Ruscha is a "gift from God" who deflects the blame she deserves, so too is Skyler a scapegoat who unjustly bears guilt. Betsey is able to convince her son of his possible complicity by exploiting the theory of lost traumatic memory—the common notion developed by psychologists and lay authors that some traumas are so devastating that victims effectively bury recollections of them.[62] Betsey uses this idea to imply, menacingly, that Skyler's wounded mind holds some dark truth "he will not divulge, for such trauma is locked inside the hippocampus— the 'seat of memory'—in a state of denial."[63] And repeatedly throughout the novel, Skyler hazily recalls a conversation with his mother on the morning of his sister's death: "Skyler you must never never tell not ever Not even Jesus, Skyler He will forgive you anyway."[64] We come to learn, however, that the scene is part of Betsey's hasty effort to implant the memory of Skyler's guilt in his own mind. Indeed, we eventually learn that his memories of the night of his sister's murder and the following morning are actually quite precise: he sleeps through his sister's death and learns of it only when his father discovers the body later in the morning. Some trauma victims object to the theory of lost traumatic memory because it makes victims susceptible to just such exploitation. Susan Brison argues that we must avoid descriptions of trauma that block the victim's access to his or her own mind, arguing that they "[make] it conceptually impossible for a survivor to bear reliable witness to the trauma."[65] In their place, we must develop a new understanding of traumatic stress that gives victims access to—and control over—memories of the wound. In *My Sister, My Love*, Oates suggests that the forces that keep us from properly mourning are tied up with atonement theology, a crucial but flawed piece of American Christian practice. And it is only after transcending atonement thinking—some of it promulgated by Betsey—that Skyler can truly mourn for his sister.

What, then, does the novel tell us about Oates's own evolving relationship with Christianity? Certainly, *Sister* betrays the author's skepticism regarding certain theological and devotional beliefs. But if one interpretation of Christianity is the problem for Skyler (and for Bliss), another form may be the solution. Fleeing his family near the end of the book, Skyler takes refuge in the parish of a man known simply as Pastor Bob, the burn-victim survivor of a car wreck that kills his family. Bob avoids the kind of pat theological speculation that produces easy belief; he says, "I have plenty of sympathy for Pilate who said, 'What is truth?'—fuck if I know."[66] Instead, Bob develops an active ministry that seeks to identify and care for the outcast, the suffering, and the lost: "Our ministry is human-sized, flawed and imperfect for we are but God's creatures, we cannot be as gods . . . my ministry is a ministry for those who dwell in hell."[67] Simply, Bob's is a church that eschews theological speculation and seeks to do the work of social justice. And its specific ministry is, it seems, care for the traumatized, for victims "who dwell in hell." As Oates suggests in a recent interview about *Sister*, she sees promise in forms of Christianity that focus simply on helping other people: "Non-charismatic, basic religion on a very human level of helping one another is a start. We need to find community in a small group of people, not in celebrity. We need other people. You can't look inside your heart all the time for the answers. You need a community."[68] In *My Sister, My Love*, Betsey looks inside her heart for religious answers and ends up killing her child. Skyler, by contrast, eventually finds spiritual solace in a community of believers devoted to helping the hurt.

Chapter 7

"Consubstantial Monstrosity," "Grim Triune"

✦

Outer Dark and Divine Child Murder

> The real culprit is violence against children.
> —McCarthy, interview with David Kushner

Literary critics often note the likenesses between Cormac McCarthy and Flannery O'Connor. Both are products of the American South; both grow up Catholic;[1] both write unvarnished tales of lives of the unlettered, marginalized poor; and both are fearless in their stark depictions of violence and death. Yet in terms of their spiritual trajectory, McCarthy more closely resembles Joyce Carol Oates. Like her, McCarthy is a lapsed Catholic who left the faith long ago, but perhaps with more animosity. In a useful feature on McCarthy's life in Knoxville, Tennessee, Mike Gibson quotes one of the author's friends, Bill Kidwell, who suspects that Catholicism "embittered him." But any residual hostility toward the religion of his youth hasn't stopped him from writing frequently about religion, and he engages spiritual themes in all of his novels and plays.[2] He does so no more explicitly than in his 2006 play *The Sunset Limited*, which takes the form of one sustained religious debate between Black, a fervent believer, and a staunch atheist called White. They meet when Black pulls White back from jumping in front of a New York City subway and coerces the suicidal academic back to his run-down apartment to try to talk him off the edge. McCarthy's works seldom end well, and *Sunset* is not an exception: the play concludes with White walking out, likely to his death. But what is perhaps surprising is that while White "wins" the argument, his victory is less a third-round knockout than a disputed split decision after the final bell. And the "bitter" Catholic McCarthy's depiction of the believer Black is sensitive, complex, sympathetic, and persuasive. Black is a reflective, progressive Christian who rejects the easy answers of fundamentalism and grapples honestly with his faith's darker corners: the problem of evil, the obscurity of the divine will, and the unlikeliness of revelation. And the fact that the "Sunset Limited" is not a New York subway but an Amtrak line that runs through not one but two of McCarthy's old hometowns—New Orleans and El Paso—suggests that the play is a very personal reflection on the beliefs that may or may not "keep you glued down to the platform when the Sunset Limited comes through at eighty mile an hour."[3] If for McCarthy, unbelief wins out over belief, it doesn't win out by much. Thus, the author is less the atheist White than the dying man sitting in a barracks in his best respected novel *Blood Meridian*: "the man who'd been shot sang church hymns and cursed God alternately."[4] This is McCarthy, hating the deity while humming his songs, a bitter believer who can't quite shake the trappings of his belief.

But whence does this "bitterness" spring? My sense is that once again—and one last time—it derives from the perceived inability of God to stop our torment, and perhaps more specifically, to protect children from abuse. Says White of the deity he cannot praise, "The clamor and din of those in torment has to be the sound most pleasing to his ear."[5] And though McCarthy is not White, perhaps he shares something of his fictional character's acrimony. In a recent *Rolling Stone* interview, David Kushner asks the author if he thinks that the apocalypse depicted in McCarthy's end-of-the-world novel *The Road* is a real possibility; the author is doubtful: "We're going to do ourselves in first," he replies.[6] As evidence of the depravity that will drive us to our own destruction, he presents the damage we do to our sons and daughters: "the real culprit is violence against children. A lot of children don't grow up well. They're being starved and sexually molested. We know how to make serial killers. You just take a Type A kid who's fairly bright and just beat the crap out of him day after day. That's how it's done."[7] Our inability to protect the innocent, the young, and the vulnerable is indicative of a kind of doomsday drive that will, for McCarthy, lead us to our own demise. Yet more important, this dark failing may be something we inherit from our Father in Heaven: McCarthy names his 1973 novel about a necrophiliac serial killer of adolescent women *Child of God* and describes its all-too-human antihero as "a child of God much like yourself perhaps."[8] The second-person pronoun "yourself" breaks the novel's fourth wall and implicates its audience in a gothic family resemblance: Lester is like God, "you" are too, and Lester kills young girls and sleeps with them. You do the math.

The God who fathers Lester Ballard makes fleeting appearances throughout McCarthy's collection of works, but he manifests himself concretely in the author's 1968 novel *Outer Dark*. In it, a trio of murderers referred to alternately as a "grim triune" or a "consubstantial monstrosity" terrorize an unidentified collection of Appalachian hamlets, killing roughly a dozen townspeople before—in a culminating act of violence—putting a knife to the throat of a tortured baby in the book's final pages. In the roughly four-and-a-half decades since the book's publication, critics have come to no reliable consensus on the identity of the three killers who haunt the italicized portions of the text and slit the throat of the child in the book's penultimate scene. John Grammer is in the minority who resist metaphysical interpretations of the three men; he sees them as purely human and calls them simply a "band of murderers."[9] For Vereen Bell, they are "evil Magi."[10] James Giles hedges, suggesting that they seem "something other than human."[11] William Schafer recalls Greek myth in naming them "crazed furies."[12] Farrell O'Gorman calls them both "unholy" and "seemingly supernatural" but nonetheless links them to what he identifies as McCarthy's "ongoing concern with prophetic messengers."[13] Steven Frye sees them as "avatars of Satan,"[14] while Russell Hillier goes in another direction entirely, likening them to the trio of angels in Bunyan's *Pilgrim's Progress*.[15] Perhaps most convincingly, William Spencer offers a sustained argument that that the trio "parodies the theological concept of the triune God."[16]

Yet here I wish to put forward a stripped-down version of Spencer's own thesis, one that I argue is both truer to the novel itself and to the author who writes it. The triune is not a parody of God; it is God. In fact, McCarthy's novel is the most accurate portrait of the God who we've been stalking throughout this project: the shadowy visage of the God of atonement, the God who saves us by forsaking his own son and letting children die. Evidence from the book's title, its content, and from the rest of McCarthy's oeuvre supports the claim. Yet to bolster the argument, I turn to David Blumenthal, who makes the case in *The Abusing God* that while the Bible's deity can be loving and protective, he is by turns also cruel and arbitrarily violent.

David Blumenthal is often referred to as a "protest theologian." A Jew writing after the Holocaust, he tackles the seminal question facing all post-Shoah theologians: how could Yahweh allow the Nazis to exterminate six million participants in the Jewish covenant? And given that he did not, how does Judaism persist and thrive in the aftermath of that cataclysm? Blumenthal's answer to these questions is as simple as it is radical: we admit that God is not wholly good, and we allow that God may abuse us. As I mention in a previous chapter, Blumenthal adopts what he calls a "personalist" theology that assigns various attributes to God. Thus, God can be angry, loving, partisan, and powerful; however, just like a human being, he needn't be all these things all the time. In similar fashion, God is—or can be—abusive. As Blumenthal writes, "*God is abusive, but not always.* God, as portrayed in our holy sources and as experienced by humans throughout the ages, acts, from time to time, in a manner that is so unjust that it can only be characterized by the term 'abusive'. In this mode, God allows the innocent to suffer greatly. In this mode, God 'caused' the holocaust, or allowed it to happen."[17] This last sentence—God "caused" the holocaust—is as striking as it is honest, and obvious. It is ridiculously difficult to defend the omnipotence or the benevolence of the Jewish God (or the Christian God or Allah, for that matter) from amid the bloodshed and death of the last century. So Blumenthal does not try. Further, he believes that Hebrew scripture both bears out his thesis and narrows its focus:

We must begin, under the seal of truth, by admitting that Scripture
does indeed portray God as an abusing person; that God, as agent in
our sacred texts, does indeed act abusively; that God, as described
in the Bible, acts like an abusing male: husband, father, and lord.
Further, we must begin by admitting that, read inter-textually with
the lives of abused persons, the impact of such scriptural texts is devastating. Reading parts of the Bible, if one is abused, is traumatic; it
is re-victimization.[18]

In brief, the God of the Bible sometimes abuses. (For support, Blumenthal
turns most frequently to the Psalms.) Yet a reading of the *Tanakh* proves to
Blumenthal that the Hebrew God not only allows the Holocaust; he is also
complicit in more personal acts of abuse—and thus perhaps authorizes such
acts for humans. Further, given that the Jewish God is most often gendered
male, his actions prefigure both a husband's spousal abuse and a father's
abuse of his child. To ignore such unsavory revelations is to misunderstand
and mischaracterize both the creator of the universe and humans' vexed
responses to him: "the texts on God's abusiveness are there. To censor them
out because they are not 'ethical' is to limit our understanding of the com-
plexity of human and divine existence."[19]

Of course, orthodox defenders of the Biblical God have a ready answer
to Blumenthal's characterization, and it is the same one Job's "friends" give
him: what you perceive as abuse is actually deserved punishment because
Jews, like Christians, see humanity as sinful. Blumenthal admits as much but
argues that God's response to sin—if it even is a "response"—is not in keeping with the size of human error: "Our sins—and we are always sinful—are
in no proportion whatsoever to the punishment meted out to us."[20] If the
Holocaust is a ready example, the story of Job is equally instructive: while
Job's friends assure him that his sin has earned him his suffering (and they
are wrong), that suffering—total impoverishment, the death of ten children,
painful boils—so vastly outweighs any perceived slight as to seem by turns
absurd and cruel. Given the abusive potential of God and the disproportionate quality of the punishments he exacts, Blumenthal believes that "faithful
defiance" is an appropriate religious approach to the deity: "Given our post-
holocaust setting and given the continued insecurity of the Jewish people in
the modern world, sustained suspicion is a religiously proper faith stance
toward God."[21] Further, for Rita Nakashima Brock, who wrote the foreword
to Blumenthal's volume, this Jewish protest theology challenges Christians
to develop an analogue: "While Blumenthal's book emerges out of the Jewish response to the holocaust, he stretches the emotional and disciplinary
envelopes and challenges Christian theologians to confront more honestly
the profound evil we find in the everyday midst of human life."[22] Simply, his
arguments stand for Christian believers as well, and followers of Jesus must
grapple with the abusing God in the same way that Jews do.

It is my contention in this chapter that Cormac McCarthy is a Catholic (or lapsed Catholic, at least) who does. And we can see evidence of his struggle in his fiction. Though McCarthy is no recluse—he ceded that title when he sat down with Oprah Winfrey in 2007—he gives interviews only infrequently and almost never discusses his own work. As his ex-wife Annie DeLisle puts it, "everything he had to say was there on the page."[23] Thus, commentary on his religious thinking must focus primarily on his novels and plays. There's no better place to start than *Suttree*, a seedy, sprawling love letter to McCarthy's hometown of Knoxville, Tennessee, and a novel that many—including the author himself—call autobiographical.[24] Gibson elicits the following admission from one of the author's old Knoxville buddies: "I think *Suttree* was totally autobiographical, moreso than anyone will ever know."[25] Thus, I wager that we may learn as much about McCarthy's theology from this book as we can from any other source. The novel tells the story of Cornelius Suttree, the educated product of a rich family who leaves wife, son, station, and home to scrape by among the vagrants and criminals who inhabit Knoxville's underbelly. Like McCarthy, Suttree is brought up Catholic and has the dubious benefit of a Catholic education. In the middle of the novel, he stumbles into one of the parishes of his youth: "A thousand hours or more he's spent in this sad chapel he."[26] Yet while he repeatedly visits churches throughout the book, Suttree often sounds as bitter as his creator when reflecting on his time in religious school; his teachers, as he recalls them, were "Grim and tireless in their orthopedic moralizing. Filled with tales of sin and unrepentant deaths and visions of hell and stories of levitation and possession and dogmas of semitic damnation for the tacking up of the paraclete. After eight years a few of their charges could read and write in primitive fashion and that was all."[27] In sum, either his Catholic schooling or his memory of it is relentlessly negative; its identifying elements are sin, death, demonic possession, damnation, and a thinly veiled anti-Judaism. Oh, and levitation. Wandering through the church again, he can still feel the sense of fear these "tales of sin" struck in him so many years ago; he is again "like the child that sat in these selfsame bones so many black Fridays in terror of his sins. Viceridden child, heart rotten with fear."[28] As an adult, Suttree embraces the vices he once fled from, yet his spiritual formation nonetheless leaves him with an unpleasant aftertaste and a vision of God as an incompetent ne'er-do-well perhaps not unlike the alcoholic delinquents he so often drinks with; he imagines God "lies sleeping in his golden cup," "a patriarchal deity in robes and beard [lurching] across the cracking plaster."[29] Perhaps the unpredictability of this God accounts for the fact that he must be "interceded with bassackwards or obliquely."[30] Neither Suttree nor McCarthy elaborates on the type of "bassackwards" intercession God requires, but I posit that it is atonement on the cross, through which Jesus intercedes for us when we cannot directly. But there is a darker side to this obliquely approached, besotted God, because Suttree also links him to the death of children, a trope that repeats quietly throughout the novel. Flipping through a browning family photo album, he sees a picture of a painted infant dead in a tiny casket and wonders why God gives only the weak human body as housing for such a vulnerable thing as a child's soul: "What deity in the realms of dementia, what rabid god decocted out of the smoking lobes of hydrophobia could have devised a keeping place for souls so poor as is this flesh. This mawky wormbent tabernacle."[31] And yet Suttree, another child of God, is a poor protector of children as well. Before the novel opens, he abandons his wife and son and returns to them—but ever so briefly—upon hearing news that his child has died. It's a painfully awkward homecoming, and he only has time to grieve over his child's body in the cemetery after his family has gone home. Leaning over the unfilled grave, he thinks, "Pale manchild were there last agonies? Were you in terror, did you know? Could you feel the claw that claimed you? And who is this fool kneeling over your bones, *choked with bitterness*? And what could a child know of the darkness of God's plan?"[32] For Suttree, a claiming claw takes his young son's life as part of the "darkness of God's plan." And that Suttree calls this deity "pederastic" later in the novel suggests that for him, God may not merely fail to protect children but may also be complicit in their abuse.[33] Drunk, incompetent, unpredictable, menacing, and sometimes abusive, Suttree's God—who, if he isn't McCarthy's God, must be a close relative of him—both is and is not the being the Catholic church peddles, and when a priest tells him "God must have been watching you" after Suttree barely survives a terrible illness near the end of the novel, he replies, "You would not believe what watches."[34]

In trying to divine McCarthy's theology, one hesitates to lean quite so heavily on *Blood Meridian* as one does on the autobiographical *Suttree*, yet we may try nonetheless, if only because the book features another notable lapsed Catholic—the "expriest" Tobin—whose views we might explore in hoping to learn more about McCarthy's own. *Blood Meridian* is a loosely historical work that focuses on the Glanton band, who descend into Mexico in the late nineteenth century to hunt "indians," and the expriest is one member of that crew. If the churches of *Suttree* are generally empty, the churches of *Blood Meridian*—and there are many—are destroyed, burned, shot-out, or filled with corpses. Or perhaps more simply, churches are not exempt from the violence and chaos that engulf the rest of the novel's fictional landscape, which is as blood-soaked and death-filled as any. Further, this landscape seems especially perilous for children. As Neil Campbell notes, infanticides pile up in the novel, especially around the Judge, the mysterious, preternatural giant who is also the de facto leader of the scalp hunters.[35] But there is no better evidence that McCarthy's God will not protect children than the tree of dead babies that is perhaps the most arresting image in recent fiction: "The way narrowed through rocks and by and by they came to a bush that was hung with dead babies. They stopped side by side, reeling in the heat. These small victims, seven, eight of them, had holes punched in their underjaws and were hung so by their throats from the broken stobs of a mesquite to stare eyeless at the naked sky. Bald and pale and bloated, *larval to some unreckonable being*."[36] We learn no more about this tree—nor about the "unreckonable being" that produces it—than this quick passage, but its presence confirms that the novel's Mexico is indeed a "terra damnata," as McCarthy calls it a few pages later.[37] Yet there is evidence that for McCarthy, God presides over this "terra" just as he does over the gates of heaven. The novel opens with an early tent-preacher delivering a sermon whose main theme is the omnipresence of God and Christ; it takes the form of a recounted conversation between the "reverend" and a skeptic:

> Neighbors, said the reverend, [Jesus] couldn't stay out of these here hell, hell, hellholes right here in Nacogdoches. I said to him, said: You goin to take the son of God in there with ye? And he said: Oh no. No I aint. And I said: Dont you know that he said I will foller ye always even unto the end of the road? Well, he said, I aint asking nobody to go nowhere. And I said: Neighbor, you dont need to ask. He's a goin to be there with ye ever step of the way whether ye ask it or ye dont. I said: neighbor, you caint get shed of him.[38]

Christ will be with us whether we request his presence or not, even as we travel to the "end of the road," or the diabolical hinterlands of *Blood Meridian*. Yet Jesus's presence notwithstanding, there is ample evidence in the novel that his presence in the "terra damnata" will do nothing to save it or its wretched denizens. As one man puts it, "This country is give much blood. This Mexico. This is a thirsty country. The blood of a thousand Christs. Nothing."[39] Jesus may follow us through hell, but he either will not or cannot rectify its myriad sins. In this, McCarthy's Mexico recalls Oates's description of *The Violent Bear It Away* cited earlier: this is a novel in which atonement doesn't work, even the blood atonement of the cross. One of the book's last images confirms the claim. Late in the novel, another of the main characters known simply as "the kid" sees a group of Christian penitents bearing a cross across the desert preparing for some sort of re-enactment of the crucifixion. When the kid happens upon them later in a kind of stone amphitheater, they are all dead:

> hacked and butchered among the stones in every attitude. Many lay about the fallen cross and some were mutilated and some were without heads. Perhaps they'd gathered under the cross for shelter but the hole into which it had been set and the cairn of rocks about its base showed how it had been pushed over and how the hooded alter-christ had been cut down and disemboweled who now lay with the scraps of rope by which he had been bound still tied about his wrists and ankles.[40]

The image's meaning is unsubtle: Christians turn to the cross quite literally for salvation and find only bloody death along with their "alter-christ." The penitents' re-creation of the crucifixion represents both the cross itself and human efforts to understand or access it, and the bloody carnage at its base suggests that either one and likely both fail quite miserably. Thus, the expriest Tobin's commentary in the middle of the book serves as an apt description of religion through its entirety: "The gifts of the Almighty are weighed and parceled out in a scale peculiar to himself. It's no fair accountin and I dont doubt but what he'd be the first to admit it and you put the query to him boldface."[41] And again, we are left with a complaint that's been rehearsed multiple times before throughout this study. For the expriest—a lapsed Catholic and a potential stand-in for McCarthy—while we expect the justice of God to be "fair accountin," it too often seems otherwise. In the cross and elsewhere, we expect a comprehensible, defensible vision of divine justice, but it is denied. And the dead bodies of children are left in its absence. On this note, we can finally turn to *Outer Dark*, where we see the abusing God alluded to in *Suttree* and *Blood Meridian* made incarnate.

McCarthy published *Outer Dark* in 1968, during what Dianne Luce calls his "Tennessee period," before he turned his attention to the American Southwest, where his later, better known novels are set. While its setting is somewhat obscure, most critics agree that the novel takes place in Appalachia, perhaps around the turn of the nineteenth century. Its protagonists are Culla and Rinthy Holme, a poor, isolated brother and sister who conceive a child that is born in the book's opening pages. For reasons that remain obscure, Culla decides to kill the child by exposing him, so while Rinthy sleeps, he takes the product of his incest into the local woods and abandons the child on the ground. When Rinthy wakes, Culla tells her the child has died, but neither knows that a wandering tinker—a traveling seller of housewares and crude pornography—has rescued the baby and taken it off. Eventually, Rinthy uncovers her brother's deception and takes off across the countryside searching for "her chap," assured that he's alive by her breasts, which leak milk throughout the novel. Learning of his sister's departure, Culla sets out in fruitless pursuit of his sister. The novel is the story of their parallel searches—both of which end in failure. Interspersed among chapters chronicling the siblings' travels are italicized passages recounting the movements of a third party—the mysterious trio of men who roam the countryside committing atrocities that seem driven only by what Mark Royden Winchell appropriately calls a "motiveless malignancy."[42] They kill, they cannibalize, they rob graves, and they incite riots. And in the book's penultimate moments, they find the tinker, hang him, and take Culla's still-living baby. Just shortly thereafter, Culla stumbles across them (for a second time) only to witness the trio's leader kill his child by slitting its throat. Yet they spare Culla, who is left—like his sister—to continue his peripatetic wandering in the closing pages.

The plot of *Outer Dark* is ostensibly driven by a number of obvious questions: is the child alive? Where has the tinker taken him? Will Rinthy find her "chap"? Will Culla track her down before she does? Yet as Christopher Nelson correctly observes, both Culla and Rinthy remain oddly listless in their questing.[43] Their searches are ill-advised and ill-planned, and both often forget or neglect their named goals. Rinthy's search for her child seems doomed to failure from the outset; she has only the vague suspicion that the tinker has something to do with her child's disappearance, she doesn't know his name, she doesn't know what he looks like, and she doesn't know where he's gone: her quest is almost totally aimless. Culla often loses track of his own "search" altogether, settling for weeks at a time in one place looking for work or getting in trouble with the locals. And any momentary successes they have—Rinthy does find the tinker and Culla does find his child—are both random and fortuitous, not the result of any focused efforts on either party's part. It is as if they are willingly ceding the stage to the trio, the mystery of whose presence is the novel's true driving force. What is this trio, and what are they doing here? Their leader also seems to know that the reader's attention is drawn to him and his bloody band. Thus, when Culla tells the leader his name, the leader replies, "I guess you'd like to know mine wouldn't ye? . . . I expect they's lots would like to know that."[44] But I argue here that though the "name" of this set of characters remains mysterious, their identity does not. They are the triune God in his "abusing" aspect, or an embodied form of the characteristics Blumenthal outlines in his book.

Some of the most compelling support for such a claim comes not from the story itself but from the title which, as multiple writers observe, is the truncation of a phrase that appears in the eighth chapter of the Gospel of Matthew: "outer darkness." But few of McCarthy's commentators (if any) point out that Jesus uses the phrase not once but three times in Matthew. And each time, he does so in the context of Bible stories that, as with Job, pose real challenges for defenders of divine justice. The first comes in chapter 8, when a centurion asks Jesus to heal his sick servant. Jesus agrees, offering to come to the centurion's house, but the centurion claims he is unworthy to have Christ under his roof and asks that Jesus "only speak the word, and my servant will be healed" (8:8). Impressed, Jesus replies, "Truly I tell you, in no one in Israel have I found such faith. I tell you, many will come from east and west and will eat with Abraham and Isaac and Jacob in the kingdom of heaven, while the heirs of the kingdom will be thrown into the *outer darkness*, where there will be weeping and gnashing of teeth" (8:10–12, italics mine). That Jesus praises the man's faith is unproblematic; that he does so at the expense of "Israel" is less so. After all, the centurion is a representative of Rome, an oppressive occupying force that on or around the time of the composition of Matthew crushes a local rebellion and destroys the temple in Jerusalem (in 70 C.E.). Jesus's praise suggests that Rome will "eat with Abraham and Isaac and Jacob" while the chosen people of Israel will be thrown to the wolves.

The Matthew author uses "outer darkness" again in the story that has come to be known as the parable of the talents. Jesus introduces the story as the second of two tales in Matthew 25 intended to reveal what "the kingdom of heaven will be like" (25:1). A man preparing for travel summons three slaves and gives each man money, "to each according to his ability" (25:15); the first receives five talents, the second two, and the third one. They receive no further instruction. In their master's absence, the first and second slaves invest the money and double it. The first returns ten talents to his master, the second four. Both are praised and "enter into the joy" of the master. By contrast, the third is financially timid; he buries his talent in the ground and gives it back upon the master's return. When speaking with the master, he defends his decision in remarkably candid terms: "Master, I knew that you were a harsh man, reaping where you did not sow, and gathering where you did not scatter seed; so I was afraid, and I went and hid your talent in the ground. Here you have what is yours" (25:14–15). The master's response seems to justify the slave's "fear" and bear out his description of the master as "harsh":

> You wicked and lazy slave! You knew, did you, that I reap where I did not sow, and gather where I did not scatter? Then you ought to have invested my money with the bankers, and on my return I would have received what was my own with interest. So take the talent from him, and give it to the one with the ten talents. For to all those who have, more will be given, and they will have an abundance; but from those who have nothing, even what they have will be taken away. As for this worthless slave, throw him into the outer darkness, where there will be weeping and gnashing of teeth. (25:26–30)

Christian apologists often characterize this parable as a story about the merits of faithfulness and preparedness.[45] Or they suggest that it is a warning about the "sin of presumption."[46] Or they tell us that it demonstrates the merits of patience."[47] But these are heavily didactic readings that do not quite iron out the text's troubling wrinkles: first, the master does not tell his slaves what they ought to do with the talents, and while the first two make him money, the third brings him no harm. Thus, while the third certainly deserves little praise, he also doesn't deserve the "outer darkness." Second, the master distributes the talents according to each man's abilities; in other words, he already expects little from the third slave. Why punish a shortcoming he's already foreseen? Third and most disturbing is what seems to be the master's own articulation of the moral of the story: "to all those who have, more will be given . . . from those who have nothing, even what they have will be taken away." Is this not the exact obverse of the Christian message of hope for the oppressed and impoverished? The incongruity of this message is more striking given what follows in the rest of Matthew 25, Jesus's most sustained support for a social justice mission to the needy and oppressed: "Come, you that are blessed by my Father, inherit the kingdom prepared for you from the foundation of the world; for I was hungry and you gave me food, I was thirsty and you gave me something to drink, I was a stranger and you welcomed me, I was naked and you gave me clothing, I was sick and you took care of me, I was in prison and you visited me" (25:34–36). By contrast, the "master" of the parable of the talents—who must certainly be a metaphor for God—seems to be exactly what the third slave says he is: harsh, unfair, and exploitative.

A third reference to "outer darkness" comes in Matthew 22, which opens with another parable about the "kingdom of heaven." A king draws up the guest list for his son's wedding but finds that none of the invited guests will come. A second effort to wrangle guests leads to bloody altercations between the king's slaves and the invitees that culminate in the monarch's burning of his enemies' city. So the king throws out the guest list: "The wedding is ready, but those invited were not worthy. Go therefore into the main streets, and invite everyone you find to the wedding banquet" (22:8–9). Yet when the king arrives at the feast, he sees one man in the crowd inappropriately attired and says to him, "How did you get in here without a wedding robe?" (22:11) The guest says nothing, and the king's response is as rash as it is hasty: "Bind him hand and foot, and throw him into the outer darkness, where there will be weeping and gnashing of teeth" (22:13). This lesson is perhaps even more unsettling than the parable of the talents, especially if one accepts its traditional allegorical interpretation, in which the king is God. As Marianne Blickenstaff writes, "God becomes a ruthless monarch who flies into a rage, kills his enemies and burns their city, then mercilessly throws out the unfortunate wedding guest who has worn improper clothing. Such a reading implies that God is no better than any of the violent earthly rulers Matthew's first-century audience knows, and that the Kingdom of Heaven merely replaces one tyranny with another."[48] Indeed, the king's "mercilessness" verges on parody, as he slaughters the members of his first guest list and then binds and physically ejects one of the new guests whose only sin is lacking ample time to change clothes.

Simply put, the image of god in the "outer darkness" passages—cruel, reckless, fickle, inconsistent, hasty, and violent—is a nearly unrecognizable version of the Christian deity preached in chapels and Catholic-school classrooms. He works according to some hazy outline of retributive justice. He perceives a slight—lacking faith, poor investment strategy, inappropriate clothing—and responds with punishment, but the offensive nature of these "slights" is unclear, and the punishment is either wildly disproportionate or wholly inappropriate.[49] And yet this God is Biblical. He is the same deity Blumenthal sees in Job and in the Psalms, translated to the gospels and thus to Christian scripture. And by titling his book *Outer Dark*, McCarthy imports Him and, I would argue, gives Him form in the bodies of the "grim triune" who ransack its benighted landscape.

Many note that McCarthy uses Christian and even Catholic language to describe the trio of killers. Most obviously, right after the three men kill an old snake wrangler by disemboweling him, McCarthy names the trio a "grim triune" as he allows them to pose in a sort of tableau as they stare down at their victim: "*His assassin smiled upon him with bright teeth, the faces of the other two peering from either shoulder in consubstantial monstrosity, a grim triune that watched wordless, affable.*"[50] "Triune" is explicitly Trinitarian language, indicating the Christian God who is both one in three and three in one: Father, Son, and Holy Spirit. And McCarthy's diction in the previous phrase is equally telling; "consubstantiality" is the Christian—and specifically Catholic—notion that the three participants in the Trinity are of the same substance, somehow comprised of the same heavenly matter.[51] That being said, most who take this Catholic language seriously adopt a position similar to Spencer's: the three men are a parody of the Godhead, a twisted mirror image of the divine.[52] And there is some textual evidence to develop this position. Early in the novel, McCarthy describes the triune as "parodic figures."[53] And yet a look at the context suggests that the parody targets something other than religion. The three men have just ransacked a barn, taking the "*crude agrarian weapons*" they will later use to slaughter their prey; thus, they are "*parodic figures transposed live and intact and violent out of a proletarian mural,*" and the subject of the satire seems not the divinity but Diego Rivera.

Other elements of the novel bolster the theory that the triune is simply the Trinity. The leader's unwillingness to give his name resembles that of the Old Testament God. When Moses asks the Lord his name in Exodus, God cagily replies, "I am who I am," and when Moses asks who he should say sends him to Egypt, God simply commands, "say to the Israelites, 'I am has sent me to you'" (Exod. 3:14). Further, Culla's first encounter with the triune, which takes place on the shores of a river, recalls Jacob's run-in with a divine figure on the shores of the river Jabbok in Genesis 32. In that story, when Jacob demands the name of his wrestling opponent, his opponent refuses (32:29). They resemble the God of the Torah once more when they descend upon a town squire (whom they'll also kill) "*attended by a constant circus of grasshoppers catapulting from the sedge*";[54] here, as Giles points out, they are like the vengeful God of Exodus bringing violence on Pharaoh, the grasshoppers like the locusts unleashed by Moses and Yahweh on the unsuspecting Egyptians.[55] Further, when they do appear, textual cues indicate that they seem to come from—and return to—another realm. Most of the time, McCarthy writes of their movements and actions in brief, italicized inter-chapters that both are and are not part of the rest of the narrative. Like the God of the Bible, they are in the text without quite being part of the text.

Yet when the trio does appear, they do so with supernatural swiftness. Before they meet and kill the tinker, they seem to take shape from thin air: "*The three men when they came might have risen from the ground. The*

tinker could not account for them."[56] Their nighttime manifestation before
the snake wrangler is similarly mysterious yet more significant; it comes
very near the novel's mid-point, and this time, when the trio step forth, they
emerge from "the outer dark"[57]—an explicit connection between the menacing God of the text and the Biblical gloom from which they derive. Of course,
that they appear so that they can kill—violently, randomly—seems the most
significant evidence for the argument that these are not divine figures but the
bloody opposite. Giles attempts to reconcile the religious language McCarthy
uses to describe the trio with the atrocities they commit by arguing that they
are the "Old Testament god of vengeance."[58] Their murders are not senseless
violence but a predictable divine response to human depravity. And a number
of other authors argue that Culla's sins in particular—which include incest
and attempted infanticide—seem to be the cause of the triune's appearance.
As Schafer puts it, "The tale is propelled by sin—from the initial incest on
through theft, murder, grave-robbing, lynching, child-maiming, and murder.
The crazed furies cross the rural culture, leaving a swath of punishment for
all manner of sin, known and unknown."[59] And Frye suggests that the triune's violence is not merely explained by the proliferation of sin in the novel
but *justified* by it; he writes, "In *Outer Dark* the evil embodied in the grisly
triune is strangely justified by Culla Holme's incest and the abandonment
of his infant child."[60] Yet "justified" seems too strong a term here, for while
there is a coincidence of sin and violence in the novel, there seems to be no
causal connection between the two. Or more simply, if *Outer Dark* is about
a sinner tracked down by a vengeful God, why does the sinner survive? And
why do so many seemingly innocent bystanders, some named, some anonymous, get massacred instead? The answer is straightforward: the triune is not
the Old Testament God of vengeance. They are the abusing God.

Recall once more the relationship between sin and divine violence in Blumenthal's description of the world as ruled by the abusing God: humans
do sin, but divine violence is seldom apparently connected to that sin and
is, in any case, an unbalanced response to that sin. Thus, while the violence
the abusing God doles out appears at first blush to be punishment because
it happens simultaneously with human sin, it is not indeed punishment but
freestanding cruelty—of which God *is* capable. Returning to *Outer Dark*, we
see the triune's murders in a new light: as divine abuse that only (and only
barely) *resembles* punishment. And we may finally turn to the most graphic,
disturbing instance of that abuse, the triune's murder of Culla's infant son in
the book's closing pages:

> The man took hold of the child and lifted it up. It was watching
> the fire. Holme saw the blade wink in the light like a long cat's eye
> slant and malevolent and a dark smile erupted on the child's throat
> and went all broken down the front of it. The child made no sound.
> It hung there with its one eye glazing over like a wet stone and the

black blood pumping down its naked belly. The mute one knelt forward. He was drooling and making little whimpering noises in his
throat. He knelt with his hands outstretched and his nostrils rimpled
delicately. The man handed him the child and he seized it up, looked
once at Holme with witless eyes, and buried his moaning face in its
throat.[61]

One can add little to McCarthy's devastating description; one can only correctly identify it—as a culminating example of divine infanticide. Yet there
are a variety of possible interpretations of this seeming crime, none much
less unsettling than the rest. From one perspective, the murder is an example
of divine abuse: the seemingly senseless violence that Blumenthal's God can
visit on the innocent and vulnerable. From another, it is collateral damage,
or a "punishment" that misses its mark. In this light, the dead child—like
Updike's Becky—recalls King David's baby, another child whose life God
ends as retribution for the father's sexual deviance. From a third angle, the
death is God finishing the job the failed filicide Culla can't quite complete in
the novel's opening pages. And yet I'd like to close my project reflecting on a
fourth possible reading of the grim Trinity's knifeplay: that the baby's death
is also a type of the crucifixion.

Critics have long sensed that Culla's newborn is a sort of Christ child.
Woodward calls *Outer Dark* a "twisted nativity story" and sees Rinthy and
her husband as dark reflections of Mary and Joseph, and Lydia Cooper is
just one critic who repeats Woodward's provocative description.[62] Yet neither
Cooper nor Woodward does much with the passage most crucial to establishing that the baby is a Christ figure; it comes early in the novel. Having
spirited the baby away from its mother, Culla takes off for the woods to
set the child out to die. He does so and deliriously flees into the wilderness,
where he wanders senselessly for hours and eventually loses his way. Yet his
path leads him back to his son, and hours later, he accidentally circles back
on the fateful clearing, where he finds his baby, a "shapeless white plasm
struggling upon the rich and incunabular moss like a lank swamp hare. He
would have taken it for some boneless cognate of his heart's dread had the
child not cried. It howled execration upon the dim camarine world of its
nativity wail on wail while he lay there gibbering with palsied jawhasps, his
hands putting back the night like some witless paraclete beleaguered with
all limbo's clamor."[63] McCarthy's use of the word "nativity" to describe the
child's earlier birth serves as some support for the suggestion that the boy is
a second Jesus, but his use of the arcane "paraclete" to describe him finishes
the deal.[64] As Frye notes, the word usually denotes the Holy Spirit, the third
member of the Trinity; however, it very occasionally refers to Jesus himself.[65]
Though such usage is infrequent, we know from *Suttree* that McCarthy is
familiar with it. In a passage quoted above, Suttree, musing on his religious
upbringing, remembers "dogmas of semitic damnation for the tacking up

of the paraclete."[66] Here, the "tacked-up" paraclete is Jesus crucified, and the "dogma of semitic damnation" is the Catholic Church's teaching—valid up until the reforms of Vatican II—that Jews are partially responsible for Christ's death and deserve punishment. Here, then, is concrete evidence that Culla's baby is explicitly a Christ child; thus, when the leader of the "grim triune" "lifts up" the paraclete and executes him, McCarthy is reenacting the crucifixion as child murder in the most explicit ways.

Thus, McCarthy's *Outer Dark* is an appropriate novel with which to end this study about the forsaken son. For the murder of Culla's child is also the cross laid bare as a moment of pure cruelty. It is the crucifixion as gratuitous violence, wrung free of any atoning merit. It is also, and finally, the death of a Christ-child as traumatic. As Serene Jones reminds us, "traumatic violence often leaves holes in the stories we tell."[67] And the end of *Outer Dark* is like the end of the Gospel of Mark: ragged, inconclusive, unfinished. Like Mark, McCarthy's novel doesn't end with the death of the son but with the confusion of those who survive him in the aftermath of his passing. The final image of the novel depicts Culla traveling along a road that abruptly trails off in the mire:

> Late in the day the road brought him into a swamp. And that was all. Before him stretched a spectral waste out of which reared only the naked trees in attitudes of agony and dimly hominoid like figures in a landscape of the damned. A faintly smoking garden of the dead that tended away to the earth's curve. He tried his foot in the mire before him and it rose in a vulvate welt claggy and sucking. He stepped back. A stale wind blew from this desolation and the marsh reeds and black ferns among which he stood clashed softly like things chained. He wondered why a road should come to such a place.[68]

Whether McCarthy intends it or not, the "naked trees in agony" recall the cross, another agony-filled "tree." And the hominoid figures around them—like the massacred penitents of *Blood Meridian*—are "damned." And if Culla wonders "why a road should come to such a place," so too do the critics of atonement addressed in this volume wonder why the way of Christianity ends at Golgotha. Why does Jesus, the beloved son of God who preaches a message of love, compassion, and justice, end up the victim of a bloody execution? And even if he does, why should we rejoice? Though he puts his foot in these muddy waters, he pulls it back, "claggy and sucking." And then he turns around and heads back from whence he came, traveling away from the "naked tree." Perhaps, implies McCarthy, we should, too.

Afterword

Post-Traumatic Christianity

> You asked me what I was driving at: you see, I'm an amateur
> and collector of certain little facts; I copy them down from
> newspapers and stories, from wherever, and save them—
> would you believe it?—certain kinds of little anecdotes. I
> already have a nice collection of them.
>
> —Ivan Karamazov

As I write this final section, the one-time NFL MVP Adrian Peterson is set to
go to trial for beating his four year-old son's bare limbs with a tree branch—so
repeatedly and energetically as to draw blood. Police photos show parallel
scars up and down the boy's legs and hands, and a jury will decide Peterson's
fate in coming months. The story of the football player's brutality recalls
another ripped-from-the-headlines tale told by Ivan Karamazov:

> An intelligent, educated gentleman and his lady flog their own daugh-
> ter, a child of seven, with a birch—I have it written down in detail.
> The papa is glad that the birch is covered with little twigs, 'it will
> smart more,' he says, and so he starts 'smarting' his own daughter. I
> know for certain that there are floggers who get more excited with
> every stroke . . . They flog for one minute, they flog for five minutes,
> they flog for ten minutes—longer, harder, faster, sharper. The child is
> crying, the child finally cannot cry, she has no breath left.[1]

The grisly anecdote is just one of the scraps Ivan adds to the "collection"
mentioned in the epigraph above, a gathering-up of stories about abused, tortured, and murdered children. Another features parents who force their tiny
daughter to eat her own excrement and sleep in the outhouse in winter after
the little girl soils her bed. In a third, a landowner sets his dogs on a serf's
son after the poor boy accidentally injures the nobleman's favorite hound
while playing; the dogs tear the lad to shreds before his mother's eyes. Yet
another has invading armies impaling infants on spears in front of their parents. For Ivan, such stories are evidence supporting his belief that a "peculiar

quality exists in much of mankind—this love of torturing children, but only children."[2] And because Ivan cannot wrap his head around the idea that a benevolent deity would create such a heinous impulse in his creatures, Ivan believes this grisly anthology is also a refutation of the goodness of God.

Turning our attention from *Karamazov* back to the novels addressed in the preceding chapters, we are tempted to wonder: are these books best understood as a few more entries in Ivan's compendium of child abuse—and thus as further support for the suggestion that no protecting God watches over us? Perhaps. And there's no denying the fact that Ivan's stories have real rhetorical force for critics of religion. Or maybe our response to his collection is even more drastic. When it was revealed early in 2014 that a Utah mother had strangled seven of her own infants, the *New York Times* called the crime "inexplicable," and there is something in the murder of a child that defies meaning.[3] Indeed, we may be drawn to respond to the most ghoulish infanticides not with atheism but with a bleaker nihilism.

Yet though O'Connor, Updike, Morrison, Oates, and McCarthy present us with child murders as wrenching as any in Ivan's "collection," I would nonetheless argue that these works do not encourage us to respond with nihilism, atheism, or despair. After all, each novel ends with what is effectively a positive spiritual message. As *The Violent Bear It Away* comes to a close, Francis's prophetic mission is just under way. Even as the *Rabbit* tetralogy winds on past *Redux*, Skeeter lives. *Beloved* ends with the unexpected reunion of the members of the Clearing. When *My Sister, My Love* wraps up, Skyler has taken refuge in the gritty mission of Pastor Bob. And while *Outer Dark*'s conclusion is certainly more ambivalent, nonetheless Culla's last encounter in the book is with an old blind man wandering the roads "at the Lord's work." In sum, if these authors write under Ivan's banner, they do not share his response to child murder. Rather, each begins to map a subtle, substantive—and, I would argue, thoroughly religious—path away from the site of tragedy. These six books are all examples of the ways spiritual struggle might persist—though transformed—even after a trauma, be it the trauma of a lost child or, indeed, the trauma of the cross.

O'Connor's path is surely the most orthodox of the five—if not the most comforting. Presenting her readers with a child murder that is also an explicit part of a divine plan, O'Connor counsels acceptance and respect for the mystery that enshrouds the Lord's will. Bishop, like Christ, is killed to fulfill God's will. So be it. O'Connor will not apologize for the creator of the universe. We may be taken aback at the hard-heartedness of her tough but durable faith, yet hers is a frank, open-eyed religious stance—and one likely shaped by the knowledge that she, too, would die young.

Updike also stays roughly within the confines of his inherited religion when handling the heartrending loss of tiny Becky. Indeed, if my surmise is correct, in channeling the theology of James Cone he turns to one of the giants of twentieth-century Christianity in seeking solace for his best-known literary creation. Yet if Cone is not heretical, he is certainly heterodox, and Updike's use of Cone's thought in his handling of atonement leads readers and believers past the faith's best-known interpretations of the crucifixion to relatively unbroken theological ground. Yet there is also something of O'Connor's refreshing bluntness in Updike's willingness to admit the dark side of the divine personality. His "God of earthquakes"—along with his surly Jesus—is not only bristling but Biblically based. The many failed theodicies of the past remind us that it is difficult to square an all-good God with this too-flawed world, and Updike's boldness in admitting that Yahweh both smiles and snarls is not only welcome; it is intellectually honest.

If Updike's theological approach resorts to addition—more, newer readings of the cross—Morrison's by contrast promotes a sort of theological subtraction: if our theories of atonement no longer serve us well, we ought to consider abandoning them. Unlike O'Connor, who would have her religion whole or not at all, Morrison suggests that some—and post-bellum African-Americans in particular—would be better served preserving the pieces of their faith that heal while discarding those that hurt. But it is worth re-emphasizing the radical nature of the subtraction her novel implies, for if Baby Suggs's Clearing-inspired faith is for Morrison a valid religious alternative, it is also, as Greisinger notes, a sort of Christianity without the cross. Yet the powerful sense of community it engenders is an unquestionably positive force in the lives of those it touches, and its efficacy in springing the exploited from the surrogacy trap is equally valuable.

Both Oates and Morrison are keenly aware of the ways theology may cause unanticipated harm; however, Oates's novel acts to warn us of those who might intentionally warp it for more immediate, nefarious ends. Yet despite the novel's dark take on the ways theology might be twisted into a bludgeon, Oates nonetheless gives its last word on religion over to Pastor Bob, a proponent of a faith-driven social justice. In doing so, the author implies that the church's mission in serving the poor, outcast, and destitute has enduring merit even when one considers the ways its belief systems might be exploited.

Admittedly, it is hardest to find a positive religious message in McCarthy's *Outer Dark*, which characterizes its Trinity as cruel, fearsome, deadly. Yet I suggest that we consider it a fledgling experiment in the type of Christian protest theology that Rita Nakashima Brock proposes in the introduction to Blumenthal's volume on the abusing God. In the wake of the Holocaust, Jews have ample reason to shake their fists at a deity they believe watched over that horror. Yet Christians, too, have borne some share of pain at the hands of a God we may cast as abusing, and the faltering Catholic McCarthy's novel may best be understood as melodramatic testimony to that reality, unappetizing as it is.

We say in closing that none of these trails leading away from the cross is particularly smooth or welcoming, and all—with the possible exception of

O'Connor's—effectively leave behind centuries of mainstream Christian theology. Yet those hoping to live past the loss of the children God forgets and forsakes don't need devout pieties. They need what works, and what helps us work through.

The sources for the book epigraphs are as follows: Jonathan Franzen, *Freedom* (New York: Farrar, Strauss, and Giroux, 2010), 221; C. G. Jung, *Answer to Job*, trans. R. F C Hull (1952; Princeton, N.J.: Princeton University Press, 1991), 56; and David Blumenthal, *Facing the Abusing God* (Louisville, Ky.: Westminster/John Knox Press, 1993), 9. Unless otherwise indicated, all biblical citations are from the New Revised Standard Version.

Chapter 1

EPIGRAPH: Rita Nakashima Brock and Rebecca Parker, *Proverbs of Ashes* (Boston: Beacon Press, 2001), 5.

1. Albert Camus, *The Fall*, trans. Justin O'Brien (1957; New York: Vintage International, 1984), 112.

2. Camus, *The Fall*, 113.

3. Ibid., 113.

4. Hans Urs von Balthasar, *Theo-Drama, Theological Dramatic Theory*, vol. 4, *The Action*, trans. Graham Harrison (1980; San Francisco: Ignatius Press, 1994), 251, 253.

5. In *The Death and Resurrection of the Beloved Son* (New Haven, Conn.: Yale University Press, 1993), Jon Levenson makes the counter-argument: that Judaism and Christianity feature both rituals and scripture stories that implicitly support the practice of child sacrifice. In her chilling chapter on maternal murder and abuse in *Of Woman Born* (1976; New York: Norton, 1986), Adrienne Rich argues that early Jews and Christians continued the practice of child sacrifice throughout the Biblical era (259).

6. Susan McReynolds identifies the effort to come to terms with Christianity as a religion that allows—or even effects—the suffering death of children as the driving force behind Dostoevsky's fiction more broadly considered: "Dostoevsky's creative biography is, among other things, a quest to make sense of Christianity as a religion of child sacrifice, a creed that thanks and praises its God for the performance of what would be abominable if committed by an individual." *Redemption and the Merchant God: Dostoevsky's Economy of Salvation and Antisemitism* (Evanston, Ill.: Northwestern University Press, 2008), 32.

7. Paula Fredriksen, *From Jesus to Christ: The Origins of the New Testament Images of Jesus* (New Haven, Conn.: Yale University Press, 1998), 44.

8. Compare Mark's unsettling "sedition" with the uncanny ability of the Christ in John 12:27 to self-soothe: "Now my soul is troubled. And what should I say—'Father, save me from this hour'? No, it is for this reason that I have come to this hour."

9. Most Biblical scholars now agree that the accepted ending of the Christian gospel of Mark (16:9–16) is not original to the book. Idiosyncrasies in style, content, and Christology indicate that the last eight verses of the gospel were added sometime in the second century, perhaps a full hundred years after the bulk of the text was initially composed. We can only speculate as to why later Christians stitched this passage onto the gospel's tail, but there is at least one simple explanation: the original ending feels incomplete, abrupt, and disturbing.

10. Serene Jones, *Trauma and Grace: Theology in a Ruptured World* (Louisville, Ky.: Westminster/John Knox Press, 2009), 94.

11. Ibid., 89.

12. John Sanders, ed., *Atonement and Violence: A Theological Conversation* (Nashville: Abingdon Press, 2006), ix.

13. Martin Hengel, *The Atonement: The Origins of the Doctrine in the New Testament*, trans. John Bowden (Philadelphia: Fortress Press, 1981).

14. Gustaf Aulén, *Christus Victor: An Historical Study of the Three Main Types of the Idea of Atonement*, trans. A. G. Hebert (1931; New York: MacMillan, 1966), 5. By contrast, God and Jesus stand united in continuous theories of atonement. Aulén's prime example of continuous atonement is what he calls the "dramatic" or "Christus Victor" model, in which God and Jesus work together in the moment of the crucifixion to defeat Satan. Aulén claims that the classic model held sway through much of Christianity's first millennium. The atonement theory that Jürgen Moltmann developed might also be called continuous: *The Crucified God: The Cross of Christ as the Foundation and Criticism of Christian Theology*, trans. R. A. Wilson and John Bowden (1973; Minneapolis: Fortress Press, 1993).

15. Quoted in Sanders, *Atonement and Violence*, 7.

16. Bernard Schweitzer, *Hating God: The Untold Story of Misotheism* (New York: Oxford University Press, 2011), 2.

17. Other recent studies of scriptural, theological, and religious allusions in modern American texts include Christopher Wheatley's *Thornton Wilder and Amos Wilder: Writing Religion in Twentieth-Century America* (South Bend, Ind.: University of Notre Dame Press, 2011); Amy Hungerford's *Postmodern Belief: American Literature and Religion since 1960* (Princeton, N.J.: Princeton University Press, 2010); Gregory Jackson's *The Word and Its Witness: The Spiritualization of American Realism* (Chicago: University of Chicago Press, 2009); John McClure's *Partial Faiths: Postsecular Fiction in the Age of Pynchon and Morrison* (Athens: University of Georgia Press, 2007), Tuire Valkeakari's *Religious Idiom and the African American Novel, 1952–1998* (Gainesville: University of Florida Press, 2007): Terry Wright's *The Genesis of Fiction: Modern Novelists as Biblical Interpreters* (Burlington, Vt.: Ashgate Publishing, 2007), and James Coleman's *Faithful Vision: Treatments of the Sacred, Spiritual, and Supernatural in Twentieth-Century African-American Fiction* (Baton Rouge: Louisiana State University Press, 2006).

18. Elie Wiesel, "The Holocaust as a Literary Inspiration," in *Dimensions of the Holocaust*, ed. Elliott Lefkovitz (Evanston, Ill.: Northwestern University Press, 1977), 9.

19. E. Ann Kaplan, *Trauma Culture* (New Brunswick, N.J.: Rutgers University Press, 2005), 24.

20. A recent review article by Eric J. Sundquist ("Witness without End?" *American Literary History* 19, no. 1 [2007]: 65–85) rounds up recent monographs on the Holocaust and trauma studies, among them Michael Bernard-Donals and Richard Glejzer's *Witnessing the Disaster* (2003), Eva Hoffman's *After Such Knowledge* (2004), and Berel Lang's *Post-Holocaust Interpretation, Misinterpretation, and the Claims of History* (2005).

21. Judith Herman, *Trauma and Recovery* (New York: Basic Books, 1992).

22. Quoted in Shelly Rambo, *Spirit and Trauma: A Theology of Remaining* (Louisville, Ky.: Westminster/John Knox Press, 2010), 63.

23. Shoshana Felman and Dori Laub, M.D., *Testimony: Crises of Witnessing in Literature, Psychoanalysis, and History* (New York: Routledge, 1992), 57–58.

24. Marianne Hirsch, "The Generation of Postmemory," *Poetics Today* 29, no. 1 (2008): 107.

25. Stephen Prothero, *American Jesus: How the Son of God Became a National Icon* (New York: Farrar, Straus and Giroux, 2003), 6.

26. Ibid., 10.

27. Ibid., 11.

28. Ibid., 148.

29. Cathy Caruth, *Unclaimed Experience* (Baltimore: Johns Hopkins University Press, 1996), 27.

30. Cathy Caruth, "An Interview with Geoffrey Hartman," *Studies in Romanticism* 35, no. 4 (1996): 641.

31. Geoffrey H. Hartman, "On Traumatic Knowledge and Literary Studies," *New Literary History* 26, no. 3 (1995): 537.

32. I include some of these insights in an essay on Cathy Caruth's theory of trauma entitled "Speak, Trauma," which appears in a 2014 issue of the journal *Narrative*.

33. Richard J. McNally, *Remembering Trauma* (Cambridge, Mass.: Harvard University Press, 2003).

Chapter 2

1. *Kapporeth* is related to the Hebrew verb *kipper*, meaning to "cover," "propitiate," or "atone."

2. See Leviticus 16:2: "The Lord said to Moses: Tell your brother Aaron not to come just at any time into the sanctuary inside the curtain before the mercy seat that is upon the ark, or he will die; for I appear in the cloud upon the mercy seat."

3. Karl Barth, *The Epistle to the Romans*, trans. Edwyn C. Hoskins (1933; Oxford: Oxford University Press, 1968), 105.

4. Jewish theologians often point out one other crucial difference between Jewish and Christian atonement: the latter requires the sacrifice of a human being. And many read the averted sacrifice of Isaac in Genesis 22 as Yahweh's dramatic repudiation of the cult of child sacrifice. However, Jon Levenson argues that the sacrificial death of the firstborn is figural continuity that Judaism and Christianity share (Levenson, *Death and Resurrection*, 200–220).

5. Clark M. Williamson notes that "theologies of atonement are rooted in the New Testament, although they develop in ways not anticipated by the New Testament" ("Atonement Theologies and the Cross," *Encounter* 71, no. 1 [2010]: 4).

6. Hengel, *Atonement*, 53–54.

7. Hengel sees another proof text for atonement in the Last Supper narrative, and it provides language still in use in Christian communion ritual: "Then he took a cup, and after giving thanks he gave it to them, and all of them drank from it. He said to them, 'This is my blood of the new covenant, which is poured out for many. Truly I tell you, I will never again drink of the fruit of the vine until that day when I drink it new in the kingdom of God'" (Mark 14:24–25) (*Atonement*, 53). One might see an incipient theory of atonement (or reconciliation) in Jesus's claim that his own blood might renew or restore the covenantal relationship between God and his people.

8. Stephen Finlan, *Problems with Atonement: The Origins of, and Controversy about, the Atonement Doctrine*, (Collegeville, Minn.: Liturgical Press, 2005). Henri Blocher offers his own summary and interpretation of atonement metaphors in a 2004 essay, "Biblical Metaphors and the Doctrine of the Atonement." *Journal of the Evangelical Theological Society* 47, no. 4 (December 2004): 629–45.

9. Finlan, *Problems*, 5, 40, 6, 55, 44, 56, respectively.

10. Balthasar, *Theo-Drama*, 237. The book features another excellent outline of the historical development of atonement theology.

11. Ibid., 317.

12. Ibid., 318.

13. Ibid., 55.

14. Aulén, *Christus Victor*, 1–5. Gordon Graham provides a parallel, succinct review of atonement theologies in "Atonement," in *The Cambridge Companion to Christian Philosophical Theology*, ed. Charles Taliaferro and Chad Meister (Cambridge, Eng.: Cambridge University Press, 2010), 123–35. Fuller treatments of the history and development of atonement can be found in Hastings Rashdall's classic *The Idea of Atonement in Christian Theology* (London: MacMillan, 1919); F. W. Dillistone's *The Christian Understanding of Atonement* (Philadelphia: Westminster Press, 1968); F. R. Barry's *The Atonement* (London: Hodder & Stoughton, 1968); Leon Morris's *The Apostolic Preaching of the Cross* (Grand Rapids, Mich.: Eerdmans, 1984); Colin E. Gunton's *The Actuality of Atonement: A Study of Metaphor, Rationality and the Christian Tradition* (London: T. & T. Clark, 1998); and Charles E. Hill and Frank A. James's *The Glory of the Atonement: Biblical, Historical, and Practical Perspectives* (Downers Grove, Ill.: InterVarsity, 2004). The first volume of the *Oxford Readings in Philosophical Theology*, edited by Michael Rea, covers recent thinking on atonement and includes an update of atonement theology by Richard Swinburne, David Lewis's essay on the logics and illogics of penal substitution, and Philip L Quinn's renovation of Abelardian atonement, among other helpful contributions. Michael Rea, ed., *Oxford Readings in Philosophical Theology*, vol. 1, *Trinity, Incarnation, and Atonement* (Oxford: Oxford University Press, 2009).

15. Aulén, *Christus Victor*, 4. The contemporary atonement critic J. Denny Weaver believes that a slightly renovated version of Aulén's model—"Narrative *Christus Victor*," he calls it—might solve some of the problems implicit in other models. "Narrative *Christus Victor*: The Answer to Anselmian Atonement Violence," in *Atonement and Violence: A Theological Conversation*, ed. John Sanders (Nashville: Abingdon Press, 2006), 1–33.

16. Timothy Gorringe, *God's Just Vengeance: Crime, Violence, and the Rhetoric of Salvation* (Cambridge, Eng.: Cambridge University Press, 1996), 91.

17. Finlan groups the Christus Victor and ransom models together under the broader rubric, "rescue theories." *Problems*, 67.

18. Aulén responds that the dualism of his theory is not "absolute"; instead, the dualism inherent in Christus Victor "constantly occurs in scripture" and is "the opposition between God and that which in his own created world resists His will; between the Divine Love and the rebellion of created wills against him." *Christus Victor*, 5n.

19. Ibid., 5, 145–47, 154.

20. Anselm, "Why God Became Man," in *Anselm of Canterbury: The Major Works*, ed. Brian Davies and G. R. Evans (Oxford: Oxford University Press, 1998), 260–357.

21. Ibid., 349.

22. Von Balthasar accentuates the voluntary nature of Jesus's decision in Anselm's characterization of the cross; "the result is that the 'command' that God addresses to the Son seems increasingly to have the form of a 'granting,' a 'ratification' of the Son's will" (*Theo-Drama*, 259).

23. Ibid., 348. The heavy weight of human sin colors Flannery O'Connor's view of the atonement, discussed in chapter 3.

24. David Bentley Hart, *The Beauty of the Infinite: The Aesthetics of Christian Truth* (Grand Rapids: Eerdmans Publishing Company, 2003), 361.

25. Sanders, *Atonement and Violence*, xiv.

26. William C. Placher, "How Does Jesus Save?" *Christian Century*, June 2, 2009, 23.

27. Quoted in Gorringe, *God's Just Vengeance*, 101.

28. Defending Anselm against such critiques, Hart argues that Harnack and others have a too-narrow understanding of the saint's conception of "honor": "it is as well to observe that in that context 'honor' certainly signified more than a sense either of one's personal dignity or of one's social position, but referred also (and more fundamentally perhaps) to the principle underlying the rather fragile governance of an entire social and economic order, sustained through the exchange of shared benefits and pledged loyalties; one's honor lay not only in the obeisance one received, but in the social covenant one upheld and to which one was obliged (ideally, at any rate)" (*Beauty*, 369).

29. Peter Abelard, *Commentary on the Epistle to the Romans*, trans. Steven R. Cartwright (Washington, D.C.: Catholic University of America Press, 2011).

30. Quoted in Finlan, *Problems*, 74.

31. Quoted in Gorringe, *God's Just Vengeance*, 110.

32. Elizabeth R. Moberly, *Suffering, Innocent and Guilty* (London: SPCK, 1978), 24.

33. Paul Tillich, *Systematic Theology, Volume II: Existence and The Christ* (1957; Chicago: University of Chicago Press, 1975), 171.

34. Alister McGrath, *Christian Theology: An Introduction* (Chichester, U.K.: Wiley-Blackwell, 2011), 67–69. Aulén also notes Enlightenment critics' contention that the atonement is an atavistic "relic of Judaism." *Christus Victor*, 7.

35. C. J. T. Talar, "The Importance of Being Ernest: Renan (1823–1892)," *Continuum* 2, nos. 2–3 (1993): 326.

36. James R. A. Merrick, review of *Saved from Sacrifice: A Theology of the Cross*, by S. Mark Heim, *Journal of the Evangelical Theological Society* 50, no. 4 (December 2007): 882.

37. Aulén, *Christus Victor*, 154.

38. Rita Nakashima Brock and Rebecca Ann Parker, *Saving Paradise: How Christianity Traded Love of this World for Crucifixion and Empire* (Boston: Beacon Press, 2008), 236.

39. In *Beyond Sacred Violence* (Baltimore: Johns Hopkins University Press, 2008), Kathryn McClymond reminds us that not all forms of sacrifice involve violence, exploring Indian religious traditions that focus on vegetal and liquid sacrifices.

40. Susan Mizruchi, *The Science of Sacrifice: American Literature and Modern Social Theory* (Princeton, N.J.: Princeton University Press, 1998), 23.

41. René Girard, *Things Hidden since the Foundation of the World*, trans. Stephen Bann and Michael Metteer (1978; Stanford: Stanford University Press, 1987), 180–81. However, in a later interview, Girard is taken to task for downplaying one New Testament interpretation of the cross that seems *patently* sacrificial—the one developed in Hebrews. Asked if he "dismissed Hebrews too quickly," Girard responds, "Yes, sure. I was completely wrong"; "I agree entirely with you that there are problems with my treatment of Hebrews. It's a problem of language: the language of the 'last sacrifice,' even though in *Things Hidden* I say, ultimately, that the word 'sacrifice' doesn't matter that much. But I say it too briefly. And I give too much importance to that word." Rebecca Adams and René Girard, "Violence, Difference, Sacrifice: A Conversation with René Girard," *Religion and Literature* 25, no. 2 (summer 1993): 28.

42. Girard, *Things*, 182. Yet in Anselm's defense, David Bentley Hart contends that the saint is simply "the victim of his own clarity of thought," suggesting that his argument is so carefully streamlined as to be susceptible to reduction (*Beauty*, 370). He indicts Harnack, Aulén, Girard, and Vladimir Lossky for oversimplifying Anselm's theories in developing critiques of his version of atonement. Hart, by contrast, calls this version "an important first step toward more considered theories" (ibid., 362). For a further analysis of the relationship between Girard and Anselm, see Michael Kirwan's essay, "Being Saved from Salvation: René Girard and the Victims of Religion," *Communio Viatorum* 52, no. 1 (2010): 27–47.

43. Girard, *Things*, 184.

44. René Girard, *The Scapegoat*, trans. Yvonne Freccero (Baltimore: the Johns Hopkins University Press, 1986).

45. S. Mark Heim, *Saved from Sacrifice: A Theology of the Cross* (Grand Rapids, Mich.: Eerdmans Publishing, 2006), 15.

46. Quoted in Girard, *Things*, 194–95.

47. Heim, *Saved from Sacrifice*, 301.

48. Ibid., 301.

49. Ibid., 306.

50. Ibid., 321.

51. Miller, "Wound," 527.

52. Heim, *Saved from Sacrifice*, 309. Miller remains unconvinced, suggesting that even continuous atonement theologies "can add divine intensity to the cry of the poor but not succor them from violence" ("Wound," 529–30).

53. Moltmann, *The Crucified God.*

54. Darby Kathleen Ray, *Deceiving the Devil: Atonement, Abuse, and Ransom* (Cleveland: Pilgrim Press, 1998), 87.

55. Ibid., 88.

56. Ibid., 41. Nonetheless, Ray is unwilling to throw out baby and bathwater. Like Aulén, Ray sees promise in what she calls "patristic" models that character-ize the atonement as a moment in which the forces of evil are duped into giving up control over humanity. She argues that updated versions of Christus Victor ("dramatic" atonement) maintain the strengths of Anselmian and Abelardian theories while answering feminist and liberationist critiques. Further, her focus on the "deceptive" quality of patristic atonement "points to the reality that any struggle against oppression and injustice that seeks to avoid violent means or that emerges from a context of relative powerlessness must rely on cunning and ingenuity rather than ascribed authority or power" (*Deceiving*, 138–39). Her atonement, then, is related to other contemporary strategies of resistance. While acknowledging the real power of evil, it also provides the weak and the oppressed with tools for fighting back. Ray's characterization of the cross is compelling, but also heavily metaphorical. She admires patristic models of atonement because of their "atheoretical character," describing them as "a loosely cohering cluster of themes and images" much like the variety of metaphors that Finlan sees laid out in the Pauline epistles. Simply, Ray is able to avoid some of the harsh realities of the crucifixion by abstracting them.

57. Weaver, "Narrative," 1.

58. Ibid., 6.

59. Ibid., 16.

60. Ibid., 7. W. Clark Gilpin agrees, writing that each of the major strands of atonement thought "placed a foundational act of violence at the center of Chris-tian ideas of salvation. And since God is the initiator of this reconciling act, not a few modern interpreters have strongly objected to the implications of the atone-ment concept for the Christian understanding of God." Quoted in Williamson, "Atonement," 23. Weaver has his critics, however. See Mark Thiessen Nation, "'Who Has Believed What We Have Heard?' A Response to Denny Weaver's *The Nonviolent Atonement*," *Conrad Grebel Review* 27, no. 2 (2009): 17–30.

61. For Weaver, Jesus's life and his resurrection—rather than his death—complete the necessary work of salvation and reconciliation. His mission on earth demonstrates that God is on humanity's side in an energetic but ultimately non-violent fight against the forces of evil. Jesus's crucifixion shows that earthly evil is a powerful force indeed, and the Romans who kill him prove that oppres-sive power is a deadly business. But God has no hand in it: "Jesus did suffer and die a violent death, but the violence was neither God's nor God directed" ("Nar-rative," 25). And the resurrection confirms that divine love overcomes the deadly machinations of human power. In Weaver's system, the cross is a bump in the road whose importance we ought not over-emphasize. Instead, we should focus on Jesus's life and rebirth, which are signs of God's support and love. Charles E. Brown shares Weaver's hope that a rehabilitated Christus Victor model might offer hope to the abused and oppressed while at the same time affirming the redemptive power of the cross. He argues that Christus Victor helps the church "speak out against the evil exploitation of the weak by the powerful and the

unjust, and embrace the suffering of the just." "The Atonement: Healing in Post-modern Society," *Interpretation* 53, no. 1 (January 1999): 42.

62. Rita Nakashima Brock and Rebecca Ann Parker, *Proverbs of Ashes: Violence, Redemptive Suffering, and the Search for What Saves Us* (Boston: Beacon Press, 2008), 5.

63. Ibid., 250.

64. Ibid.

65. Williamson also notes that the God of the Bible is a complex character who is by turns cruel and nonviolent. However, he often accentuates God's peacefulness: "The nonviolent God of the Torah is a God of distributive justice, not of retributive (violent) justice; God provides for the equitable distribution of land, the ability to provide for families, forgiving debts, freeing slaves, and reversing homelessness and poverty. God's especial concern is for the vulnerable—widows, orphans and strangers" ("Atonement," 17).

66. Blumenthal, *Facing*, 155.

67. Ibid., xii.

68. James H. Cone, *God of the Oppressed* (San Francisco: Harper and Row, 1975), 175.

69. Ibid., 177.

70. Ibid., 183.

71. Ibid.

72. Ibid., 231.

73. Ibid.

74. Ibid.

75. Ibid., 192.

76. See Mary Daly, *Beyond God the Father: Toward a Philosophy of Women's Liberation* (Boston: Beacon Press, 1973), 25; Sarah L. Darter, "Response to 'Does Feminist Theology Liberate?'" *Foundations* 19 (January–March 1976): 50–52; and Jacquelyn Grant, "Black Christology : Interpreting Aspects of the Apostolic Faith," *Mid-Stream* 24, no. 4 (1985): 366–75.

77. Delores S. Williams, *Sisters in the Wilderness: The Challenge of Womanist God-Talk* (Maryknoll, N.Y.: Orbis Books, 1993).

78. Daly, *Beyond*, 75.

79. Ibid., 77.

80. Ibid., 75.

81. Ibid., 76. Robert J. Daly concurs, noting that the *imitatio* tradition may be understood as encouraging violence in believers set on patterning their behavior on divine action: "If God, whose perfection Christians are supposed to imitate—see Matthew 5:48: 'Be perfect, therefore, as your heavenly Father is perfect (*teleios*)'—is violent, can we expect Christians to be nonviolent?" ("Images of God and the Imitation of God: Problems with Atonement," *Theological Studies* 68 [2007]: 37).

82. Joanne Carlson Brown and Rebecca Parker, "For God So Loved the World?" in *Christianity, Patriarchy, and Abuse: A Feminist Critique*, ed. Joanne Carlson Brown and Carole R. Bohn (New York: Pilgrim Press, 1989), 13.

83. Ibid., 2.

84. Ibid., 9.

85. Miller, "Wound," 536.

86. Ibid., 545.

87. Ibid., 533.

88. Jones, *Trauma*, 92.

89. In *God and the Victim* (New York: Oxford University Press, 2007), a more properly devotional volume, Jennifer Erin Beste grapples with the debilitating effects of trauma on potential believers and argues that the deleterious effects of trauma may hinder the individual's ability to accept God. She further argues that believers have an ethical responsibility to reach out to trauma victims in helping them realize God's love and his healing power.

90. Caruth, *Unclaimed*, 4.

91. Rambo, *Spirit*, 62–64.

92. Serene Jones, *Trauma*, 124.

93. Cathy Caruth, ed., *Trauma: Explorations in Memory* (Baltimore: Johns Hopkins University Press, 1995), 4–5.

94. Rambo, *Spirit*, 37–40.

95. Ibid., 40.

96. Ibid., 41–42.

97. Felman and Laub, *Testimony*, 80.

98. Ibid., 80.

99. Patrick H. Hutton, "The Art of Memory Reconceived: From Rhetoric to Psychoanalysis," *Journal of the History of Ideas* 48, no. 3 (1987): 388.

100. Ibid., 390.

101. Richard King, "Memory and Phantasy," *Comparative Literature* 98, no. 5 (December 1983): 1207–1208.

102. John Milbank and Slavoj Žižek, *The Monstrosity of Christ* (Cambridge: MIT Press, 2009), 27. Žižek claims that a plurality of Hegel critics have fallen under the influence of a screen memory that amounts to a simplistic understanding of the philosopher's message: "This is to say: something happens in Hegel, a breakthrough into a unique dimension of thought, which is obliterated, rendered invisible in its true dimension, by postmetaphysical thought. This obliteration leaves an empty space which has to be filled in so that the continuity of the development of philosophy can be reestablished—filled in with what? The index of this obliteration is the ridiculous image of Hegel as the absurd 'Absolute Idealist' who 'pretended to know everything,' to possess Absolute Knowledge, to read the mind of God, to deduce the whole of reality out of the self-movement of (his) mind— the image which is an exemplary case of what Freud called *Deck-Erinnerung* (screen-memory), a fantasy formation intended to cover up a traumatic truth" (26–27).

103. Ibid., 53.

104. Susan Brison, *Aftermath: Violence and the Remaking of a Self* (Princeton, N.J.: Princeton University Press, 2002), 71.

105. Kaplan, *Trauma Culture*, 20.

Chapter 3

EPIGRAPH: Flannery O'Connor, *The Habit of Being*, ed. Sally Fitzgerald (New York: Vintage Books, 1979), 394.

1. Brad Gooch, *Flannery: A Life of Flannery O'Connor* (New York: Little, Brown, and Co., 2009), 327–28.

2. O'Connor, *Habit*, 394.

3. Ibid., 421.

4. Ibid., 540.

5. Ibid., 442, italics mine.

6. Ibid., 394.

7. Flannery O'Connor, *Collected Works* (New York: Library of America, 1988), 28.

8. O'Connor, *Habit*, 90. For Marshall Bruce Gentry, critics trying to make sense of the relationship between O'Connor's faith and the content of her fiction fall into four camps: those who find no theological intent in the fiction; those who see the fiction as compatible with orthodox Catholic theology; those who see it as a vehicle of a "harsh" orthodoxy; and those who understand her writing as unorthodox or even demonic (*Flannery O'Connor's Religion of the Grotesque* [Jackson: University Press of Mississippi, 1986], 3). Joanne Halleran McMullen counts herself as a member of a fifth "school" of O'Connor criticism, one that "emphasizes the deliberate mystery O'Connor has so cleverly and abstractly concealed throughout her fiction" (*Writing against God: Language as Message in the Literature of Flannery O'Connor* [Macon, Ga.: Mercer University Press, 1996], 2).

9. Flannery O'Connor, *Mystery and Manners: Occasional Prose*, ed. Sally and Robert Fitzgerald (New York: Farrar, Straus and Giroux, 1969), 226–27.

10. O'Connor, *Habit*, 147.

11. O'Connor, *Mystery*, 185.

12. Other critics argue convincingly that the theological notion of Incarnation—the idea that in Jesus, God takes human or earthly form—is of equal importance. For more, see Brian Abel Ragen's *A Wreck on the Road to Damascus: Innocence, Guilt, and Conversion in Flannery O'Connor* (Chicago: Loyola University Press, 1989); McMullen's *Writing against God*; Susan Srigley's *Flannery O'Connor's Sacramental Art* (South Bend, Ind.: University of Notre Dame Press, 2004); and Peter Candler's "The Anagogical Imagination of Flannery O'Connor," *Christianity and Literature* 60, no. 1 (autumn 2010): 11–33.

13. O'Connor, *Collected Works*, 805.

14. Jill Peláez Baumgaertner, "Flannery O'Connor and the Cartoon Catechism," in *Inside the Church of Flannery O'Connor*, eds. Joanne Halleran McMullen and Jon Parrish Peede (Macon, Ga.: Mercer University Press, 2007): 104.

15. To refine our understanding of O'Connor's Redemption, Gentry turns to *The Catholic Encyclopedia*, which defines Redemption as "the restoration of man from the bondage of sin to the liberty of the children of god through the satisfactions and merits of Christ" (*Flannery*, 4).

16. W. A. Sessions, "Real Presence: Flannery O'Connor and the Saints," in *Inside the Church of Flannery O'Connor*, eds. Joanne Halleran McMullen and Jon Parrish Peede (Macon, Ga.: Mercer University Press, 2007), 24. Arthur Kinney catalogs the contents of her collection in *Flannery O'Connor's Library: Resources of Being*. (Athens: University of Georgia Press, 1985).

17. O'Connor, *Habit*, 81, 93.

18. Gooch, *Flannery*, 114.

19. Helen R. Andretta, "The Hylomorphic Sacramentalism of 'Parker's Back,'" in *Inside the Church of Flannery O'Connor*, ed. Joanne Halleran McMullen and Jon Parrish Peede (Macon, Ga.: Mercer University Press, 2007), 42.

20. Thomas Aquinas, *An Aquinas Reader*, ed. Mary T. Clark (Garden City, N.Y.: Image Books, 1972), 469. Eleanor Stump sees Aquinas's version of atonement as both subtler and more convincing than Anselm's; nonetheless, she describes it in terms that would be familiar to those who know Anselm: "To understand Aquinas's account of this function of the Atonement [satisfaction], it is important to be clear about what he means by satisfaction and what importance he attaches to it. Satisfaction, he says, removes the debt of punishment for sin. Now if God had willed to free humans from sin without any satisfaction, he would not have acted against justice; for if he forgives sin without satisfaction—without removal (that is) of the debt of punishment—he wrongs no one, just as anyone who overlooks a trespass against himself acts mercifully and not unjustly. Nonetheless, there was no more suitable way of healing our nature than by making satisfaction." "Atonement According to Aquinas," in *Oxford Readings in Philosophical Theology*, vol. 1, *Trinity, Incarnation, and Atonement*, ed. Michael Rea (Oxford: Oxford University Press, 2009), 271.

21. The theologian uses Anselmian language to make a similar point in his commentary on Paul's letter to the Romans: "If in fact it be asked why Christ died for the wicked, the answer is that God in this way commends his charity toward us. He shows us in this way that he loves us with a love that knows no limits, for while we were as yet sinners Christ died for us. The very death of Christ for us shows the love of God, for it was his Son whom he gave to die that satisfaction might be made for us." Aquinas, *An Aquinas Reader*, 532–33.

22. O'Connor, *Habit*, 99. As one sign of its persistent popularity in Catholic circles, Cardinal Joseph Ratzinger—later Pope Benedict XVI—wrote the introduction for a 1982 rerelease.

23. Sessions argues that Guardini's writings have a singular effect in shaping O'Connor's Christology ("Real Presence," 24).

24. Romano Guardini, *The Lord*, trans. Elinor Castendyk Briefs (1954; Chicago: Regnery Gateway, 1982), 398. Elsewhere in the same section, Guardini argues that sin begins with the individual's failing efforts to be independent from God: "Thus God created man, who had no coherence, no life save in his Creator. Then man sinned; he attempted to free himself from this fundamental truth of his existence; attempted to be sufficient unto himself. And he fell away from God—in the terrible, literal sense of the word. He fell from genuine being towards nothingness—and not back to the positive, creative pure nothingness from which God had lifted him, but towards the negative nothingness of sin, destruction, death, senselessness and the abyss [. . . yet] God not only glanced down at him and summoned him lovingly to return, he personally entered into that vacuous dark to fetch him, as St. John so powerfully expresses it in his opening gospel." Ibid., 398. In *A Wreck on the Road to Damascus*, Brian Abel Ragen argues that the tension created by humans' misguided efforts to stand alone without God drives much of O'Connor's fiction.

25. Kinney, *Library*, 29.

26. O'Connor, *Collected Works*, 820, italics mine.

27. O'Connor, *Mystery*, 112.

28. Ralph C. Wood, "'God May Strike You Thisaway': Flannery O'Connor and Simone Weil on Affliction and Joy," *Renascence* 59, no. 3 (spring 2007): 191.

29. O'Connor, *Collected Works*, 632.

30. Ibid., 546.

31. We may also hear echoes of Deuteronomy 33:26 in "riding majestically": "There is none like God, O Jeshurun, / who rides through the heavens to your help, / majestic through the skies."

32. O'Connor, *Collected Works*, 385.

33. It is worth noting that for O'Connor, the death of an adult can also provoke a religious turn; as an example, take "The Displaced Person," in which the passing of Mr. Guizac spurs Mrs. McIntyre's conversion.

34. Richard Giannone, *Flannery O'Connor, Hermit Novelist* (Urbana: University of Illinois Press, 2000), 145.

35. O'Connor, *Collected Works*, 332.

36. Ibid., 333.

37. Ibid., 333. As John R. May points out, Jesus's parable of the sower underpins the novel; accordingly, Rayber is like the hard soil on which the seed of the Word falls but fails to take root. *The Pruning Word: the Parables of Flannery O'Connor* (South Bend, Ind.: University of Notre Dame Press, 1976), 137 ff.

38. Joseph Zornado, "A Becoming Habit: Flanner O'Connor's Fiction of Unknowing," *Religion and Literature* 29, no. 2 (summer 1997): 51.

39. John F. Desmond, "Flannery O'Connor and the Displaced Sacrament," in *Inside the Church of Flannery O'Connor*, ed. Joanne Halleran McMullen and Jon Parrish Peede (Macon, Ga.: Mercer University Press, 2007), 74.

40. O'Connor, *Collected Works*, 389.

41. The "bread of life" imagery that grounds this final vision supports P. Travis Kroeker's argument that O'Connor borrows much of *Violent*'s language and vision from the gospel of John: "'Jesus Is the Bread of Life': Johannine Sign and Deed in *The Violent Bear It Away*," in *Dark Faith: New Essays on Flannery O'Connor's "The Violent Bear It Away*," ed. Susan Srigley (South Bend, Ind.: University of Notre Dame Press, 2012).

42. O'Connor, *Collected Works*, 478.

43. Ibid., 479.

44. Ronald L. Grimes argues that O'Connor's staging of the baptism/drowning forces upon the reader the uncomfortable task of discerning how the murder and the baptism are related: "If readers merely reject the baptism-drowning, they are in trouble, because O'Connor anticipates this response and forces those who choose it to identify with Rayber. On the other hand, if readers merely accept the gesture, they are complicit with homicide, no matter how much it may resemble a ritual sacrifice. If we say yes to the baptism we imply our approval of murder." "Anagogy and Ritualization: Baptism in Flannery O'Connor's *The Violent Bear It Away*," *Religion and Literature* 21, no. 1 (spring 1989): 12. In Grimes's reading, affirming the baptism is tantamount to affirming the murder, while if we reject the crime, we also lose the saving grace of baptism and fall into the schoolteacher's sterile intellectualism.

45. O'Connor, *Collected Works*, 456.

46. Ibid., 458.

47. Ibid.

48. Ibid., 465.

49. Ibid.

50. Giannone, *Hermit*, 159, 153.

51. Gary M. Ciuba, "'Not His Son': Violent Kinship and the Spirit of Adoption in *The Violent Bear It Away*," in *Dark Faith: New Essays on Flannery O'Connor's "The Violent Bear It Away*," ed. Susan Srigley (South Bend, Ind.: University of Notre Dame Press, 2012), 78.

52. Susan Srigley, *Sacramental*, 96.

53. Joyce Carol Oates, *New Heaven, New Earth: The Visionary Experience in Literature* (New York: Vanguard, 1974), 157.

54. O'Connor, *Habit*, 536, italics mine.

55. Ibid., 358.

56. Ibid., 343, italics mine.

57. O'Connor, *Collected Works*, 329.

58. O'Connor, *Habit*, 382. As examples, see Srigley, *Sacramental*, 100; Karl E. Martin, "Suffering Violence in the Kingdom of Heaven: *The Violent Bear It Away*," in *Dark Faith: New Essays on Flannery O'Connor's "The Violent Bear It Away*," ed. Susan Srigley (South Bend, Ind.: University of Notre Dame Press, 2012), 150; and Jolly Kay Sharp, *"Between the House and the Chicken Yard": The Masks of Mary Flannery O'Connor* (Macon, Ga.: Mercer University Press, 2011), 73.

59. O'Connor, *Mystery*, 113.

60. Of course, the notion that the barrel of a gun might effect grace might strike some as unnatural; yet O'Connor is perfectly willing to admit the strangeness of this state of affairs. In the same letter to Hester in which she describes Bishop's murder as "forgotten by God," she notes that "the violent are not natural" while acknowledging that she's "much more interested in the nobility of unnaturalness than in the nobility of naturalness." For O'Connor as perhaps for us, it is a strange truth that violence may be both unnatural and noble. Yet as she continues in the same letter, "it is the business of the artist to uncover the strangeness of truth." O'Connor, *Habit*, 343.

61. O'Connor, *Habit*, 116. O'Connor echoes this sentiment in "The Catholic Novelist in the Protestant South," writing, "Our response to life is different if we have been taught only a definition of faith than if we have trembled with Abraham as he held the knife over Isaac." *Mystery*, 203.

62. In drawing attention to the trope of child sacrifice in both the Old and New Testaments, O'Connor anticipates the arguments of Jon Levenson, who in *The Death and Resurrection of the Beloved Son* traces the hidden Biblical history of child sacrifice in both Judaism and Christianity.

63. O'Connor, *Mystery*, 202.

64. Jack Mulder, Jr., *Kierkegaard and the Catholic Tradition: Conflict and Dialogue* (Bloomington: Indiana University Press, 2010), 57.

65. Ibid.

66. O'Connor, *Mystery*, 116.

67. O'Connor, *Habit*, 100.

68. O'Connor, *Mystery*, 178, italics mine.

69. O'Connor, *Habit*, 191.

70. Martin, "Suffering," 164. Christina Bieber Lake describes the similarity provocatively and concisely: "Jesus is God's grotesque . . . Bishop is O'Connor's grotesque. He is the cause of conflict, the generator of violence, the locus of the sacred." *The Incarnational Art of Flannery O'Connor* (Macon, Ga.: Mercer University Press, 2005), 147.

71. O'Connor, *Collected Works*, 400, 379.

72. Ibid., 401.

73. Ibid., 427.

74. Ibid., 421.

75. Ibid., 456.

76. As Giannone argues, "the distant din is Bishop's death roar; the cry of suffering is the voice of God." *Hermit*, 160.

77. O'Connor, *Collected Works*, 393.

78. O'Connor, *Habit*, 488.

79. Farrell O'Gorman speculates—convincingly—that O'Connor's distaste for Rayber's reductive philosophy springs from her own bad experiences with secular education; her novels "mercilessly satirized the secular pseudoscientific 'schoolteachers,' such as Rayber of *The Violent Bear It Away*, who attempt to reduce individual human beings to rationally comprehensible types. It is difficult not to see in her dubious experience with modern education—as opposed to her earlier training at Catholic schools—the roots of [this] major theme." *Peculiar Crossroads: Flannery O'Connor, Walker Percy, and Catholic Vision in Postwar Southern Fiction* (Baton Rouge: Louisiana State University Press, 2004), 39.

80. O'Connor, *Habit*, 359.

81. O'Connor, *Mystery*, 227. Srigley also notes the similarity (*Sacramental*, 96).

82. O'Connor, *Collected Works*, 413.

83. Ibid., 413.

84. Desmond, "Displaced," 68.

85. O'Connor, *Collected Works*, 419.

86. Ibid., 419.

87. Gentry, *Flannery*, 154.

88. Giannone, *Hermit*, 159.

89. John F. Desmond, "Stalking Joy: Flannery O'Connor and the Dangerous Quest," *Christianity and Literature* 60, no. 1 (autumn 2010): 107.

90. O'Connor, *Collected Works*, 435.

91. See Henry Friedlander, *The Origins of Nazi Genocide: From Euthanasia to the Final Solution* (Chapel Hill: University of North Carolina Press, 1997).

92. Martin, "Suffering," 168.

93. O'Connor, *Habit*, 379.

94. Mulder, *Kierkegaard*, 57.

Chapter 4

EPIGRAPHS: Charlie Reilly, "An Interview with John Updike," *Contemporary Literature* 43, no. 2 (2002): 227; John Updike, *More Matter* (New York: Alfred A. Knopf, 1999), 60.

1. Charles Thomas Samuels, "The Art of Fiction XLIII: John Updike," in *Conversations with John Updike*, ed. James Plath (Jackson: University Press of Mississippi, 1994), 37.

2. Jeff Campbell, "Interview with John Updike," in *Conversations with John Updike*, ed. James Plath (Jackson: University Press of Mississippi, 1994), 90.

3. Reilly, "Interview," 226–27, italics mine.

4. Jan Nunley, "Thoughts of Faith Infuse Updike's Novels," in *Conversations with John Updike*, ed. James Plath (Jackson: University Press of Mississippi,

1994), 253. Somewhat unexpectedly, O'Connor would seem to agree. In a letter to Father McCown, she calls *Rabbit, Run* "the product of a real religious consciousness" (O'Connor, *Habit*, 420).

5. Updike, *More Matter*, 464.

6. Larry Woiwode, *Words Made Fresh: Essays on Literature and Culture* (Wheaton, Ill.: Crossway, 2011), 94.

7. Ibid., 59.

8. John Updike, *Higher Gossip* (New York: Alfred A. Knopf, 2011), 479.

9. Elinor Stout, "Interview with John Updike," in *Conversations with John Updike*, ed. James Plath (Jackson: University Press of Mississippi, 1994), 75. Among the many critics who argue for the influence of Barth's theology on Updike's work are Hedda Ben-Bassat, *Prophets without Vision: Subjectivity and the Sacred in Contemporary American Writing* (Lewisburg, Pa.: Bucknell University Press, 2000); George W. Hunt, *John Updike and the Three Great Things: Sex, Religion, and Art* (Grand Rapids, Mich.: Eerdmans, 1980); Marshall Boswell, "The Black Jesus: Racism and Redemption in John Updike's *Rabbit Redux*," *Contemporary Literature* 39, no. 1 (1998): 99–132; Stephen H. Webb, "Writing as a Reader of Karl Barth: What Kind of Religious Writer Is John Updike Not?" in *John Updike and Religion: The Sense of the Sacred and the Motions of Grace*, ed. James Yerkes (Grand Rapids: Eerdmans, 1999), 145–61; and James Wood, *The Broken Estate: Essays on Literature and Belief*, (New York: Random House, 1999).

10. Jack De Bellis, *The John Updike Encyclopedia* (Westport: Greenwood Press, 2000), 378.

11. A significant number of authors have also written on Kierkegaard and Updike; see Ralph Wood, *The Comedy of Redemption: Christian Faith and Comic Vision in Four American Novelists* (South Bend, Ind.: University of Notre Dame Press, 1988); John M. Neary, "'Ah: Runs': Updike, Rabbit, and Repetition," *Religion and Literature* 21, no. 1 (1989): 89–110; Avis Hewitt, "Intimations of Immortality: Mastered Irony in John Updike's 'Pigeon Feathers,'" *Christianity and Literature* 49, no. 4 (2000): 499–509; Marshall Boswell, *John Updike's Rabbit Tetralogy: Mastered Irony in Motion* (Columbia: University of Missouri Press, 2001); and Peter J. Bailey, *Rabbit (Un)Redeemed: The Drama of Belief in John Updike's Fiction* (Madison, N.J.: Fairleigh Dickinson University Press, 2006).

12. John Updike, *Self-Consciousness* (New York: Alfred A. Knopf, 1989), 230.

13. Nunley, "Thoughts," 254.

14. Wood, *Comedy*, 209.

15. John Updike, *Roger's Version* (New York: Alfred A. Knopf, 1986), 321.

16. John Updike, *In the Beauty of the Lilies* (New York: Fawcett Columbine, 1996), 61.

17. John Updike, *A Month of Sundays* (New York: Alfred A. Knopf, 1975), 207.

18. Nunley, "Thoughts," 254.

19. Updike, *Self-Consciousness*, 233, italics mine.

20. Ibid., 206, italics mine.

21. That he rejects both these orthodox models lends credence to Edward P. Vargo's claim that "the God affirmed in *Rabbit, Run* is not representative of traditional Christianity" (*Rainstorms and Fire: Ritual in the Novels of John Updike* [Port Washington, N.Y.: Kennikat Press, 1973], 53).

22. John Updike, *Picked-Up Pieces* (New York: Alfred A. Knopf, 1975), 508.

23. Updike, *Higher Gossip*, 453.

24. As Bailey puts it, Rabbit is Updike's "by-some-standards wildly inappropriate interrogator of the promises of religious belief" (*[Un]Redeemed*, 66).

25. De Bellis notes that Kruppenbach is based on Updike's own Lutheran pastor, the Reverend Victor Kroninger (*Encyclopedia*, 376).

26. John Updike, *Rabbit, Run* (1960; New York: Fawcett Crest, 1988), 159.

27. Ibid., 139.

28. Ralph C. Wood, *Comedy*, 216. We might sense in this religious egoism hints of what Bellah identifies in *Habits of the Heart* as "expressive individualism," which "holds that each person has a unique core of feeling and intuition that should unfold or be expressed if individuality is to be realized" (1985; Berkeley: University of California Press, 2008) (334). Charles Taylor (who, like Bellah, sees the roots of expressive individualism in nineteenth-century Romanticism) sees its flourishing in America in the sixties and seventies—when *Rabbit, Run* and *Rabbit Redux* are set—in calls to "find yourself, realize yourself, release your true self, and so on" (*A Secular Age* [Cambridge: Harvard University Press, 2007], 475). Certainly, the critical consensus has long acknowledged Rabbit's devotion to his own self, and for a critic like Thomas F. Haddox, Rabbit's "individualism"—or egoism—threatens to collapse into a kind of religious narcissism (*Hard Sayings: The Rhetoric of Christian Orthodoxy in Late Modern Fiction* [Columbus: Ohio State University Press, 2013], 85–125). Yet, as I will argue below, Rabbit's self-worship is shaped by his creator's theological training; said differently, when Rabbit expresses himself, he frequently does so in recognizable, established theological vocabularies.

29. John Updike, *Assorted Prose* (New York: Alfred A. Knopf, 1965), 273–82.

30. Updike, *Rabbit, Run*, 259.

31. Ibid., 219.

32. Lewis A. Lawson, "Rabbit Angstrom," 244.

33. William C. Placher, "Christ Takes Our Place," 7.

34. Updike, *Rabbit, Run*, 183.

35. Ibid., 141.

36. Ibid., 183.

37. Ibid., 263.

38. Ibid., 264.

39. Ibid., 271.

40. Ibid., 272.

41. Placher, "Christ Takes Our Place," 7.

42. David Lewis, "Do We Believe in Penal Substitution?" in *Oxford Readings in Philosophical Theology*, vol. 1, *Trinity, Incarnation, and Atonement*, ed. Michael Rea (New York: Oxford University Press, 2009), 308.

43. Bailey, *(Un)Redeemed*; Stephen H. Webb, "John Updike and the Waning of Mainline Protestantism," *Christianity and Literature* 57, no. 4 (2008); Suzanne Henning Uphaus, *John Updike* (New York: Frederick Ungar Publishing, 1980).

44. Uphaus, *John Updike*, 82. If Rabbit "rejects" religion in *Redux*, such rejection conforms with Bailey's central argument, in *Rabbit (Un)Redeemed*, that the Rabbit tetralogy maps Harry's slow but inexorable movement away from faith.

45. John Updike, *Rabbit Redux* (New York: Fawcett Crest, 1971), 112.

46. Ralph C. Wood, *Comedy*, 220.

47. Bailey, *(Un)Redeemed*, 93.

48. Kyle A. Pasework, "The Troubles with Harry: Freedom, America, and God in John Updike's Rabbit Novels," *Religion and American Culture: A Journal of Interpretation* 6, no. 1 (1996): 7.

49. Vargo, *Rainstorms*, 160.

50. Updike, *Redux*, 187. Exceptions to this rule include Joyce B. Markle (*Fighters and Lovers: Theme in the Novels of John Updike* [New York: New York University Press, 1973]) and, to a lesser extent, Boswell and Hunt. The last of these rounds up Biblical evidence to support Skeeter's claim. Hunt, *Updike*, 179.

51. Updike, *Picked-Up Pieces*, 510.

52. Updike, *Rabbit Redux*, 191.

53. Patrick Allitt, *Religion in America Since 1945: A History* (New York: Columbia University Press, 2003), 113.

54. Will Herzfeld, "Words of Liberation" (review of *Black Theology and Black Power*, by James H. Cone), *Christian Century* (December 17, 1969): 1620.

55. Glenn R. Bucher, review of *God of the Oppressed*, by James H. Cone, *Theology Today* 33, no. 1 (1976): 119, 116.

56. James H. Cone, *Black Theology and Black Power* (New York: Seabury Press, 1969), 68.

57. Ibid., 36.

58. Ibid., 124.

59. Ibid., 150.

60. Updike, *Redux*, 187.

61. Ibid., 214.

62. Ibid., 205–6.

63. Ibid., 247.

64. Ibid., 241. Robert Alter credits Rabbit's brush with Skeeter's gospel of chaos and confusion with advancing Rabbit's racial education and establishing a sense of "complicity" between himself and the oppressed other: "What emerges most prominently from Rabbit's confusions is a sense of complicity. He can no longer see the nation altogether as a division between 'we' who are right and 'they' who make the trouble, for he has reached some inner knowledge that we all have a hand in the trouble." "Updike, Malamud, and the Fire This Time," in *John Updike: A Collection of Critical Essays*, ed. David Thorburn and Howard Eiland (Englewood Cliffs, N.J.: Prentice-Hall, 1979), 48.

65. A preliminary but partial answer invokes the two authors' shared theological influences. Like Updike, Cone frequently cites both Barth and Kierkegaard in developing his own theory of religion.

66. As mentioned in a previous chapter, in *God of the Oppressed*, Cone rejects Anselm's atonement because he approaches the cross from "a rationalistic viewpoint that was meaningless for the oppressed. [. . . Anselmian atonement is] a neat rational theory but useless as a leverage against political oppression. It dehistoricizes the work of Christ, separating it from God's liberating act in history" (*Oppressed*, 231). He objects to subjective atonement theologies for similar reasons: "Abelard not only de-emphasized the objective reality of divine reconciliation, he apparently failed to grasp the radical quality of evil and oppression" (ibid).

67. Cone, *Black Theology*, 36.

68. Ibid., 46.

69. In his preference for a Christology that affirms God's participation in human agony, Cone echoes the atonement Moltmann outlines in *The Crucified God*; not coincidentally, Cone cites Moltmann in *Black Theology and Black Power*, 37.

70. Updike, *More Matter*, 329, italics mine.

71. Here, we may hear echoes again of von Balthasar, who argues that the Son's kenosis—or self-emptying—mirrors or finds its origin in that of God himself: "It is possible to say, with Bulgakov, that the Father's self-utterance in the generation of the Son is an initial 'kenosis' within the Godhead that underpins all subsequent kenosis. For the Father strips himself, without remainder, of his Godhead and hands it over to the Son" (*Theo-Drama*, 323).

72. Thomas M. Dicken, "God and Pigment: John Updike on the Conservation of Meaning," *Religion and Literature* 36, no. 3 (2004): 70.

73. Updike, *Assorted Prose*, 182.

74. John Updike, *Odd Jobs*, 259.

75. Updike, *Rabbit, Run*, 120.

76. Updike, *More Matter*, 819.

77. Updike, *Rabbit, Run*, 236.

78. Ibid., 244.

79. Ibid., 243; Boswell, *Updike's Rabbit Tetralogy*, 66.

80. John Stephen Martin, "Rabbit's Faith: Grace and the Transformation of the Heart," *Pacific Coast Philology* 17, nos. 1–2 (1982): 106.

81. Updike, *Redux*, 261–64, 334–35. Boswell develops his reading of an elusive God's presence watching over Jill and Skeeter in "The Black Jesus." Boswell, "Black Jesus," 126.

82. It is worth noting at this point that the notion of *a God* who suffers (rather than the human Jesus) is non-traditional, if not heterodox. Christian tradition usually affirms a deity who is impassible, or unsusceptible to human pain, suffering, and passion. To support this characterization, Gilles Emery cites a Roman counsel of 382: "If anyone says that in the passion of the cross it is God himself who felt the pain and not the flesh and the soul which Christ, the Son of God, had taken to himself—the 'form of a servant' which he had accepted as scripture says [cf. Phil. 2:7]—he is mistaken." "The Immutability of the God of Love and the Problem of Language concerning the 'Suffering of God,' " in *Divine Impassibility and the Mystery of Human Suffering*, ed. James F. Keating and Thomas Joseph White (Grand Rapids, Mich.: Eerdmans, 2009), 29. In the same volume, Gary Culpepper shows how the proclamations of the Council of Chalcedon (451 C.E.) are often interpreted as suggesting that only the human element of Jesus can and does suffer on the cross; they "[suggest] to many Christians that God should be said to suffer, not according to his divine nature, but only in the human nature that is assumed by the divine person of the Son." " 'One Suffering, in Two Natures': An Analogical Inquiry into Divine and Human Suffering," in ibid., 78.

83. Updike, *Rabbit, Run*, 243.

84. Updike, *Picked-Up Pieces*, 504.

85. Wood, *Comedy*, 201.

86. Campbell, "Interview," 93.

87. Ibid., 85.

88. John Updike, *The Rabbit Novels, Vol. 2: Rabbit Is Rich; Rabbit at Rest* (New York: Ballantine, 2003), 394, 444.

89. Nunley, "Thoughts," 251.

90. Updike, *Roger's Version*, 41.

91. Karl Barth, *The Word of God and the Word of Man*, trans. Douglas Horton (New York: Harper and Row, 1957), 80.

92. Ibid., 38–39.

93. Samuels, "Art of Fiction," 36.

94. Søren Kierkegaard, *Fear and Trembling and the Sickness unto Death*, trans. Walter Lowrie (Princeton, N.J.: Princeton University Press, 1954), 41.

95. Ibid., 67.

96. Wood, *Comedy*, 210.

97. Updike, *More Matter*, 60, italics mine. Of course, Kierkegaard would disagree. In *Fear and Trembling*, he makes a clear distinction between Abraham and the tragic child killers of Greek myth. Kierkegaard, *Fear and Trembling*, 69.

98. John Updike, *Hugging the Shore* (New York: Alfred A. Knopf, 1983), 858–59.

Chapter 5

EPIGRAPH: Cecil Brown, "Interview with Toni Morrison," *Massachusetts Review* 36, no. 3 (1995): 466.

1. David Kocieniewski and Gary Gately, "Man Shoots 11, Killing 5 Girls, in Amish School," *New York Times*, October 3, 2006; http://www.nytimes .com/2006/10/03/us/03amish.html.

2. Toni Morrison, "Goodness: Altruism and the Literary Imagination," Ingersoll Lecture on Immortality, Harvard University, December 6, 2012 (video); http://www.youtube.com/watch?v=PJmVpYZnKTU.

3. Zia Jaffrey, "Toni Morrison," in *Toni Morrison: Conversations*, ed. Carolyn C. Denard (Jackson: University of Mississippi Press, 2008), 141.

4. Toni Morrison, *Paradise* (New York: Alfred A. Knopf, 1998), 295.

5. Antonio Monda, *Do You Believe? Conversations on God and Religion* (New York: Vintage, 2007), 118.

6. Ibid., 122.

7. In the introduction to his interview with Morrison on religion and belief, Monda writes that God and faith are subjects "she would never have imagined discussing publicly" (ibid., 116).

8. Emma Brockes, "Toni Morrison: 'I Want to Feel What I Feel. Even if It's Not Happiness'" *The Guardian*, April 13, 2012. http://www.theguardian.com/books /2012/apr/13/toni-morrison-home-son-love.

9. Ibid., 117.

10. Ibid., 118.

11. Pam Houston, "Pam Houston Talks with Toni Morrison," in *Toni Morrison: Conversations*, ed. Carolyn C. Denard (Jackson: University of Mississippi Press, 2008), 254.

12. Elissa Schappell, "Toni Morrison: The Art of Fiction No. 134." *Paris Review* 128 (fall 1993); http://www.theparisreview.org/interviews/1888/the-art-of-fiction-no -134-toni-morrison.

13. Charles Ruas, "Toni Morrison," in *Conversations with Toni Morrison*, ed. Danille Taylor-Guthrie (Jackson: University Press of Mississippi, 1994), 97.

14. Sheldon Hackney, "'I Come from People Who Sang All the Time': A Conversation with Toni Morrison," in *Toni Morrison: Conversations*, ed. Carolyn C. Denard (Jackson: University of Mississippi Press, 2008), 131.

15. Ann Hostetler, "Interview with Toni Morrison: 'The Art of Teaching,'" in *Toni Morrison: Conversations*, ed. Carolyn C. Denard (Jackson: University of Mississippi Press, 2008), 199.

16. Bessie W. Jones and Audrey Vinson, "An Interview with Toni Morrison," in *Conversations with Toni Morrison*, ed. Danille Taylor-Guthrie (Jackson: University Press of Mississippi, 1994), 177–78.

17. Jaffrey, "Toni Morrison," 168. Though purely theological readings of Morrison's novels are not common, Susan Corey Everson develops one in her analysis of *Tar Baby*: "Toni Morrison's *Tar Baby*: A Resource for Feminist Theology," *Journal of Feminist Studies in Religion* 5, no. 2 (1989): 65–78.

18. As just one early example, see Rosemary Ruether, "Crisis in Sex and Race: Black Theology vs. Feminist Theology," *Christianity and Crisis* 34 (1974): 67–73.

19. Williams, *Sisters*, 60–61.

20. Ibid., 61.

21. Ibid., 164.

22. Ibid., 162.

23. In her essay on Biblical allusions in *Beloved*, Carolyn Mitchell cites Mary Daly, who—as mentioned elsewhere in this volume—believes that the male Christ is an ineffective model for women regardless of gender. "'I Love to Tell the Story': Biblical Revisions in *Beloved*," *Religion and Literature* 23, no. 3 (1991): 30.

24. Robert Stepto, "Intimate Things in Place: A Conversation with Toni Morrison," in *Conversations with Toni Morrison*, ed. Danille Taylor-Guthrie (Jackson: University Press of Mississippi, 1994), 17, italics mine.

25. Susan Bowers writes, "*The Black Book* contains what became the germ of *Beloved*: the story of a slave woman in Cincinnati who killed one child and tried to kill the other three, to, in her words, 'end their sufferings, [rather] than have them taken back to slavery, and murdered by piecemeal.'" "*Beloved* and the New Apocalypse," in *Toni Morrison's Fiction: Contemporary Criticism*, ed. David L. Middleton (New York: Garland Publishing, 1997), 213. *The Black Book* also features a news item that inspires Morrison's later novel *Jazz*.

26. Toni Morrison, *Beloved* (1987; New York: Plume, 1988), 60. Andrea O'Reilly notes that "Slave women were defined as not-mothers and thus denied the right to mother their own children. Viewed only as breeders, slave women were separated from their own children and forced to work the fields or on behalf of the master's children." *Toni Morrison and Motherhood: A Politics of the Heart* (Albany: State University of New York Press, 2004), 128.

27. Morrison, *Beloved*, 200.

28. Ibid., 62.

29. Ibid., 232–33.

30. Ibid., 209.

31. Ibid., 240.

32. Ibid., 144.

33. Ibid., 5.

34. Ibid., 251.
35. Ibid., 23.
36. Ibid., 226.
37. Ibid., 198. Florens, the main character of Morrison's *A Mercy*, feels similar anguish when she is stripped and physically analyzed by white men trying to determine if she is a demon: "Without touching they tell me what to do. To show them my teeth, my tongue. They frown at the candle burn on my palm . . . They look under my arms, between my legs. They circle me, lean down to inspect my feet. Naked under their examination I watch for what is in their eyes. No hate is there or scare or disgust but they are looking at me my body across distances without recognition." Later, she speaks of that moment as the instant her "withering" was born. *A Mercy* (New York: Alfred A. Knopf, 2008), 112–13, 160.
38. Morrison, *Beloved*, 196.
39. Ibid., 77.
40. Ibid., 185.
41. Ibid.
42. Ibid.
43. Ibid., 61.
44. Ibid.
45. Stepto, "Intimate Things," 17.
46. See Acts 5:30, 10:39, and 13:29.
47. As just one example, see Mitchell, who argues that the tree/cross on Sethe's back makes her a Christ figure. "'I Love to Tell the Story,'" 30.
48. Morrison, *Beloved*, 21.
49. Ibid., 22.
50. Ibid., 6.
51. Williams, *Sisters*, 167.
52. Morrison, *Beloved*, 87.
53. Emily Griesinger, "Why Baby Suggs, Holy, Quit Preaching the Word: Redemption and Holiness in Toni Morrison's *Beloved*," *Christianity and Literature* 50, no. 4 (2001): 693.
54. Ibid., 692.
55. Williams, *Sisters*, 4.
56. Ruas, "Toni Morrison," 115.
57. Morrison, *Beloved*, 88–89.
58. Ibid., 95.
59. Bowers, "*Beloved* and the New Apocalypse," 215.
60. Morrison, *Beloved*, 95.
61. Ibid., 162.
62. Ibid., 179.
63. Ibid., 177.
64. Deborah Guth, "'Wonder What God Had in Mind': *Beloved*'s Dialogue with Christianity," *The Journal of Narrative Technique* 24, no. 2 (1994): 87–88.
65. As just a few examples, see 2 Cor. 11:2, Eph. 5:25, and Rev. 19:7–9.
66. Morrison, *Beloved*, 188.
67. Ibid., 205.
68. Ibid., 256.
69. Ibid., 62.

70. Brooks J. Bouson, *Quiet As It's Kept: Shame, Trauma, and Race in the Novels of Toni Morrison* (Albany: State University of New York Press, 2000), 139.

71. Morrison, *Beloved*, 256.

72. Ibid., 234. Stamp's reading of the filicide lends credence to Kathleen Marks's suggestion that the murder is apotropaic; writes Marks, "apotropaic gestures anticipate, mirror, and put into effect that which they seek to avoid" (*Toni Morrison's "Beloved" and the Apotropaic Imagination* [Columbia: University of Missouri Press, 2002], 2). Thus Sethe, sensing that her children's lives are in danger, seeks to kill her children.

73. Morrison, *Beloved*, 163.

74. Ibid., 164.

75. Ibid.

76. Ibid., 165.

77. Ibid., 149.

78. Yvette Christiansë, *Toni Morrison: An Ethical Poetics* (New York: Fordham University Press, 2013), 141.

79. Morrison, *Beloved*, 149.

80. Ibid., 200.

81. Ibid., 251.

82. Ibid.

83. Ibid., 261.

84. Ibid., 271.

85. Ibid., 271–72.

86. Ibid., 272.

87. Ibid., 163.

88. McNally, *Remembering Trauma*, 180.

89. For more sustained trauma-theoretical readings of *Beloved*, see Evelyn Jaffe Schreiber, *Race, Trauma, and Home in the Novels of Toni Morrison* (Baton Rouge: Louisiana State University Press 2010); and Bouson, *Quiet*.

90. Morrison, *Beloved*, 273.

Chapter 6

EPIGRAPH: Joyce Carol Oates, *My Sister, My Love: The Intimate Story of Skyler Rampike* (New York: Harper Perennial, 2008), 344.

1. A 2013 tweet on Egyptian Islam, however, landed her in hot water. "Where 99.3% of women report having been sexually harassed & rape is epidemic—Egypt—natural to inquire: what's the predominant religion?"; as Liz Bury writes in *The Guardian*, many perceived the comments as "linking rape culture to Islam." Liz Bury, "Joyce Carol Oates Sparks Twitter Storm over Egypt Remarks," *The Guardian*, July 8, 2013; http://www.theguardian.com/books/2013/jul/08/joyce-carol-oates-twitter-egypt-islam.

2. Fyodor Dostoevsky, *The Brothers Karamazov*, trans. Richard Pevear and Larissa Volokhonsky (1880; New York: Farrar, Straus and Giroux, 1990), 292.

3. Ibid., 292.

4. Joyce Carol Oates, *The Edge of Impossibility: Tragic Forms in Literature* (New York: Vanguard Press, 1972), 208.

5. Dostoevsky, *Brothers Karamazov*, 245. Susan McReynolds's interpretation of this contrast is worth considering; she argues that both Ivan and Zossima have

essentially the same understanding of God: "Ivan and Zosima both believe that redemption is an economic transaction between the merchant God and his adult customers. The choice between these two characters is not between different conceptions of God and redemption but between acceptance or rejection of God as a merchant and redemption as an item for sale for the right price in innocent suffering in general and dead children specifically. Zosima accepts a relationship between humanity and the divine founded on the exchange of children; Ivan rejects it." McReynolds, *Redemption and the Merchant God*, 157.

6. Joyce Carol Oates, *Where I've Been, and Where I'm Going*, (New York: Plume, 1999), 244.

7. Lawrence Grobel, "An Interview with Joyce Carol Oates," in *Joyce Carol Oates: Conversations 1970–2006*, ed. Greg Johnson (Princeton, N.J.: Ontario Review Press, 2006), 159.

8. She explores the relationship between art and victimhood in an early essay entitled "Art and 'Victim Art.'" In it, she writes, "there is a long and honorable tradition of art that bears witness to human suffering, but this is not 'victim art' as the current term would have it, still less an art that manipulates or intimidates its audience to a perverse degree . . . That a human being has been in some way 'victimized' doesn't reduce his or her humanity, but may in fact amplify it." Oates, *Where I've Been*, 69.

9. Joyce Carol Oates, *A Widow's Story: A Memoir* (New York: Ecco, 2011), 221.

10. Oates, *Edge of Impossibility*, 4.

11. Lee Milazzo, ed., *Conversations with Joyce Carol Oates* (Jackson: University Press of Mississippi, 1989), xiii.

12. Like so many of Oates's novels, *My Sister, My Love* earned polarizing reviews. In *Harper's*, John Leonard writes that Oates "writes brilliantly for JonBenét, against our pulpy molestations." "New Books," *Harper's Magazine*, December 2008, 81. By contrast, Sarah Churchwell, writing in the *New York Times*, finds the book repetitive and clichéd, claiming that despite Oates's "unquestionable genius," she "is capable of so much more." Sarah Churchwell, "The Death of Innocence," *New York Times*, August 10, 2008, BR8.

13. Grobel, "Interview with Joyce Carol Oates," 159.

14. Greg Johnson, *Invisible Writer: A Biography of Joyce Carol Oates* (New York: Dutton, 1998), 40.

15. Ibid., 28.

16. Ibid., 40, 263.

17. Grobel, "Interview with Joyce Carol Oates," 159.

18. Johnson, *Invisible Writer*, 41.

19. Ibid., 206.

20. In her own spiritual wanderings, however, she has never confined herself to Western or Judeo-Christian sources. In an interview with John Alfred Avant, she speaks of her long-standing interest in Asian religion. And throughout her life, she has occasionally dabbled in both Zen and various meditative practices. John Alfred Avant, "An Interview with Joyce Carol Oates," in *Conversations with Joyce Carol Oates*, ed. Lee Milazzo (Jackson: University Press of Mississippi, 1989), 28–31.

21. Oates, *Widow's Story*, 207.

22. Ibid., 262.

23. Robert Phillips, "Joyce Carol Oates: The Art of Fiction," in *Joyce Carol Oates: Conversations 1970–2006*, ed. Greg Johnson (Princeton, N.J.: Ontario Review Press, 2006), 83.

24. Timothy P. Schilling, "The Shape of Our Despair: The Fiction of Joyce Carol Oates," *Commonweal* 132, no. 13 (July 15, 2005): 21.

25. Johnson, *Invisible Writer*, 286.

26. Judith Applebaum, "Joyce Carol Oates," in *Conversations with Joyce Carol Oates*, ed. Lee Milazzo (Jackson: University Press of Mississippi, 1989), 60.

27. Leif Sjoberg, "An Interview with Joyce Carol Oates," in *Conversations with Joyce Carol Oates*, ed. Lee Milazzo (Jackson: University Press of Mississippi, 1989), 106, italics mine.

28. Oates, *New Heaven*, 132.

29. Linda Kuehl, "An Interview with Joyce Carol Oates," in *Conversations with Joyce Carol Oates*, ed. Lee Milazzo, (Jackson: University Press of Mississippi, 1989), 10. The book focuses on a woman named Karen Herz and explores her tortured relationship with her father and her doomed romance with a race-car driver. Though the parallels aren't immediately apparent, Oates describes the book as a reworking of the Biblical story of Abraham and Isaac. Brenda Daly works through the connections between Genesis and *Shuddering* in the opening chapter of her book-length study of Oates's novels, *Lavish Self-Divisions: The Novels of Joyce Carol Oates* (Jackson: University Press of Mississippi, 1996).

30. Sanford Pinsker, "Speaking about Short Fiction: An Interview with Joyce Carol Oates," in *Joyce Carol Oates: Conversations 1970–2006*, ed. Greg Johnson (Princeton, N.J.: Ontario Review Press, 2006), 101.

31. Applebaum, "Joyce Carol Oates," 61.

32. In interviews, Oates speaks of a moment in her development as a writer—shortly after the production of her early novel *Wonderland* (1971)—at which she intended to "move toward a more articulate moral position" in her novels, rendering her fictions not merely descriptive but prescriptive. Walter Clemons, "Joyce Carol Oates: Love and Violence," in *Conversations with Joyce Carol Oates*, ed. Lee Milazzo, (Jackson: University Press of Mississippi, 1989), 39. In an interview published in 2006, she persists in affirming the ethical function of the novel, arguing that it can be a "vehicle for [. . .] moral guidance." Gavin Cologne-Brookes, "Written Interviews and a Conversation with Joyce Carol Oates," *Studies in the Novel* 38, no. 4 (winter 2006): 547.

33. Cologne-Brooks, "Written Interviews," 547.

34. Oates, *Where I've Been*, 34.

35. Oates, *New Heaven*, 157.

36. Oates, *Edge of Impossibility*, 110.

37. Sharon Oard Warner argues that in these novels, Oates is rendering what Warner calls "metaphorical truth." "The Fairest in the Land: *Blonde* and *Black Water*, the Nonfiction Novels of Joyce Carol Oates," *Studies in the Novel* 38, no. 4 (winter 2006): 513.

38. As it features a murder that rips through the sprawling lawns and capacious houses of a rich neighborhood, *Sister* recalls *Expensive People*, another novel that depicts a mother-child relationship that turns violent.

39. Kierkegaard, *Fear and Trembling*, 230.

40. David J. Gouwens, *Kierkegaard as Religious Thinker* (Cambridge, Eng.: Cambridge University Press, 1996), 147.

41. Oates, *My Sister*, 10–11.

42. Ibid., 11.

43. Ibid., 549.

44. Ibid. Here, Pastor Bob sounds much like Oates herself, writing again in *The Edge of Impossibility*. In that book, Oates distinguishes between the existentialist, who freely takes responsibility for all his or her actions, and the Christian "essentialist," a childish figure whose engagement in the logic of forgiveness and expiation allows him or her to evade personal accountability: "The existentialist accepts all responsibility for his actions and does not beg forgiveness, but he accepts absolutely no responsibility for actions that are not his own. The essentialist (in this context, the ideal Christian) accepts all guilt for all actions, is morally ubiquitous, has no singular identity, and can be forgiven for any sin, no matter how terrible, because he ultimately has no freedom and no responsibility, not simply for his own sins but for the sins of mankind; he is a 'creature'. To recognize oneself as a 'creature' is, then, to submit gratefully to the condition of having no responsibility for one's actions . . . and to remain forever a child" (107).

45. Oates, *My Sister*, 551.

46. Ibid., 115.

47. Ibid.

48. Ibid., 253.

49. Ibid., 92.

50. Ibid.

51. Ibid., 95.

52. Ibid., 231.

53. Ibid., 403.

54. Ibid., 344.

55. Daly, *Beyond*, 76.

56. Ibid., 77.

57. Oates, *My Sister*, 541–42.

58. Ibid., 541.

59. Ibid., 313.

60. Ibid., 231.

61. Ibid., 545.

62. See Herman, *Trauma and Recovery*, and Bessel A. van der Kolk, Alexander C. McFarlane, and Lars Weisaeth, *Traumatic Stress: The Effects of Overwhelming Experience on Mind, Body, and Society* (New York: The Guilford Press, 1996).

63. Oates, *My Sister*, 413.

64. Ibid., 330.

65. Brison, *Aftermath*, 71.

66. Oates, *My Sister*, 552.

67. Ibid., 548, 552.

68. Arsen Kashkashian, "Oates Writes on JonBenet Ramsey," *Kash's Book Corner*, August 1, 2008; http://kashsbookcorner.blogspot.com/2008/08/oates-writes-on-jonbenet-ramsey.html.

Chapter 7

EPIGRAPH: David Kushner, "Cormac McCarthy's Apocalypse," *Rolling Stone*, December 27, 2007, 44–51.

1. McCarthy's literary biographer Steven Frye writes, "McCarthy was raised a Roman Catholic and was educated in Catholic schools until he entered the University of Tennessee." *Understanding Cormac McCarthy* (Columbia: University of South Carolina Press, 2009), 2.

2. Frye continues, "McCarthy in all his works engages the ultimate questions—the nature of the real, the possibility of the divine, the source of ethics and identity—but always in a richly philosophical context and with an active interest in secular science." Ibid., 3.

3. Cormac McCarthy, *Sunset Limited* (New York: Vintage, 2006), 26.

4. Cormac McCarthy, *Blood Meridian; or, The Evening Redness in the West* (1985; New York: Vintage, 1992), 119.

5. McCarthy, *Sunset*, 137.

6. Kushner, "Cormac McCarthy's Apocalypse," 50.

7. Ibid., 50.

8. Cormac McCarthy, *Child of God* (1973; New York: Vintage, 1993), 4.

9. John M. Grammer, "A Thing Against Which Time Will Not Prevail: Pastoral and History in Cormac McCarthy's South," in *Perspectives on Cormac McCarthy*, ed. Edwin T. Arnold and Dianne C. Luce (Jackson: University Press of Mississippi, 1993), 33.

10. Vereen M. Bell, "The Ambiguous Nihilism of Cormac McCarthy," *Southern Literary Journal* 15, no. 2 (1983): 37.

11. James R. Giles, *The Spaces of Violence* (Tuscaloosa: University of Alabama Press, 2006), 20.

12. William J. Schafer, "Cormac McCarthy: The Hard Wages of Original Sin," *Appalachian Journal* 4, no. 2 (1977): 111.

13. Farrell O'Gorman, "Violence, Nature, and Prophecy in Flannery O'Connor and Cormac McCarthy," in *Flannery O'Connor in the Age of Terrorism: Essays on Violence and Grace*, ed. Robert Donahoo (Knoxville: University of Tennessee Press, 2010), 146.

14. Frye, *Understanding Cormac McCarthy*, 36.

15. Russell M. Hillier, "'In a Dark Parody' of John Bunyan's *The Pilgrim's Progress*: The Presence of Subversive Allegory in Cormac McCarthy's *Outer Dark*," *American Notes and Queries* 19, no. 4 (2006): 56.

16. William C. Spencer, "Cormac McCarthy's Unholy Trinity: Biblical Parody in *Outer Dark*," in *Sacred Violence: A Reader's Companion to Cormac McCarthy*, ed. Wade Hall and Rick Wallach (El Paso: Texas Western Press, 1995), 69.

17. Blumenthal, *Facing*, 247.

18. Ibid., 242.

19. Ibid., 245.

20. Ibid., 248.

21. Ibid., 256.

22. Ibid., xi–xii.

23. Richard B. Woodward, "Cormac McCarthy's Venomous Fiction," *New York Times*, April 19, 1992; http://www.nytimes.com/books/98/05/17/specials/mccarthy-venom.html.

24. Woodward, the only person to score two interviews with the author, claims in the first of them that Suttree "is also McCarthy" (Woodward, "Venomous"). And the author himself admits as much in his *Rolling Stone* interview with David Kushner (Kushner, "Cormac McCarthy's Apocalypse," 48).

25. Mike Gibson, "He Felt at Home Here," *Metro Pulse*, March 1, 2001.

26. Cormac McCarthy, *Suttree* (1979; New York: Vintage, 1986), 253.

27. Ibid., 254.

28. Ibid., 253.

29. Ibid., 253, 254.

30. Ibid., 246.

31. Ibid., 130.

32. Ibid., 154, italics mine.

33. Ibid., 460.

34. Ibid., 461.

35. Neil Campbell, "'Beyond Reckoning': Cormac McCarthy's Version of the West in *Blood Meridian or The Evening Redness in the West*," *Critique* 39, no. 1 (1997): 60. He adds, "Infanticides abound in the novel, but always around the Judge . . . That gruesome renewal defeats time and keeps the Judge 'child like' and powerful, as if he has stepped outside time by being both father and son— killing both to steal their power and prolong himself" (60).

36. McCarthy, *Blood Meridian*, 57, italics mine.

37. Ibid., 61.

38. Ibid., 6.

39. Ibid., 102.

40. Ibid., 315.

41. Ibid., 123.

42. Mark Royden Winchell, "Inner Dark: or, The Place of Cormac McCarthy," *Southern Review* 26, no. 2 (1990): 299.

43. Christopher R. Nelson, "A Style of Horror: Is Evil Real in Cormac McCarthy's *Outer Dark?*" *Critique* 53, no. 1 (2012): 34.

44. Cormac McCarthy, *Outer Dark* (1968; New York: Vintage, 1993), 174–75.

45. As just one example, see John F. Walvoord, "Christ's Olivet Discourse on the End of the Age: The Parable of the Talents," *Bibliotheca Sacra* 129, no. 515 (1972): 206–10.

46. See Carolyn Dipboye, "Matthew 25:14–30: To Survive or to Serve," *Review and Expositor* 92, no. 4 (1995): 507–12.

47. E. Carson Brisson, "Matthew 25:14–30," *Interpretation* 56, no. 3 (2002): 307–10.

48. Marianne Blickenstaff, "Matthew's Parable of the Wedding Feast (Matt 22:1–14)," *Review and Expositor* 109, no. 2 (2012): 261. To skirt this characterization, Blickenstaff reads the gospel story against the grain and tries to wrest meaning from a more literal interpretation of the text.

49. If the God of these parables defies our expectations, John Dominic Crossan memorably argues that overturning expectations is the very function of parabolic literature. As one example, he argues that the "parable" of the Biblical book of Ruth is about undermining ancient Jews' assumption that God disapproves of marriage to foreigners (*The Dark Interval* [Allen, Tx.: Argus Communications, 1975], 68–72). Later, Crossan notes that Jesus's parable of the mustard

seed—and the humble mustard bush—destabilizes one of the prophets' tradi-tional images for imperial power: the cedars of Lebanon (ibid., 93–96). And yet Crossan demurs when he arrives at the destruction of the enemies' city in the parable of the wedding feast in Matthew 22, arguing that the event is "unlikely," "incredible," and "narrative overkill" (ibid., 117). Even for Crossan, it seems as if this image of God defies not expectation but belief.

50. McCarthy, *Outer Dark*, 129.

51. Michael Rea explains consubstantiality in the introduction to the Trin-ity in the first volume of *Oxford Readings in Philosophical Theology*: "In God, there are three *genuinely distinct* persons, Father, Son, and Holy Spirit. The persons are not to be viewed as mere *manifestations* or *aspects* of a single sub-stance; rather, each is a substance, and is *consubstantial* with the Father. To say that the persons are consubstantial is *at least* to say that they share a common nature. Whatever else it means, then, it means that all three persons are equally divine: no one is superior to or any more divine than any of the others. Thus, Father, Son, and Holy Spirit are three distinct divine beings. *And yet*, says the Athanasian Creed, *They are not three gods, but there is one god*." Rea, *Oxford Readings*, 3.

52. As another example, O'Gorman borrows a phrase from the title of Spen-cer's essay and calls them a "clearly unholy trinity" (O'Gorman, "Violence," 146).

53. McCarthy, *Outer Dark*, 35.

54. Ibid., 51.

55. Giles, *Spaces of Violence*, 27.

56. McCarthy, *Outer Dark*, 229.

57. Ibid., 129.

58. Giles, *Spaces of Violence*, 28.

59. Schafer, "Hard Wages," 111.

60. Frye, *Understanding Cormac McCarthy*, 14–15.

61. McCarthy, *Outer Dark*, 236.

62. Lydia R. Cooper, *No More Heroes: Narrative Perspective and Morality in Cormac McCarthy* (Baton Rouge: Louisiana State University Press, 2011), 37.

63. McCarthy, *Outer Dark*, 18.

64. The shifting pronoun in the previous passage—from "it" to "he"—leaves room for the suggestion that Culla is the paraclete, not the baby. Yet the rest of McCarthy's description (the "witless" "gibbering" thing pushes back his the night with his hands) seems to apply better to an infant than to a grown man. Further, the metaphorical location, limbo, makes more sense for the son than the father; in Dante's *Inferno*, limbo is hell's highest circle, reserved for unbaptized babies.

65. Frye, *Understanding Cormac McCarthy*, 34.

66. McCarthy, *Suttree*, 254.

67. Jones, *Trauma*, 92.

68. McCarthy, *Outer Dark*, 242.

Afterword

EPIGRAPH: Dostoevsky, *Brothers Karamazov*, 239.

1. Ibid., 241.

2. Ibid., 241.

3. Jack Healy and Serge F. Kovaleski, "One Mother, 7 Dead Newborns and a Stunned Community in Utah," *New York Times*, April 26, 2014; http://www
.nytimes.com/2014/04/27/us/one-mother-7-dead-newborns-and-a-stunned
-community-in-utah.html.

BIBLIOGRAPHY

Abelard, Peter. *Commentary on the Epistle to the Romans*. Translated by Steven R. Cartwright. Washington, D.C.: Catholic University of America Press, 2011.

Adams, Rebecca, and René Girard. "Violence, Difference, Sacrifice: A Conversation with René Girard." *Religion and Literature* 25, no. 2 (summer 1993): 9–33.

Allitt, Patrick. *Religion in America Since 1945: A History*. New York: Columbia University Press, 2003.

Alter, Robert. "Updike, Malamud, and the Fire This Time." In *John Updike: A Collection of Critical Essays*, edited by David Thorburn and Howard Eiland, 39–49. Englewood Cliffs, N.J.: Prentice-Hall, 1979.

Anderson, Donald R. "Eccles Redux." *Journal of Modern Literature* 24, no. 2 (2000–2001): 327–36.

Andretta, Helen R. "The Hylomorphic Sacramentalism of 'Parker's Back.'" In *Inside the Church of Flannery O'Connor*, edited by Joanne Halleran McMullen and Jon Parrish Peede, 41–63. Macon, Ga.: Mercer University Press, 2007.

Anselm. "Why God Became Man." In *Anselm of Canterbury: The Major Works*, edited by Brian Davies and G. R. Evans, 260–357. Oxford: Oxford University Press, 1998.

Applebaum, Judith. "Joyce Carol Oates." In *Conversations with Joyce Carol Oates*, edited by Lee Milazzo, 59–61. Jackson: University Press of Mississippi, 1989.

Aquinas, Thomas. *An Aquinas Reader*. Edited by Mary T. Clark. Garden City, N.Y.: Image Books, 1972.

Arnold, Edwin T. "Naming, Knowing and Nothingness: McCarthy's Moral Parables." In *Perspectives on Cormac McCarthy*, edited by Edwin T. Arnold and Dianne C. Luce, 43–68. Jackson: University Press of Mississippi, 1993.

Aulén, Gustaf. *Christus Victor: An Historical Study of the Three Main Types of the Idea of Atonement*. 1931. Translated by A. G. Hebert. New York: MacMillan, 1966.

Avant, John Alfred. "An Interview with Joyce Carol Oates." In *Conversations with Joyce Carol Oates*, edited by Lee Milazzo, 28–31. Jackson: University Press of Mississippi, 1989.

Bailey, Peter J. *Rabbit (Un)Redeemed: The Drama of Belief in John Updike's Fiction*. Madison, N.J.: Fairleigh Dickinson University Press, 2006.

Balthasar, Hans Urs von. *Theo-Drama, Theological Dramatic Theory*. Vol. 4, *The Action*. 1980. Translated by Graham Harrison. San Francisco: Ignatius Press, 1994.

Barry, F. R. *The Atonement*. London: Hodder & Stoughton, 1968.

Barth, Karl. *The Epistle to the Romans*. 1933. Translated by Edwyn C. Hoskins. Oxford: Oxford University Press, 1968.

————. *The Word of God and the Word of Man*. Translated by Douglas Horton. New York: Harper and Row, 1957.

Bassard, Katherine Clay. "The Race for Faith: Justice, Mercy and the Sign of the Cross in African American Literature." *Religion and Literature* 38, no. 1 (2006): 95–114.

Bate, Nancy Berkowitz. "Toni Morrison's *Beloved*: Psalm and Sacrament." In *Toni Morrison and the Bible: Contested Intertextualities*, edited by Shirley A. Stave, 26–70. New York: Peter Lang, 2006.

Baumgaertner, Jill Peláez. *Flannery O'Connor: A Proper Scaring*. Wheaton: Harold Shaw Publishers, 1988.

————. "Flannery O'Connor and the Cartoon Catechism." In *Inside the Church of Flannery O'Connor*, edited by Joanne Halleran McMullen and Jon Parrish Peede, 102–16. Macon, Ga.: Mercer University Press, 2007.

Bell, Vereen M. "The Ambiguous Nihilism of Cormac McCarthy." *Southern Literary Journal* 15, no. 2 (1983): 31–41.

Bellah, Robert N. *Habits of the Heart: Individualism and Commitment in American Life*. 1985. Berkeley: University of California Press, 2008.

Ben-Bassat, Hedda. *Prophets without Vision: Subjectivity and the Sacred in Contemporary American Writing*. Lewisburg, Pa.: Bucknell University Press, 2000.

Beste, Jennifer Erin. *God and the Victim*. New York: Oxford University Press, 2007.

Billings, J. Todd. "John Updike as Theologian of Culture: *Roger's Version* and the Possibility of Embodied Redemption." *Christianity and Literature* 52, no. 2 (2003): 203–12.

Blickenstaff, Marianne. "Matthew's Parable of the Wedding Feast (Matt 22:1–14)." *Review and Expositor* 109, no. 2 (2012): 261–68.

Blocher, Henri. "Biblical Metaphors and the Doctrine of the Atonement." *Journal of the Evangelical Theological Society* 47, no. 4 (December 2004): 629–45.

Blumenthal, David R. *Facing the Abusing God: A Theology of Protest*. Louisville, Ky.: Westminster/John Knox Press, 1993.

Boswell, Marshall. "The Black Jesus: Racism and Redemption in John Updike's *Rabbit Redux*." *Contemporary Literature* 39, no. 1 (1998): 99–132.

————. *John Updike's Rabbit Tetralogy: Mastered Irony in Motion*. Columbia: University of Missouri Press, 2001.

Bouson, J. Brooks. *Quiet As It's Kept: Shame, Trauma, and Race in the Novels of Toni Morrison*. Albany: State University of New York Press, 2000.

Bowers, Susan. "*Beloved* and the New Apocalypse." In *Toni Morrison's Fiction: Contemporary Criticism*, edited by David L. Middleton, 209–30. New York: Garland Publishing, 1997.

Breit, Harvey. "Galley Proof: *A Good Man Is Hard to Find*." In *Conversations with Flannery O'Connor*, edited by Rosemary M. Magee, 5–10. Jackson: University Press of Mississippi, 1987.

Brewton, Vince. "The Changing Landscape of Violence in Cormac McCarthy's Early Novels and the Border Trilogy." *The Southern Literary Journal* 37, no. 1 (2004): 121–43.

Brison, Susan. *Aftermath: Violence and the Remaking of a Self*. Princeton, N.J.: Princeton University Press, 2002.

Brisson, E. Carson. "Matthew 25:14–30." *Interpretation* 56, no. 3 (2002): 307–10.

Brock, Rita Nakashima, and Rebecca Ann Parker. *Proverbs of Ashes: Violence, Redemptive Suffering, and the Search for What Saves Us.* Boston: Beacon Press, 2001.

———. *Saving Paradise: How Christianity Traded Love of this World for Crucifixion and Empire.* Boston: Beacon Press, 2008.

Brockes, Emma. "Toni Morrison: 'I Want to Feel What I Feel. Even If It's Not Happiness.'" *The Guardian*, April 13, 2012. http://www.theguardian.com/books/2012/apr/13/toni-morrison-home-son-love.

Broncano, Manuel. *Religion in Cormac McCarthy's Fiction: Apocryphal Borderlands.* New York: Routledge, 2013.

Brown, Cecil. "Interview with Toni Morrison." *Massachusetts Review* 36, no. 3 (1995): 455–73.

Brown, Charles E. "The Atonement: Healing in Postmodern Society." *Interpretation* 53, no. 1 (January 1999): 34–43.

Brown, Joanne Carlson, and Rebecca Parker. "For God So Loved the World?" In *Christianity, Patriarchy, and Abuse: A Feminist Critique*, edited by Joanne Carlson Brown and Carole R. Bohn, 1–30. New York: Pilgrim Press, 1989.

Bucher, Glenn R. Review of *God of the Oppressed*, by James H. Cone. *Theology Today* 33, no. 1 (1976): 116–19.

Bury, Liz. "Joyce Carol Oates Sparks Twitter Storm over Egypt Remarks." *The Guardian*, July 8, 2013. http://www.theguardian.com/books/2013/jul/08/joyce-carol-oates-twitter-egypt-islam.

Campbell, Jeff. "Interview with John Updike." In *Conversations with John Updike*, edited by James Plath, 84–104. Jackson: University Press of Mississippi, 1994.

Campbell, Neil. "'Beyond Reckoning': Cormac McCarthy's Version of the West in *Blood Meridian or The Evening Redness in the West.*" *Critique* 39, no. 1 (1997): 55–64.

Camus, Albert. *The Fall.* 1957. Translated by Justin O'Brien. New York: Vintage International, 1984.

Candler, Peter M., Jr. "The Anagogical Imagination of Flannery O'Connor." *Christianity and Literature* 60, no. 1 (autumn 2010): 11–33.

Caruth, Cathy. "An Interview with Geoffrey Hartman." *Studies in Romanticism* 35, no. 4 (1996): 630–52.

———. *Trauma: Explorations in Memory.* Baltimore: Johns Hopkins University Press, 1995.

———. *Unclaimed Experience.* Baltimore: Johns Hopkins University Press, 1996.

Charles, Pepsi. "An Interview with Toni Morrison." In *Toni Morrison: Conversations*, edited by Carolyn C. Denard, 17–23. Jackson: University of Mississippi Press, 2008.

Christiansë, Yvette. *Toni Morrison: An Ethical Poetics.* New York: Fordham University Press, 2013.

Churchwell, Sarah. "The Death of Innocence." Review of *My Sister, My Love*, by Joyce Carol Oates. *New York Times*, August 10, 2008.

Ciuba, Gary M. "'Not His Son': Violent Kinship and the Spirit of Adoption in *The Violent Bear It Away.*" In *Dark Faith: New Essays on Flannery O'Connor's* The Violent Bear It Away, edited by Susan Srigley, 57–86. South Bend, Ind.: University of Notre Dame Press, 2012.

Clemons, Walter. "Joyce Carol Oates: Love and Violence." In *Conversations with Joyce Carol Oates*, edited by Lee Milazzo, 32–41. Jackson: University Press of Mississippi, 1989.

Coleman, James. *Faithful Vision: Treatments of the Sacred, Spiritual, and Supernatural in Twentieth-Century African-American Fiction*. Baton Rouge: Louisiana State University Press, 2006.

Cologne-Brookes, Gavin. "Written Interviews and a Conversation with Joyce Carol Oates." *Studies in the Novel* 38, no. 4 (winter 2006). 547–65.

Cone, James H. *Black Theology and Black Power*. New York: Seabury Press, 1969.

———. *God of the Oppressed*. San Francisco: Harper and Row, 1975.

"Conversation with Alice Childress and Toni Morrison." In *Conversations with Toni Morrison*, edited by Danille Taylor-Guthrie, 3–9. Jackson: University Press of Mississippi, 1994.

Cooper, Lydia R. *No More Heroes: Narrative Perspective and Morality in Cormac McCarthy*. Baton Rouge: Louisiana State University Press, 2011.

Corey, Susan. "Toward the Limits of Mystery: The Grotesque in Toni Morrison's *Beloved*." In *The Aesthetics of Toni Morrison*, edited by Mark C. Connor, 31–48. Jackson: University Press of Mississippi, 2000.

Crossan, John Dominic. *The Dark Interval*. Allen, Tx.: Argus Communications, 1975.

Cullinan, Colleen Carpenter. "A Maternal Discourse of Redemption: Speech and Suffering in Morrison's *Beloved*." *Religion and Literature* 34, no. 2 (2002): 77–104.

Culpepper, Gary. "'One Suffering, in Two Natures': An Analogical Inquiry into Divine and Human Suffering." In *Divine Impassibility and the Mystery of Human Suffering*, edited by James F. Keating and Thomas Joseph White, 77–98. Grand Rapids, Mich.: Eerdmans, 2009.

Daly, Brenda. *Lavish Self-Divisions: The Novels of Joyce Carol Oates*. Jackson: University Press of Mississippi, 1996.

Daly, Mary. *Beyond God the Father: Toward a Philosophy of Women's Liberation*. Boston: Beacon Press, 1973.

Daly, Robert J. "Images of God and the Imitation of God: Problems with Atonement." *Theological Studies* 68 (2007): 36–51.

Darling, Marsha Dean. "In the Realm of Responsibility: A Conversation with Toni Morrison." *Women's Review of Books* 5, no. 6 (1988): 5–6.

Darter, Sarah L. "Response to 'Does Feminist Theology Liberate?'" *Foundations* 19 (January–March 1976): 50–52.

De Bellis, Jack. *The John Updike Encyclopedia*. Westport, Conn.: Greenwood Press, 2000.

Denard, Carolyn. "Blacks, Modernism, and the American South: An Interview with Toni Morrison." *Studies in the Literary Imagination* 31, no. 2 (1998): 1–16.

Desmond, John F. "Flannery O'Connor and the Displaced Sacrament." In *Inside the Church of Flannery O'Connor*, edited by Joanne Halleran McMullen and Jon Parrish Peede, 64–78. Macon, Ga.: Mercer University Press, 2007.

———. "Stalking Joy: Flannery O'Connor and the Dangerous Quest." *Christianity and Literature* 60, no. 1 (autumn 2010): 97–111.

Dicken, Thomas M. "God and Pigment: John Updike on the Conservation of Meaning." *Religion and Literature* 36, no. 3 (2004): 69–87.

Dillistone, F. W. *The Christian Understanding of Atonement.* Philadelphia: Westminster Press, 1968.

Dipboye, Carolyn. "Matthew 25:14–30: To Survive or to Serve." *Review and Expositor* 92, no. 4 (1995): 507–12.

Donner, Robert. "She Writes Powerful Fiction." In *Conversations with Flannery O'Connor,* edited by Rosemary M. Magee, 44–50. Jackson: University Press of Mississippi, 1987.

Doody, Terrence A. "Updike's Idea of Reification." *Contemporary Literature* 20, no. 2 (1979): 204–20.

Dostoevsky, Fyodor. *The Brothers Karamazov.* 1880. Translated by Richard Pevear and Larissa Volokhonsky. New York: Farrar, Straus and Giroux, 1990.

Edelberg, Cynthia Dubin. "Morrison's Voices: Formal Education, the Work Ethic, and the Bible." *American Literature* 58, no. 2 (1986): 217–37.

Emery, Gilles. "The Immutability of the God of Love and the Problem of Language concerning the 'Suffering of God.'" In *Divine Impassibility and the Mystery of Human Suffering,* edited by James F. Keating and Thomas Joseph White, 27–76. Grand Rapids, Mich.: Eerdmans, 2009.

Everson, Susan Corey. "Toni Morrison's *Tar Baby*: A Resource for Feminist Theology." *Journal of Feminist Studies in Religion* 5, no. 2 (1989): 65–78.

Felman, Shoshana, and Dori Laub, M.D. *Testimony: Crises of Witnessing in Literature, Psychoanalysis, and History.* New York: Routledge, 1992.

Finlan, Stephen. *Problems with Atonement: The Origins of, and Controversy about, the Atonement Doctrine.* Collegeville, Minn.: Liturgical Press, 2005.

Franzen, Jonathan. *Freedom.* New York: Farrar, Straus and Giroux, 2010.

Fredriksen, Paula. *From Jesus to Christ: The Origins of the New Testament Images of Jesus.* New Haven, Conn.: Yale University Press, 1998.

Freud, Sigmund. "Screen Memories." In *The Standard Edition of the Complete Psychological Works of Sigmund Freud,* vol. 3, translated by James Strachey, 300–322. London: Hogarth Press, 1962.

Frias, Maria, Wayne Pond, and Trudier Harris. "An Interview with Toni Morrison, and a Commentary about Her Work." *Atlantis* 16, nos. 1/2 (1994): 273–83.

Friedlander, Henry. *The Origins of Nazi Genocide: From Euthanasia to the Final Solution.* Chapel Hill: University of North Carolina Press, 1997.

Frye, Steven. *Understanding Cormac McCarthy.* Columbia: University of South Carolina Press, 2009.

Fugin, Katherine, Faye Rivard, and Margaret Sieh. "An Interview with Flannery O'Connor." In *Conversations with Flannery O'Connor,* edited by Rosemary M. Magee, 58–60. Jackson: University Press of Mississippi, 1987.

Gauthier, Marni. "The Other Side of *Paradise*: Toni Morrison's (Un)Making of Mythic History." *African American Review* 39, no. 3 (2005): 395–414.

Gentry, Marshall Bruce. *Flannery O'Connor's Religion of the Grotesque.* Jackson: University Press of Mississippi, 1986.

Giannone, Richard. *Flannery O'Connor, Hermit Novelist.* Urbana: University of Illinois Press, 2000.

Gibson, Mike. "He Felt at Home Here." *Metro Pulse,* March 1, 2001.

Giles, James R. *The Spaces of Violence*. Tuscaloosa: University of Alabama Press, 2006.

Girard, René. *The Scapegoat*. Translated by Yvonne Freccero. Baltimore: Johns Hopkins University Press, 1986.

———. *Things Hidden since the Foundation of the World*. 1978. Translated by Stephen Bann and Michael Metteer. Stanford, Calif.: Stanford University Press, 1987.

Gooch, Brad. *Flannery: A Life of Flannery O'Connor*. New York: Little, Brown, 2009.

Gorringe, Timothy. *God's Just Vengeance: Crime, Violence, and the Rhetoric of Salvation*. Cambridge, Eng.: Cambridge University Press, 1996.

Gouwens, David J. *Kierkegaard as Religious Thinker*. Cambridge, Eng.: Cambridge University Press, 1996.

Graham, Gordon. "Atonement." In *The Cambridge Companion to Christian Philosophical Theology*, edited by Charles Taliaferro and Chad Meister, 123–35. Cambridge, Eng.: Cambridge University Press, 2010.

Grammer, John M. "A Thing against Which Time Will Not Prevail: Pastoral and History in Cormac McCarthy's South." In *Perspectives on Cormac McCarthy*, edited by Edwin T. Arnold and Dianne C. Luce, 27–42. Jackson: University Press of Mississippi, 1993.

Grant, Jacquelyn. "Black Christology: Interpreting Aspects of the Apostolic Faith." *Mid-Stream* 24, no. 4 (1985): 366–75.

Griesinger, Emily. "Why Baby Suggs, Holy, Quit Preaching the Word: Redemption and Holiness in Toni Morrison's *Beloved*." *Christianity and Literature* 50, no. 4 (2001): 689–702.

Grimes, Ronald L. "Anagogy and Ritualization: Baptism in Flannery O'Connor's *The Violent Bear It Away*." *Religion and Literature* 21, no. 1 (spring 1989): 9–26.

Grobel, Lawrence. "An Interview with Joyce Carol Oates." In *Joyce Carol Oates: Conversations 1970–2006*, edited by Greg Johnson, 142–71. Princeton, N.J.: Ontario Review Press, 2006.

Guardini, Romano. *The Lord*. 1954. Translated by Elinor Castendyk Briefs. Chicago: Regnery Gateway, 1982.

Gunton, Colin E. *The Actuality of Atonement: A Study of Metaphor, Rationality and the Christian Tradition*. London: T & T Clark, 1998.

Guth, Deborah. "'Wonder What God Had in Mind': *Beloved*'s Dialogue with Christianity." *Journal of Narrative Technique* 24, no. 2 (1994): 83–97.

Hackney, Sheldon. "'I Come from People Who Sang All the Time': A Conversation with Toni Morrison." In *Toni Morrison: Conversations*, edited by Carolyn C. Denard, 126–38. Jackson: University of Mississippi Press, 2008.

Haddox, Thomas F. *Hard Sayings: The Rhetoric of Christian Orthodoxy in Late Modern Fiction*. Columbus: Ohio State University Press, 2013.

Hage, Erik. *Cormac McCarthy: A Literary Companion*. Jefferson, Mo.: McFarland, 2010.

Hamilton, Robert. "Liturgical Patterns in Cormac McCarthy's *Blood Meridian*." *The Explicator* 71, no. 2 (2013): 140–43.

Hartman, Geoffrey H. "On Traumatic Knowledge and Literary Studies." *New Literary History* 26, no. 3 (1995): 537–63.

Healy, Jack, and Steve F. Kovaleski. "One Mother, 7 Dead Newborns and a Stunned Community in Utah. *New York Times*, April 26, 2014. http://www .nytimes.com/2014/04/27/us/one-mother-7-dead-newborns-and-a-stunned-community-in-utah.html.

Heim, S. Mark. *Saved from Sacrifice: A Theology of the Cross*. Grand Rapids, Mich.: Eerdmans, 2006.

Hengel, Martin. *The Atonement: The Origins of the Doctrine in the New Testament*. Translated by John Bowden. Philadelphia: Fortress Press, 1981.

Herman, Judith. *Trauma and Recovery*. New York: Basic Books, 1992.

Herzfeld, Will. "Words of Liberation." Review of *Black Theology and Black Power*, by James H. Cone. *Christian Century*, December 17, 1969: 1619–20.

Hewitt, Avis. "Intimations of Immortality: Mastered Irony in John Updike's 'Pigeon Feathers.'" *Christianity and Literature* 49, no. 4 (2000): 499–509.

———. "The Obligation to Live: Duty and Desire in John Updike's *Self-Consciousness*." In *John Updike and Religion: The Sense of the Sacred and the Motions of Grace*, edited by James Yerkes, 31–49. Grand Rapids, Mich.: Eerdmans, 1999.

Higgins, Therese E. *Religiosity, Cosmology, and Folklore: The African Influence in the Novels of Toni Morrison*. New York: Routledge, 2001.

Hill, Charles E., and Frank A. James, eds. *The Glory of the Atonement: Biblical, Historical, and Practical Perspectives*. Downers Grove, Ill.: InterVarsity, 2004.

Hillier, Russell M. "'In a Dark Parody' of John Bunyan's *The Pilgrim's Progress*: The Presence of Subversive Allegory in Cormac McCarthy's *Outer Dark*." *American Notes and Queries* 19, no. 4 (2006): 52–59.

Hirsch, Marianne. "The Generation of Postmemory." *Poetics Today* 29, no. 1 (2008): 103–28.

Hostetler, Ann. "Interview with Toni Morrison: 'The Art of Teaching.'" In *Toni Morrison: Conversations*, edited by Carolyn C. Denard, 196–205. Jackson: University of Mississippi Press, 2008.

Houston, Pam. "Pam Houston Talks with Toni Morrison." In *Toni Morrison: Conversations*, edited by Carolyn C. Denard, 228–59. Jackson: University of Mississippi Press, 2008.

Howard, Jane. "Can a Nice Novelist Finish First?" In *Conversations with John Updike*, edited by James Plath, 9–17. Jackson: University Press of Mississippi, 1994.

Hungerford, Amy. *Postmodern Belief: American Literature and Religion since 1960*. Princeton, N.J.: Princeton University Press, 2010.

Hunt, George W. *John Updike and the Three Great Things: Sex, Religion, and Art*. Grand Rapids, Mich.: Eerdmans, 1980.

Hutton, Patrick H. "The Art of Memory Reconceived: From Rhetoric to Psychoanalysis." *Journal of the History of Ideas* 48, no. 3 (1987): 371–92.

Jackson, Gregory. *The Word and Its Witness: The Spiritualization of American Realism*. Chicago: University of Chicago Press, 2009.

Jaffrey, Zia. "Toni Morrison." In *Toni Morrison: Conversations*, edited by Carolyn C. Denard, 139–54. Jackson: University of Mississippi Press, 2008.

Jennings, La Vinia Delois. *Toni Morrison and the Idea of Africa*. Cambridge, Eng.: Cambridge University Press, 2008.

Jesser, Nancy. "Violence, Home, and Community in Toni Morrison's *Beloved*." *African American Review* 33, no. 2 (1999): 325–45.

Johnson, Greg. *Invisible Writer: A Biography of Joyce Carol Oates*. New York: Dutton, 1998.

Johnson, Hannibal B. *Acres of Aspiration: The All-Black Towns of Oklahoma*. Fort Worth, Tx.: Eakin Press, 2007.

Jones, Bessie W., and Audrey Vinson. "An Interview with Toni Morrison." In *Conversations with Toni Morrison*, edited by Danille Taylor-Guthrie, 171–87. Jackson: University Press of Mississippi, 1994.

Jones, Serene. *Trauma and Grace: Theology in a Ruptured World*. Louisville, Ky.: Westminster/John Knox Press, 2009.

Jung, C. G. *Answer to Job*. 1952. Translated by R. F C Hull. Princeton, N.J.: Princeton University Press, 1991.

Jürgensen, John. "Hollywood's Favorite Cowboy." *Wall Street Journal*, November 20, 2009. http://online.wsj.com/news/articles/SB10001424052748704576 204574529703577274572.

Kaplan, E. Ann. *Trauma Culture: The Politics of Terror and Loss in Media and Literature*. New Brunswick, N.J.: Rutgers University Press, 2005.

Kashkashian, Arsen. "Oates Writes on JonBenet Ramsey." *Kash's Book Corner*, August 1, 2008. http://kashsbookcorner.blogspot.com/2008/08/oates-writes-on -jonbenet-ramsey.html

Kessler, Edward. *Flannery O'Connor and the Language of the Apocalypse*. Princeton, N.J.: Princeton University Press, 1986.

Kierkegaard, Søren. *Fear and Trembling and the Sickness unto Death*. 1843. Translated by Walter Lowrie. Princeton, N.J.: Princeton University Press, 1954.

King, Richard. "Memory and Phantasy." *Comparative Literature* 98, no. 5 (December 1983): 1197–1213.

Kinney, Arthur F. "Flannery O'Connor and the Fiction of Grace." *Massachusetts Review* 27, no. 1 (spring 1986): 71–96.

———. *Flannery O'Connor's Library: Resources of Being*. Athens: University of Georgia Press, 1985.

Kirwan, Michael. "Being Saved from Salvation: René Girard and the Victims of Religion." *Communio Viatorum* 52, no. 1 (2010): 27–47.

Kocieniewski, David, and Gary Gately. "Man Shoots 11, Killing 5 Girls, in Amish School." *New York Times*, October 3, 2006. http://www.nytimes .com/2006/10/03/us/03amish.html.

Kroeker, P. Travis. "'Jesus Is the Bread of Life': Johannine Sign and Deed in *The Violent Bear It Away*." In *Dark Faith: New Essays on Flannery O'Connor's "The Violent Bear It Away*," edited by Susan Srigley, 136–56. South Bend, Ind.: University of Notre Dame Press, 2012.

Kuehl, Linda. "An Interview with Joyce Carol Oates." In *Conversations with Joyce Carol Oates*, edited by Lee Milazzo, 7–13. Jackson: University Press of Mississippi, 1989.

Kushner, David. "Cormac McCarthy's Apocalypse." *Rolling Stone*, December 27, 2007: 44–51.

Lake, Christina Bieber. "The Demonic in Service of the Divine: Toni Morrison's *Beloved*." *South Atlantic Review* 69, nos. 3-4 (2004): 51–80.

————. *The Incarnational Art of Flannery O'Connor*. Macon, Ga.: Mercer University Press, 2005.

Lawson, Lewis A. "Rabbit Angstrom as Religious Sufferer." *Journal of the American Academy of Religion* 42, no. 2 (1974): 232–46.

Leonard, John. "New Books." Review of *My Sister, My Love*, by Joyce Carol Oates. *Harper's Magazine*, December 2008.

Levenson, Jon D. *The Death and Resurrection of the Beloved Son: The Transformation of Child Sacrifice in Judaism and Christianity*. New Haven, Conn.: Yale University Press, 1993.

Lewis, David. "Do We Believe in Penal Substitution?" In *Oxford Readings in Philosophical Theology*, vol. 1, *Trinity, Incarnation, and Atonement*, edited by Michael Rea, 308–14. New York: Oxford University Press, 2009.

Lochridge, Betsy. "An Afternoon with Flannery O'Connor." In *Conversations with Flannery O'Connor*, edited by Rosemary M. Magee, 37–40. Jackson: University Press of Mississippi, 1987.

Luce, Dianne C. *Reading the World: Cormac McCarthy's Tennessee Period*. Columbia: University of South Carolina Press, 2009.

Maritain, Jacques. *Art and Scholasticism and the Frontiers of Poetry*. 1930. Translated by Joseph W. Evans. New York: Charles Scribner's Sons, 1962.

Marius, Richard. "*Suttree* as Window into the Soul of Cormac McCarthy." In *Sacred Violence: A Reader's Companion to Cormac McCarthy*, edited by Wade Hall and Rick Wallach, 1–16. El Paso: Texas Western Press, 1995.

Markle, Joyce B. *Fighters and Lovers: Theme in the Novels of John Updike*. New York: New York University Press, 1973.

Marks, Kathleen. *Toni Morrison's "Beloved" and the Apotropaic Imagination*. Columbia: University of Missouri Press, 2002.

Martin, John Stephen. "Rabbit's Faith: Grace and the Transformation of the Heart." *Pacific Coast Philology* 17, nos. 1–2 (1982): 103–11.

Martin, Karl E. "Flannery O'Connor's Prophetic Imagination." *Religion and Literature* 26, no. 3 (autumn 1994): 33–58.

————. "Suffering Violence in the Kingdom of Heaven: *The Violent Bear It Away*." In *Dark Faith: New Essays on Flannery O'Connor's "The Violent Bear It Away*," edited by Susan Srigley, 157–84. South Bend, Ind.: University of Notre Dame Press, 2012.

May, John R. "Flannery O'Connor and the Discernment of Catholic Fiction." In *Inside the Church of Flannery O'Connor*, edited by Joanne Halleran McMullen and Jon Parrish Peede, 205–20. Macon, Ga.: Mercer University Press, 2007.

————. *The Pruning Word: The Parables of Flannery O'Connor*. South Bend, Ind.: University of Notre Dame Press, 1976.

McCarthy, Cormac. *Blood Meridian; or, The Evening Redness in the West*. 1985. New York: Vintage, 1992.

————. *Child of God*. 1973. New York: Vintage, 1993.

————. *Outer Dark*. 1968. New York: Vintage, 1993.

————. *Sunset Limited*. New York: Vintage, 2006.

————. *Suttree*. 1979. New York: Vintage, 1986.

McClure, John. *Partial Faiths: Postsecular Fiction in the Age of Pynchon and Morrison*. Athens: University of Georgia Press, 2007.

McCluskey, Audrey T. "A Conversation with Toni Morrison." In *Toni Morrison: Conversations*, edited by Carolyn C. Denard, 38–44. Jackson: University of Mississippi Press, 2008.

McClymond, Kathryn. *Beyond Sacred Violence: A Comparative Study of Sacrifice*. Baltimore: Johns Hopkins University Press, 2008.

McGrath, Alister. *Christian Theology: An Introduction*. Chichester, U.K.: Wiley-Blackwell, 2011.

McKay, Nellie. "An Interview with Toni Morrison." *Contemporary Literature* 24, no. 4 (1983): 314–429.

McLaughlin, Frank. "A Conversation with Joyce Carol Oates." In *Conversations with Joyce Carol Oates*, edited by Lee Milazzo, 123–28. Jackson: University Press of Mississippi, 1989.

McMullen, Joanne Halleran. "Christian but Not Catholic: Baptism in Flannery O'Connor's 'The River.'" In *Inside the Church of Flannery O'Connor*, edited by Joanne Halleran McMullen and Jon Parrish Peede, 167–88. Macon, Ga.: Mercer University Press, 2007.

———. *Writing against God: Language as Message in the Literature of Flannery O'Connor*. Macon, Ga.: Mercer University Press, 1996.

McNally, Richard J. *Remembering Trauma*. Cambridge, Mass.: Harvard University Press, 2003.

McReynolds, Susan. *Redemption and the Merchant God: Dostoevsky's Economy of Salvation and Antisemitism*. Evanston, Ill.: Northwestern University Press, 2008.

Merrick, James R. A. Review of *Saved from Sacrifice: A Theology of the Cross*, by S. Mark Heim. *Journal of the Evangelical Theological Society* 50, no. 4 (December 2007): 882–87.

Metress, Christopher. "Via Negativa: The Way of Unknowing in Cormac McCarthy's *Outer Dark*." *Southern Review* 37, no. 1 (2001): 147–54.

Milazzo, Lee, ed. *Conversations with Joyce Carol Oates*. Jackson: University Press of Mississippi, 1989.

Milbank, John, and Slavoj Žižek. *The Monstrosity of Christ*. Cambridge, Mass.: MIT Press, 2009.

Miller, Jerome. "Wound Made Fountain: Toward a Theology of Redemption." *Theological Studies* 70 (2009): 525–54.

Mitchell, Carolyn A. "'I Love to Tell the Story': Biblical Revisions in *Beloved*." *Religion and Literature* 23, no. 3 (1991): 27–42.

Mizruchi, Susan. *The Science of Sacrifice: American Literature and Modern Social Theory*. Princeton, N.J.: Princeton University Press, 1998.

Moberly, Elizabeth R. *Suffering, Innocent and Guilty*. London: SPCK, 1978.

Moltmann, Jürgen. *The Crucified God: The Cross of Christ as the Foundation and Criticism of Christian Theology*. 1973. Translated by R. A. Wilson and John Bowden. Minneapolis: Fortress Press, 1993.

Monda, Antonio. *Do You Believe? Conversations on God and Religion*. New York: Vintage, 2007.

Morey, Ann-Janine. "Margaret Atwood and Toni Morrison: Reflections on Postmodernism and the Study of Religion and Literature." In *Toni Morrison's Fiction: Contemporary Criticism*, edited by David L. Middleton, 247–68. New York: Garland Publishing, 1997.

Morris, Leon. *The Apostolic Preaching of the Cross*. Grand Rapids, Mich.: Eerdmans, 1984.

Morrison, Toni. *Beloved*. 1987. New York: Plume, 1988.

———. "Goodness: Altruism and the Literary Imagination." Ingersoll Lecture on Immortality, Harvard University. December 6, 2012. Video. http://www.youtube.com/watch?v=PJmVpYZnKTU.

———. *A Mercy*. New York: Alfred A. Knopf, 2008.

———. *Paradise*. New York: Alfred A. Knopf, 1998.

———. *Playing in the Dark: Whiteness and the Literary Imagination*. Cambridge, Mass.: Harvard University Press, 1992.

———. *What Moves at the Margin: Selected Nonfiction*. Edited by Carolyn Denard. Jackson: University Press of Mississippi, 2008.

Mulder, Jack Jr. *Kierkegaard and the Catholic Tradition: Conflict and Dialogue*. Bloomington: Indiana University Press, 2010.

Mullins, C. Ross. "Flannery O'Connor: An Interview." In *Conversations with Flannery O'Connor*, edited by Rosemary M. Magee, 103–7. Jackson: University Press of Mississippi, 1987.

Nation, Mark Thiessen. "'Who Has Believed What We Have Heard?' A Response to Denny Weaver's *The Nonviolent Atonement*." *Conrad Grebel Review* 27, no. 2 (2009): 17–30.

Neary, John M. "'Ah: Runs': Updike, Rabbit, and Repetition." *Religion and Literature* 21, no. 1 (1989): 89–110.

Nelson, Christopher R. "A Style of Horror: Is Evil Real in Cormac McCarthy's *Outer Dark?*" *Critique* 53, no. 1 (2012): 30–48.

Noudelmann, François. "Interview with Toni Morrison." *Black Renaissance* 12, no. 1 (2012):

Nunley, Jan. "Thoughts of Faith Infuse Updike's Novels." In *Conversations with John Updike*, edited by James Plath, 248–59. Jackson: University Press of Mississippi, 1994.

O'Connor, Flannery. *Collected Works*. New York: Library of America, 1988.

———. *The Habit of Being*. Edited by Sally Fitzgerald. New York: Vintage Books, 1979.

———. *Mystery and Manners: Occasional Prose*. Edited by Sally and Robert Fitzgerald. New York: Farrar, Straus and Giroux, 1969.

O'Gorman, Farrell. *Peculiar Crossroads: Flannery O'Connor, Walker Percy, and Catholic Vision in Postwar Southern Fiction*. Baton Rouge: Louisiana State University Press, 2004.

———. "Violence, Nature, and Prophecy in Flannery O'Connor and Cormac McCarthy." In *Flannery O'Connor in the Age of Terrorism: Essays on Violence and Grace*, edited by Robert Donahoo, 143–68. Knoxville: University of Tennessee Press, 2010.

O'Reilly, Andrea. *Toni Morrison and Motherhood: A Politics of the Heart*. Albany: State University of New York Press, 2004.

Oates, Joyce Carol. *Dear Husband*. New York: Ecco, 2009.

———. *The Edge of Impossibility: Tragic Forms in Literature*. New York: Vanguard Press, 1972.

———. *My Sister, My Love: The Intimate Story of Skyler Rampike*. New York: Harper Perennial, 2008.

———. *The Mysteries of Winterthurn*. New York: Dutton, 1984.

———. "The Mystery of JonBenét Ramsey." *New York Review of Books*, June 24, 1999.

———. *New Heaven, New Earth: The Visionary Experience in Literature*. New York: Vanguard, 1974.

———. *Where Are You Going, Where Have You Been?: Selected Early Stories*. Princeton, N.J.: Ontario Review Press, 1993.

———. *Where I've Been, and Where I'm Going*. New York: Plume, 1999.

———. *A Widow's Story: A Memoir*. New York: Ecco, 2011.

———. *Zombie*. New York: Dutton, 1995.

Ochoa, Peggy. "Morrison's *Beloved*: Allegorically Othering 'White' Christianity." *MELUS* 24, no. 2 (1999): 107–23.

Page, Philip. "Furrowing All the Brows: Interpretation and the Transcendent in Toni Morrison's *Paradise*." *African American Review* 35, no. 4 (2001): 637–49.

Pasewark, Kyle A. "The Troubles with Harry: Freedom, America, and God in John Updike's Rabbit Novels." *Religion and American Culture: A Journal of Interpretation* 6, no. 1 (1996): 1–33.

Pederson, Joshua. "Speak, Trauma: Toward a Revised Understanding of Literary Trauma Theory." *Narrative* 22, no. 3 (2014): 333–53.

Phillips, Robert. "Joyce Carol Oates: The Art of Fiction." In *Joyce Carol Oates: Conversations 1970–2006*, edited by Greg Johnson, 64–84. Princeton, N.J.: Ontario Review Press, 2006.

Pinsker, Sanford. "Speaking about Short Fiction: An Interview with Joyce Carol Oates." In *Joyce Carol Oates: Conversations 1970–2006*, edited by Greg Johnson, 98–104. Princeton, N.J.: Ontario Review Press, 2006.

Placher, William C. "Christ Takes Our Place: Rethinking Atonement." *Interpretation* 53, no. 1 (1999): 5–20.

———. "How Does Jesus Save?" *Christian Century*, June 2, 2009.

Pritchard, William H. *Updike: America's Man of Letters*. South Royalton, Vt.: Steerforth Press, 2000.

Prothero, Stephen. *American Jesus: How the Son of God Became a National Icon*. New York: Farrar, Straus and Giroux, 2003.

Ragen, Brian Abel. *A Wreck on the Road to Damascus: Innocence, Guilt, and Conversion in Flannery O'Connor*. Chicago: Loyola University Press, 1989.

Rambo, Shelly. *Spirit and Trauma: A Theology of Remaining*. Louisville, Ky.: Westminster/John Knox Press, 2010.

Rashdall, Hastings. *The Idea of Atonement in Christian Theology*. London: MacMillan, 1919.

Ray, Darby Kathleen. *Deceiving the Devil: Atonement, Abuse, and Ransom*. Cleveland: Pilgrim Press, 1998.

Rea, Michael, ed. *Oxford Readings in Philosophical Theology*, vol. 1, *Trinity, Incarnation, and Atonement*. Oxford: Oxford University Press, 2009.

"Recent Southern Fiction: A Panel Discussion." In *Conversations with Flannery O'Connor*, edited by Rosemary M. Magee, 61–78. Jackson: University Press of Mississippi, 1987.

Reilly, Charlie. "An Interview with John Updike." *Contemporary Literature* 43, no. 2 (2002): 217–48.

Rich, Adrienne. *Of Woman Born: Motherhood as Experience and Institution.* 1976. New York: W. W. Norton, 1986.

Romero, Channette. "Creating the Beloved Community: Religion, Race, and Nation in Toni Morrison's *Paradise.*" *African American Review* (2005): 415–30.

Ruas, Charles. "Toni Morrison." In *Conversations with Toni Morrison,* edited by Danille Taylor-Guthrie, 93–118. Jackson: University Press of Mississippi, 1994.

Ruether, Rosemary. "Crisis in Sex and Race: Black Theology vs. Feminist Theology." *Christianity and Crisis* 34 (1974): 67–73.

Rushdie, Salman. "An Interview with Toni Morrison." In *Toni Morrison: Conversations,* edited by Carolyn C. Denard, 51–61. Jackson: University of Mississippi Press, 2008.

Samuels, Charles Thomas. "The Art of Fiction XLIII: John Updike." In *Conversations with John Updike,* edited by James Plath, 22–45. Jackson: University Press of Mississippi, 1994.

Sanders, John, ed. *Atonement and Violence: A Theological Conversation.* Nashville: Abingdon Press, 2006.

Schafer, William J. "Cormac McCarthy: The Hard Wages of Original Sin." *Appalachian Journal* 4, no. 2 (1977): 105–19.

Schappell, Elissa. "Toni Morrison: The Art of Fiction No. 134." *Paris Review* 128, fall 1993. http://www.theparisreview.org/interviews/1888/the-art-of-fiction-no -134-toni-morrison.

Schiff, James A. "The Pocket Nothing Else Will Fill: Updike's Domestic God." In *John Updike and Religion: The Sense of the Sacred and the Motions of Grace,* edited by James Yerkes, 50–63. Grand Rapids, Mich.: Eerdmans, 1999.

Schilling, Timothy P. "The Shape of Our Despair: The Fiction of Joyce Carol Oates." *Commonweal* 132, no. 13 (July 15, 2005): 21.

Schreiber, Evelyn Jaffe. *Race, Trauma, and Home in the Novels of Toni Morrison.* Baton Rouge: Louisiana State University Press, 2010.

Schweitzer, Bernard. *Hating God: The Untold Story of Misotheism.* New York: Oxford University Press, 2011.

Sessions, W. A. "Real Presence: Flannery O'Connor and the Saints." In *Inside the Church of Flannery O'Connor,* edited by Joanne Halleran McMullen and Jon Parrish Peede, 15–40. Macon, Ga.: Mercer University Press, 2007.

Sharp, Jolly Kay. *"Between the House and the Chicken Yard": The Masks of Mary Flannery O'Connor.* Macon, Ga.: Mercer University Press, 2011.

Silverblatt, Michael. "'Things We Find in Language': A Conversation with Toni Morrison." In *Toni Morrison: Conversations,* edited by Carolyn C. Denard, 171–77. Jackson: University of Mississippi Press, 2008.

Sjoberg, Leif. "An Interview with Joyce Carol Oates." In *Conversations with Joyce Carol Oates,* edited by Lee Milazzo, 101–18. Jackson: University Press of Mississippi, 1989.

Smith, H. Shelton. *In His Image, But . . : Racism in Southern Religion, 1780– 1910.* Durham, N.C.: Duke University Press, 1972.

Spencer, William C. "Cormac McCarthy's Unholy Trinity: Biblical Parody in *Outer Dark.*" In *Sacred Violence: A Reader's Companion to Cormac McCarthy,* edited by Wade Hall and Rick Wallach, 69–76. El Paso, Tx.: Texas Western Press, 1995.

Spivey, Ted. *Flannery O'Connor: The Woman, the Thinker, the Visionary*. Macon, Ga.: Mercer University Press, 1995.

Srigley, Susan. "Asceticism and Abundance: The Communion of the Saints in *The Violent Bear It Away*." In *Dark Faith: New Essays on Flannery O'Connor's "The Violent Bear It Away*," edited by Susan Srigley, 185–212. South Bend, Ind.: University of Notre Dame Press, 2012.

———. *Flannery O'Connor's Sacramental Art*. South Bend, Ind.: University of Notre Dame Press, 2004.

———. "The Violence of Love: Reflections on Self-Sacrifice through Flannery O'Connor and René Girard." *Religion and Literature* 39, no. 3 (autumn 2007): 31–45.

Stave, Shirley, ed. *Toni Morrison and the Bible: Contested Intertextualities*. New York: Peter Lang, 2006.

———. "Toni Morrison's *Beloved* and the Vindication of Lilith." *Atlantic Review* 58, no. 1 (1993): 49–66.

Stepto, Robert. "Intimate Things in Place: A Conversation with Toni Morrison." In *Conversations with Toni Morrison*, edited by Danille Taylor-Guthrie, 10–29. Jackson: University Press of Mississippi, 1994.

Stout, Elinor. "Interview with John Updike." In *Conversations with John Updike*, edited by James Plath, 74–83. Jackson: University Press of Mississippi, 1994.

Stump, Eleanor. "Atonement According to Aquinas." In *Oxford Readings in Philosophical Theology*, vol. 1, *Trinity, Incarnation, and Atonement*, edited by Michael Rea, 267–93. Oxford: Oxford University Press, 2009.

Sundquist, Eric J. "Witness without End?" *American Literary History* 19, no. 1 (2007): 65–85.

Talar, C. J. T. "The Importance of Being Ernest: Renan (1823–1892)." *Continuum* 2, nos. 2–3 (1993): 325–32.

Taylor, Charles. *A Secular Age*. Cambridge, Mass.: Harvard University Press, 2007.

Taylor-Guthrie, Danille. "Who Are the Beloved? Old and New Testaments, Old and New Communities of Faith." *Religion and Literature* 27, no. 1 (1995): 119–29.

Third Plenary Council of Baltimore. *A Catechism of Christian Doctrine, No. 1*. New York, 1885. Kindle edition.

Tillich, Paul. *Systematic Theology, Volume 2: Existence and the Christ*. 1957. Chicago: University of Chicago Press, 1975.

Updike, John. *Assorted Prose*. New York: Alfred A. Knopf, 1965.

———. *Higher Gossip*. New York: Alfred A. Knopf, 2011.

———. *Hugging the Shore*. New York: Alfred A. Knopf, 1983.

———. *In the Beauty of the Lilies*. New York: Fawcett Columbine, 1996.

———. *A Month of Sundays*. New York: Alfred A. Knopf, 1975.

———. *More Matter*. New York: Alfred A. Knopf, 1999.

———. *Odd Jobs*. New York: Alfred A. Knopf, 1991.

———. *Picked-Up Pieces*. New York: Alfred A. Knopf, 1975.

———. *Pigeon Feathers and Other Stories*. 1959. New York: Random House, 1996.

———. *The Poorhouse Fair*. 1958. New York: Alfred A. Knopf, 1977.

———. *The Rabbit Novels, Vol. 2: Rabbit Is Rich; Rabbit at Rest.* New York: Ballantine, 2003.

———. *Rabbit Redux.* New York: Fawcett Crest, 1971.

———. *Rabbit, Run.* 1960. New York: Fawcett Crest, 1988.

———. *Roger's Version.* New York: Alfred A. Knopf, 1986.

———. *Self-Consciousness.* New York: Alfred A. Knopf, 1989.

Uphaus, Suzanne Henning. *John Updike.* New York: Frederick Ungar Publishing, 1980.

Valkeakari, Tuire. *Religious Idiom and the African American Novel, 1952–1998.* Gainesville: University of Florida Press, 2007.

Van der Kolk, Bessel A., Alexander C. McFarlane, and Lars Weisaeth. *Traumatic Stress: The Effects of Overwhelming Experience on Mind, Body, and Society.* New York: Guilford Press, 1996.

Vargo, Edward P. *Rainstorms and Fire: Ritual in the Novels of John Updike.* Port Washington, N.Y.: Kennikat Press, 1973.

Verdelle, A. J. "Loose Magic: A. J. Verdelle Interviews Toni Morrison." In *Toni Morrison: Conversations,* edited by Carolyn C. Denard, 159–70. Jackson: University of Mississippi Press, 2008.

Walker, Melissa. *Down from the Mountaintop: Black Women's Novels in the Wake of the Civil Rights Movement, 1966–1989.* New Haven, Conn.: Yale University Press, 1991.

Walvoord, John F. "Christ's Olivet Discourse on the End of the Age: The Parable of the Talents." *Bibliotheca Sacra* 129, no. 515 (1972): 206–10.

Warner, Sharon Oard. "The Fairest in the Land: *Blonde* and *Black Water,* the Nonfiction Novels of Joyce Carol Oates." *Studies in the Novel* 38, no. 4 (winter 2006): 513–24.

Watson, James. "'The Only Words I Know Are the Catholic Ones': Sacramental Existentialism in Cormac McCarthy's *Suttree.*" *Southwestern American Literature* 38, no. 2 (2013): 7–24.

Weaver, J. Denny. "Narrative *Christus Victor*: The Answer to Anselmian Atonement Violence." In *Atonement and Violence: A Theological Conversation,* edited by John Sanders, 1–33. Nashville: Abingdon Press, 2006.

———. *The Nonviolent Atonement.* Grand Rapids, Mich.: Eerdmans, 2001.

Webb, Stephen H. "John Updike and the Waning of Mainline Protestantism." *Christianity and Literature* 57, no. 4 (2008): 583–93.

———. "Writing as a Reader of Karl Barth: What Kind of Religious Writer Is John Updike Not?" In *John Updike and Religion: The Sense of the Sacred and the Motions of Grace,* edited by James Yerkes, 145–61. Grand Rapids, Mich.: Eerdmans, 1999.

Wheatley, Christopher. *Thornton Wilder and Amos Wilder: Writing Religion in Twentieth-Century America.* South Bend, Ind.: University of Notre Dame Press, 2011.

Wiesel, Elie. "The Holocaust as a Literary Inspiration." In *Dimensions of the Holocaust,* edited by Elliott Lefkovitz, 5–90. Evanston, Ill.: Northwestern University Press, 1977.

Wieviorka, Annette. *The Era of the Witness.* Translated by Jared Stark. Ithaca, N.Y.: Cornell University Press, 2006.

Williams, Delores S. *Sisters in the Wilderness: The Challenge of Womanist God-Talk*. Maryknoll, N.Y.: Orbis Books, 1993.

Williamson, Clark M. "Atonement Theologies and the Cross." *Encounter* 71, no. 1 (2010): 1–25.

Winchell, Mark Royden. "Inner Dark: or, The Place of Cormac McCarthy." *Southern Review* 26, no. 2 (1990): 293–309.

Woiwode, Larry. *Words Made Fresh: Essays on Literature and Culture*. Wheaton, Ill.: Crossway Books, 2011.

Wood, James. *The Broken Estate: Essays on Literature and Belief*. New York: Random House, 1999.

Wood, Ralph C. *The Comedy of Redemption: Christian Faith and Comic Vision in Four American Novelists*. South Bend, Ind.: University of Notre Dame Press, 1988.

———. "'God May Strike You Thisaway': Flannery O'Connor and Simone Weil on Affliction and Joy." *Renascence* 59, no. 3 (spring 2007): 181–95.

Woodward, Richard B. "Cormac McCarthy's Venomous Fiction." *New York Times*, April 19, 1992. http://www.nytimes.com/1992/04/19/magazine/cormac-mccarthy-s-venomous-fiction.html.

———. "Cormac McCarthy Would Rather Hang Out with Physicists than Other Writers." *Vanity Fair*, August 2005.

Wright, Terry. *The Genesis of Fiction: Modern Novelists as Biblical Interpreters*. Burlington, Vt.: Ashgate Publishing, 2007.

Wyatt, Jean. "Giving Body to the Word: The Maternal Symbolic in Toni Morrison's *Beloved*." *PMLA* 108, no. 3 (1993): 474–88.

Zornado, Joseph. "A Becoming Habit: Flannery O'Connor's Fiction of Unknowing." *Religion and Literature* 29, no. 2 (summer 1997): 27–59.

INDEX

Abbott, Shirley, 43
Abelard, Peter, 8, 20–22, 28, 31–32, 61, 94, 95, 139n66
Albee, Edward, 4
Allitt, Patrick, 64
Alter, Robert, 139n64
Andretta, Helen, 44
Anselm, 8, 18, 19–21, 23, 25, 26–28, 31, 33, 44, 59, 61, 92, 127n28, 128n42, 139n66
Applebaum, Judith, 91
Aquinas, Thomas, 44–45, 50–51, 59, 91, 133nn20–21
Arnold, Matthew, 91
atonement theology, 5–12, 15–34, 39, 124n14, 125n5, 126n7, 128n52, 129n56, 129n60, 139n66; Aquinas and, 44, 133nn20–21; Jewish vs. Christian, 16–17, 125n4, 127n34; McCarthy and, 105, 107, 109, 117; Morrison and, 73, 75, 77, 82, 84–85, 121; Oates and, 87, 92, 94–95, 97–100; O'Connor and, 44–45, 50, 53, 127n23; Updike and, 59–63, 66–68, 97, 121
Augustine, 91
Aulén, Gustaf, 8, 18–19, 22, 23, 28, 32, 124n14, 127n18

Bailey, Peter J., 63, 64, 138n24, 138n44
Balthasar, Hans Urs von, 4, 12, 17–18, 35, 127n22, 140n71
Baltimore Catechism, 43–44
baptism, 48, 68, 134n44
Barth, Karl, 16, 59, 61, 69–70
Baumgaertner, Jill Peláez, 43
Beckett, Samuel, 89, 90
Béguin, Albert, 45, 52
Bell, Vereen, 105
Bellah, Robert N., 138n28

Beste, Jennifer Erin, 35, 131n89
Bible: African Americans and, 73–74, 80; parables in, 112–13; 149n48–49. *See also* atonement theology; black theology
—Old Testament, 13, 38, 69–70, 92, 105–6, 130n65; Genesis, 5, 50–51, 70, 96, 114, 125n4, 146n29; Exodus, 47, 48, 68, 114; Leviticus, 16, 25, 125n2; Deuteronomy, 134n31; Ruth, 149n49; 1 Samuel, 62, 116; 1 Kings, 70; 2 Kings, 48; Job, 38–39, 88, 106, 111, 113; Psalms, 30, 106, 113; Song of Songs, 93; Jeremiah, 3–4; Ezekiel, 47; Daniel, 48; Hosea, 24; Habakkuk, 46
—New Testament, 7, 13, 69, 81, 96; Matthew, 3–4, 5, 8, 24, 49–50, 52, 72, 96, 111–13; Mark, v, 4, 6–7, 8, 17, 35, 117, 123–24nn8–9, 126n7; Luke, 4, 81, 96; John, 4, 6, 7, 81, 95, 96, 123n8, 134n41; Acts, 36, 79; Romans, 16, 17, 133; 2 Corinthians, 17; Hebrews, 128n41; 1 John, 96–97. *See also* Slaughter of the Innocents
Black Book, The, 75, 142n25
black theology, 31, 32, 63–69
Blickenstaff, Marianne, 113, 149n48
Blumenthal, David, v, 29–30, 105–6, 111, 113, 116, 121
Bouson, Brooks J., 82–83
Bowers, Susan, 75, 80, 142n25
Brison, Susan, 39, 100
Brock, Rita Nakashima, 29–30, 106, 121; and Rebecca Ann Parker, 3, 8, 23, 29, 97
Brown, Charles E., 129n61
Brown, Joanne Carlson, and Rebecca Ann Parker, 33–34
Bucher, Glenn R., 64–65
Bultmann, Rudolf, 59